Table of Contents

3   Dedication
4   Preface

Chapter 1: Introduction
5   Embracing Shadows

Chapter 2: Hoodoo
8   Unveiling the Mysteries of Hoodoo
8   Spiritual Practice Not a Religion
9   Africa's Influence on Hoodoo?
10 Animism in Hoodoo
12 Native American Influences
13 European Occultism Influences
14 Christian Influences

Chapter 3: Being Called
16 Being Called
18 What is Being Called?
19 How Do I Know I'm Called?
20 Ida "Seven Sisters" Carter
21 Self-Initiation Ritual

Chapter 4: Ancestors
24 Honor Your Ancestors
25 Misconceptions of Ancestral Veneration
26 Ancestral Altar
28 Being Contacted by an Ancestor
29 Connecting with an Ancestor
32 Common Ancestor Offerings
33 My Very First Altar

Chapter 5: Conjure
35 Conjure in Hoodoo
37 What is Conjure?
38 Common Aspects of Spirit Work
39 Common Types of Hoodoo Spirits
40 Hoodoo Ancestors
43 Safety Disclaimer for Spirit Work

Chapter 6: Rootworker Kye
45 Rootwork in Hoodoo
46 What is Rootwork?
48 From Kye to Rootworker Kye
52 Aja The "Wild Wind" of the Forest
54 Grounding Yourself
55 Grounding & Centering Ritual

Chapter 7: Orishas
58 Orishas in Hoodoo
59 The Controversy of Orishas in Hoodoo
60 Orishas Found in Hoodoo
62 Ways To Honor Orishas in Hoodoo
63 Safety Protocols for Orisha Work

Chapter 8: Rootworkin'
65 Let's get to Rootworkin'
66 Hoodoo Herbs
67 45 Commonly Used Herbs
72 Holistic Remedies
73 Simple & Easy Remedies
76 One Herb Remedies
79 Semi-Advanced Remedies
83 Charms, Mojos, & Sachets
84 Containment Recipes
87 How to Use Containments
88 Spiritual Baths
89 Spiritual Bath Recipes
91 How to Use Spiritual Baths
93 Hoodoo Oils
95 Hoodoo Oil Recipes
98 How to Use Hoodoo Oils
98 Hoodoo Floor Washes
101 Floor Wash Recipes
103 How to Use Floor Washes
105 Hoodoo Sprays, Waters, Colognes
107 Hoodoo Liquid Recipes
110 How to Use Hoodoo Liquids
111 Hoodoo Incense Blends
112 Incense Recipes
115 How to Use Hoodoo Incense
116 Hoodoo Candles
117 Hoodoo Candle Recipes
120 How to Use Hoodoo Candles

Chapter 9: Two-Headed
122 Journey to Two-Headed Doctor
124 What is a Two-Headed Doctor?
125 Lightwork Vs Dark Work
126 Karma in Hoodoo
129 Consent, Harm Reduction, & Accountability
130 Take Care of Yourself
131 After work Cleanse
132 Father Simms The Two-Headed Doctor

Chapter 10: Workin'

134	Workings of a Two-Headed Doctor
135	Covering Your Head in White
136	Rootworker Kye's 7 Day Cleanse
139	Cleanse Your Space
140	Additional Cleansing Tips
141	Return To Sender
141	Rootworker Kye's 7 Day Return to Sender
143	Candle Working with Hot Foot Powder
144	Herb Sachet with Mirror
144	Evocation W/Banishing
145	Protection
146	Protection Candle W/Bay Leaf
146	Herb Bath for Protection
147	Evocation W/Protection
148	Energy Shielding & Cleansing
149	Ritual Cleansing & Protection
149	Ritual Energy Shielding
150	Psalms 91 Shielding

Chapter 11: Enhancing

152	Living in My Power
153	Enhancing Your Power
154	Meditation in Hoodoo
155	Rootworker Kye's Meditation
156	Chakra Work in Hoodoo
158	Chakra Unbalanced?
159	Simple Chakra Balancing
161	Crystals & Stones in Hoodoo
163	Crystals of Hoodoo
165	Crystal Workings
166	Crystal Chakra Balancing Ritual
168	Shadow Work in Hoodoo
169	Shadow Work Ritual
171	The Purple Place
173	Kyesha The Dreamwalker
173	Dream Warnings: Struggle Of Being Heard
175	Dream Interpretation
177	Dream Symbols
179	Colors of Dreams
182	Enhance Your Dreams

Chapter 12: Christianity

185	Christianity in Hoodoo
186	The Power of the Psalms
188	The Use of Psalms
187	Psalms Commonly Used
190	Bible Verses of Hoodoo
193	Saints of Hoodoo
194	Gospel Music in Hoodoo
196	Commonly Used Gospel
197	Biblical Figures Used in Hoodoo
198	Biblical Figure Petition
198	Misconceptions: Christianity Vs. Hoodoo

Additional Information

201	Hoodoo Sigils
202	Hoodoo Candle Color Meanings
203	Types of Candles in Hoodoo
204	Candle Interpretation
208	Divination Practices in Hoodoo
210	Astrology in Hoodoo
211	The Moon & The Sun
212	Bodies of Water in Hoodoo
213	Dirt in Hoodoo
215	Container Workings
216	The Ring Shout
217	Additional Rituals
230	Closing Remarks
231	My Hoodoo Startup Journal
232	Introduction
233	My Thoughts
259	My Recipes
275	My Rituals
292	My Dreams
323	About the Author
324	Introduction to Ref Page
325	Reference Page

Within these pages, you will find not only captivating stories but also a wealth of valuable information and resources. Use this table of contents as your trusted index page, allowing you to effortlessly navigate through the book and easily refer to any section you may need on your own Hoodoo journey. Embrace the power of this ancient tradition as you explore the chapters, unlocking the transformative experiences that lie within.

Dedication

To the one who took the leap,
To the one who faced their fears,
To the one who embarked on a journey,
This book is dedicated to you.

For so long, I sought validation in the presence of others,
I hesitated to start projects on my own,
But now, I stand here, having conquered that fear.

To the one who discovered the strength within,
To the one who embraced solitude,
To the one who walked the path of self discovery,
This book is dedicated to your unwavering spirit.

In this journey of spiritual growth,
I found solace in my own company,
I listened to the whispers of my soul,
And I learned to trust my intuition.

To the one who embarked on this sacred quest,
To the one who persevered,
To the one who nurtured their own growth,
This book is dedicated to your courage and resilience.

May it serve as a reminder,
That you are capable of greatness,
That you are deserving of love and self acceptance,
And that your journey is uniquely beautiful.

This dedication is not meant to boast,
But to celebrate the triumphs of self discovery,
To honor the strength it takes to walk alone,
And to remind you that you are enough.

With deepest gratitude and love,
This book is dedicated to me.

- Rootworker Kye

PREFACE

I just want to share a little of me and my journey with the hopes that this book will help others. Hoodoo became not just a spiritual practice for me, but a way to provide readers with more understanding of Hoodoo. My journey has allowed me to pass on what knowledge I have gained to those who are on the same journey.

This book will not only serve as a memoir of my life on my journey to Rootwork, but I will also be delving into the realm of ancestors, plants, and animism. I will explore the significance of various herbs, roots, and flowers in Hoodoo rituals and what we call "work". I will discuss their properties, correspondences, and how they can be utilized to enhance spiritual practices. From traditional recipes passed down through generations to modern adaptations, readers will learn how to infuse their life with intentions, using Hoodoo practices as a conduit for spiritual nourishment and manifestation.

Additionally, I will delve into the world of spiritual tools and curios, exploring the significance of items such as candles, crystals, symbols, and containments in Hoodoo practices. Readers will gain insight into how these objects can be used to amplify energy, focus intention, and create sacred space for spiritual rituals. It will also serve as a guide, providing readers with practical exercises, rituals, and meditations to deepen their spiritual connection and understand the principles of Hoodoo firsthand. Through these practices, readers will be able to integrate the teachings of Hoodoo into their own lives and cultivate a personal relationship with the divine.

Furthermore, I will address the importance of ethics and responsibility in Hoodoo. With great power comes great responsibility, and it is crucial for practitioners to approach their spiritual work with integrity, respect, and a deep understanding of the consequences of their actions. I will emphasize the importance of consent, harm reduction, and accountability in Hoodoo practices, ensuring that readers are equipped with the knowledge and tools to navigate their spiritual path responsibly.

Lastly, I will explore the history and cultural context of Hoodoo, shedding light on its African diasporic roots and how it has evolved over time. By understanding the cultural significance and historical context of Hoodoo, readers will gain a deeper appreciation for its traditions and the wisdom it holds. In this book, I aim to provide a comprehensive and accessible resource for those seeking to explore Hoodoo and incorporate its teachings into their spiritual journey. Whether readers are new to Hoodoo or have an existing practice, I hope to inspire and empower them to embrace their spirituality, cultivate a deeper connection with the divine, and create positive change in their lives and communities.

Copyright © 2024 Rootworker Kye.

All rights reserved. No part of this publication may be reproduced, distributed, or transmitted in any form or by any means, including photocopying, recording, or other electronic or mechanical methods, without the prior written permission of the publisher, except in the case of brief quotations embodied in critical reviews and certain other noncommercial uses permitted by copyright law. For permission requests, write to the publisher, addressed "Attention: Permissions Coordinator," at the email address below.

ISBN: 979-8-987-89483-5 (Hard Cover)
ISBN: 979-8-987-89485-9 (Ebook)

Any references to historical events, real people, or real places are used fictitiously. Names, characters, and places are products of the author's imagination.

Front cover image by Rootworker Kye
Book design by Rootworker Kye
Printed by IngramSpark, in the United States of America.

First printing edition 2024.

Paved Visions
New York
info@pavedvisions.com

CHAPTER 1
Embracing Shadows

Isolation is often seen as a period of solitude, a time of soul-searching and self-discovery. It can be a sanctuary, a place where we can delve deep into our thoughts and emotions. But what happens when isolation is not our choice, but rather a consequence of our spiritual journey? My journey into Hoodoo began innocently enough, sparked by a genuine search for truth and a more personal relationship with God, the divine.

From an early age, I was taught to believe in the teachings of the church and to trust in the wisdom of its leaders. However, as I grew older, doubts started to creep into my mind. I couldn't help but notice how some people in the church treated others. Instead of embracing love, acceptance, and inclusivity, there were instances of judgment, exclusion, and hypocrisy. It didn't align with the values I believed God stood for.

These discrepancies began to weigh heavily on my heart. I found myself questioning the teachings I had been brought up with. Was this really the path to spiritual enlightenment? Was this the true essence of God's love? Feeling anxious and conflicted, I decided to embark on a journey of seeking God on my own terms. I delved into books, explored different religious philosophies, and engaged in deep self-analysis. It was during this soul-searching process that I stumbled upon the path of Hoodoo. As I delved deeper into the practices and beliefs of this ancient African American spiritual practice, I discovered a profound connection to the spiritual realm.

Hoodoo, with its rich history and profound symbolism, resonated with me on a soul level. Little did I know that this newfound spiritual path would lead me down a path of isolation, estrangement from the very people I held dear. Friends and family, who once stood by my side, now stood in judgment, casting their doubts and fears upon me. Rumors quickly spread like wildfire, whispered words painting me as a worshipper of demons, a person who had strayed too far from the comforts of societal norms.

In the beginning, I tried to explain, to help them understand the beauty and depth of Hoodoo. I spoke of its roots in African spirituality, its connection to nature, and its emphasis on personal empowerment. But my words fell on deaf ears, overshadowed by their preconceived notions and misunderstandings. They saw my rituals and practices through the narrow lens of fear and ignorance, unable to grasp the true essence of what I had found. As the whispers grew louder and the judgments became more pronounced, I found solace in the shadows. I retreated into myself, seeking refuge in the very isolation that had been thrust upon me.

Alone, I began to unravel the threads of my spiritual awakening, navigating the deep recesses of my soul with a newfound sense of clarity and purpose. In this solitude, I discovered the strength to embrace my journey fully, to confront the demons of doubt that resided within me. I realized that the judgment and rejection from those around me were not a reflection of my worth, but rather a reflection of their own fears and insecurities. Their inability to accept my path obscured their ability to see the light that Hoodoo brought into my life. Through the trials of isolation, I learned the importance of self-acceptance and resilience.

I recognized that my spiritual journey was not meant to be understood or validated by others but by my own heart and spirit. It was a personal exploration, a sacred pilgrimage into what would eventually shape and transform my very being. As I delved deeper into the teachings of Hoodoo, I discovered a world that went beyond rituals and what people would call "spell work". It was a spiritual path that embraced the interconnectedness of all things, a recognition that we are all part of a greater cosmic tapestry.

Hoodoo taught me to honor the natural world and its divine energies, to find harmony and balance within myself and my surroundings. I often wonder how such a beautiful belief system became a whisper of devil worship and dark magic. How was it painted as a vessel for evil forces. That answer soon came to me the more I have dived into the belief system, and will be addressed in this book, but my pursuit of spirituality had unleashed a storm of fear and prejudice that tore through the fabric of my relationships. Their rejection and condemnation cut deep, and at first, they left wounds that festered in the depths of my soul.

However, the isolation that followed became both a refuge and a battleground. In the solitude, I grappled with the pain of losing connections that had once been so dear. Within the isolation, I found strength. I discovered a resilience that I didn't know existed within me. I realized that my spiritual journey was not meant to be defined by the opinions and expectations of others. It was a personal exploration, a sacred dance between my spirit and the divine.

As I embraced the shadows, I began to shed the layers of societal conditioning and fear that had held me captive for so long. I found solace in the quiet moments, the stillness that allowed me to hear the whispers of my own intuition. I learned to trust in my own spiritual experiences, to honor the guidance that came from deep within.

In the depths of isolation, I discovered a sense of liberation. I no longer felt bound by the judgments of others or the need for external validation. I realized that my journey into Hoodoo was a path of empowerment, a reclaiming of my own spiritual sovereignty. I emerged stronger, more resilient, and with a deeper sense of self.

Hoodoo, with its roots in African and African American traditions, spoke to me in a way that the rigid dogmas of the church couldn't. It emphasized personal empowerment, connection with nature, and the use of spiritual tools to manifest positive change. It allowed for a personal connection to God that I wasn't afforded in Christianity. It felt like the missing piece of the puzzle in my spiritual quest.

Then, through social media, I discovered a community of like-minded individuals who embraced Hoodoo as a powerful tool and a connection to our Ancestors who created this practice so we as African Americans wouldn't forget where we came from. My Isolation had ended, and I found a new tribe.

Through Hoodoo, I found a way to honor my ancestors, tap into my own inner strength, and cultivate a deeper relationship with the divine. It provided me with a sense of agency and allowed me to explore a spirituality that felt authentic to me.

While my journey from the church to Hoodoo was not without challenges and moments of doubt, it ultimately led me to a place of peace and self-discovery. I realized that spirituality is a deeply personal journey, and it is essential to find a path that resonates with our own beliefs and values. As I continue to walk this path, I strive to embrace love, compassion, and inclusivity in all aspects of my life. I am grateful for the lessons I learned in the church, but I am equally grateful for the courage to seek my own truth and find solace in the practice of Hoodoo.

CHAPTER 2

Unveiling the Mysteries of Hoodoo

Hoodoo essentially is a collection of historical memories linking previous generations of African Americans to their African past. It is a spiritual and physical healing, protective, and hope bringing belief system that originated with the ancestors of African Americans who were victims of the Transatlantic Slave Trade. It allows us as African Americans to experience our past, and present simultaneously through the spirituality and rituals that were taken from us. It is home to some of the most ancient African principals, values, and beliefs. Some of those beliefs include animism, spirit possession, ancestor veneration, water immersion, sacred dances, music, sounds, symbols, and natural medicine among many other things.

Hoodoo is a practice that is ever changing and evolving, which makes it powerful, and is one of the many reasons it's so hard to put a single definition on it. This belief system was once the only thing that kept our ancestors protected and filled with hope. Over time it has suffered many regressions and at one point was almost completely erased and would be today if it wasn't for authors like Zora Neale Hurston.

Let us take a step back from my personal journey to delve into the rich history and origins of Hoodoo. I want to provide an informative overview of how Hoodoo emerged as a spiritual practice, tracing its roots in African and African American traditions, while exploring the cultural influences of Native American spirituality, European occultism, and Christianity that contributed to the development of Hoodoo as a unique and powerful form of spiritual expression.

Spiritual Practice Not a Religion

The origins of Hoodoo can be traced back to West African spiritual practices and religions brought to the Americas during the Transatlantic Slave Trade and incorporates elements of animism, ancestor veneration, and a belief in the power of spirits and natural forces. Central to Hoodoo is the belief in a divine power, often referred to as "The Creator," "The Most High," Olodumare, "The Universe," or God. It really depends on you. Hoodoo is not a religion; it is a practice.

What do I mean by this? A Spiritual practice involves a personal quest and personal connection to a higher power, while religion involves an organized entity with rituals and practices focusing on a higher power or higher powers. People who engage in spiritual practices learn and develop their beliefs based on their own experience while religious people learn based on the experiences they are told about. That is why if you are a Hoodoo practitioner you also can practice other religions. It depends on your spiritual path.

There are many Hoodoo practitioners who also practice Voodoo, and there are some who practice Christianity. That is why you will find that when speaking to Hoodoo practitioners the name they decide to call their divine power will vary from person to person. Hoodoo practitioners believe in the interconnectedness of all things and the ability to harness spiritual energy for practical purposes. They view the world to be saturated with spiritual forces that can be accessed and influenced through rituals, metaphysical work, and the use of specific objects like herbs, roots, and charms.

Ancestors also hold a significant place in Hoodoo, as they are seen as spiritual guides and protectors. Practitioners may communicate with their ancestors through prayers, offerings, and rituals, seeking their wisdom and assistance in various aspects of life.

Hoodoo also places great emphasis on the power of intention and personal responsibility. Practitioners believe that through focused intent, they can manifest desired outcomes and influence their own destinies. Rituals that are performed with the intention of bringing about positive change, protection, healing, love, or success are exceedingly popular in Hoodoo. I will say this often in this book, but it is always important to remember that Hoodoo is not a religion but a spiritual practice that can be adapted and incorporated into different belief systems. Its flexibility and accessibility has allowed it to evolve and thrive, serving as a source of empowerment, healing, and cultural preservation for generations.

What is Africa's influence on Hoodoo?

African Traditional Religions (ATRs): Hoodoo draws heavily from the practices of various African ethnic groups. These practices often involve the use of herbs, roots, and other natural materials for spiritual purposes, such as healing, protection, and divination. In ATRs, the belief in the spiritual properties of plants and their ability to affect various aspects of life is deeply ingrained. This belief is also central to Hoodoo.

In Hoodoo, practitioners utilize a wide range of herbs, roots, and natural materials for various purposes, including healing, protection, love, and luck. Each herb and root possess specific spiritual properties and energies that can be harnessed. For example, the use of herbs like basil, rosemary, and lavender for purification and spiritual cleansing is a widespread practice in both ATRs and Hoodoo. The knowledge of specific herbs and roots and their spiritual properties has been passed down through generations in both ATRs and Hoodoo, demonstrating the continuity of these practices and their influence on one another.

Animism:

Animism is a core belief system that underlies many spiritual practices in Africa and has become a core belief in Hoodoo, animism refers to the belief that all things, including plants, animals, natural elements, and even inanimate objects, possess a spirit or essence. Many call it Ashay or Ashe, I have seen it spelled in so many ways.

In the context of Hoodoo, animism influences the way practitioners interact with and perceive the world around them. It recognizes the interconnectedness and interdependence of all living beings and the spiritual energy that flows through them. Animism in Hoodoo is deeply tied to the concept of sympathetic metaphysics, which is the idea that like attracts like. We as practitioners believe that by harnessing the spiritual energy present in various objects and beings, they can influence and manifest our desired outcomes.

For example, in Hoodoo, practitioners may believe that a specific plant or animal possesses certain qualities or energies that can be utilized in work or rituals. They might use the feathers of a specific bird, such as a crow or owl, for their protective or intuitive properties. Similarly, they might work with plants like rosemary or bay leaves for their purification or clarity properties. However, it is important to remember that animism in Hoodoo extends beyond just the physical elements. It acknowledges the presence of ancestral spirits and the importance of honoring and connecting with them. Ancestors are seen as powerful spiritual guides and protectors, and practitioners often seek their guidance and assistance in their workings.

Animism in Hoodoo also emphasizes the importance of reciprocity and respect for the spirits and energies involved. Practitioners understand that they must establish and maintain a harmonious relationship with the spiritual forces they work with. This includes offering gratitude, making offerings, and engaging in rituals and practices that honor and acknowledge the spirits.

Overall, animism plays a significant role in Hoodoo by recognizing and working with the spiritual essence present in all things. It guides practitioners to develop a deep reverence for the interconnectedness of the natural world and to harness its energies for personal and collective transformation.

Key Beliefs Surrounding Animism Within Hoodoo

Interconnectedness: Animism in Hoodoo acknowledges the interconnectedness of all living beings and the natural world. It emphasizes that everything is part of a larger web of spiritual energy, and that actions and energies have ripple effects throughout this interconnected system.

Spirits in Nature: Hoodoo practitioners believe that everything in nature, including plants, animals, crystals/stones, rivers, and even weather phenomena, has a spiritual essence or a spirit. These spirits can be communicated with, worked with, and influenced through rituals, offerings, and other forms of spiritual practice.

Sympathetic Metaphysics: Animism in Hoodoo is closely tied to the concept of sympathetic metaphysics, which is the belief that like attracts like. Practitioners believe that certain plants, animals, or objects possess specific qualities or energies that can be harnessed for metaphysical purposes. For example, using a rabbit's foot for luck or carrying a protective amulet made from specific herbs.

Ancestral Spirits: Hoodoo places a strong emphasis on ancestral veneration and communication. Practitioners believe that their ancestors continue to exist in the spirit world and can offer guidance, protection, and assistance in their daily lives. Ancestral spirits are seen as powerful allies and are honored through rituals, offerings, and the keeping of ancestral altars. They are an energy source that never dies.

Ancestor veneration is a fundamental aspect of many African spiritual traditions, and it is also a significant element in Hoodoo. Practitioners honor their ancestors through offerings, prayers, libations "pouring liquids for your dead homies" and rituals, seeking their guidance and protection. Ancestors are believed to have the power to influence the living and can provide wisdom, support, and blessings.

Reciprocity and Respect: Animism in Hoodoo emphasizes the importance of maintaining a harmonious relationship with the spirits and energies involved. Practitioners understand that they must show respect and gratitude to the spirits they work with, and that this reciprocal relationship is vital for successful metaphysical workings.

Personal Connection: Hoodoo practitioners believe in the power of personal connection and intuition. They are encouraged to develop their own relationships with the spirits and energies they work with, trusting their instincts and adapting practices to their unique needs and circumstances.

Other African Influences:

African Divination Systems: Various divination systems originating from Africa have been incorporated into Hoodoo. For example, the practice of reading bones, known as "throwing bones," is common in many African cultures and is also utilized in Hoodoo. Divination tools like cowrie shells are also used to gain insights and guidance from the spiritual realm.

Spirit Work: Hoodoo practitioners work closely with spirits and spiritual entities. This tradition finds its roots in African belief systems that acknowledge the existence of spirits and their influence on human lives. Spirits, such as ancestors, deities, and nature spirits, are communicated with, honored, and sometimes petitioned for assistance or guidance in Hoodoo rituals. In Hoodoo this is called conjure or conjuring.

Rituals and Ceremonies: Many African spiritual traditions involve elaborate rituals and ceremonies to connect with the divine and harness spiritual energy. Hoodoo incorporates various ritual practices very similar to those found in Africa such as "The Ring Shout" and water immersion.

What are the Native American influences in Hoodoo?

It is important to recognize that Native American spiritual practices and Hoodoo are distinct and separate traditions. However, it is true that Native American traditions have influenced certain aspects of Hoodoo, particularly because of cultural exchange and intermingling in the United States.

Herbal Knowledge: Native American cultures have a deep understanding of the medicinal and spiritual properties of various plants. This herbal knowledge, including the use of specific plants for healing, purification, and spiritual purposes, has been incorporated into Hoodoo practice. Some herbs and plants used in Native American traditions, such as sage or sweetgrass, have also become common in Hoodoo rituals and cleansing practices.

Sacred Spaces and Land Spirits: Native American spiritual traditions often emphasize the sacredness of the land and the presence of spirits in natural elements. This awareness of the spiritual significance of certain places and the reverence for land spirits have influenced Hoodoo practitioners who also recognize the power of specific locations, such as crossroads or graveyards, and work with spirits associated with those spaces.

Animal Symbolism and Totems: Native American traditions often incorporate animal symbolism and totems for guidance and spiritual connection. Hoodoo practitioners have also adopted some of these beliefs and practices, working with animal spirits and incorporating animal parts (such as feathers or bones) into rituals or charms for specific purposes.

Ritualistic Practices: While Hoodoo primarily draws from the African diaspora traditions, it is important to note that Native American rituals and ceremonial practices have also influenced certain aspects of Hoodoo.

For example, the use of smudging with sacred herbs, drumming, or chanting have been incorporated into Hoodoo rituals to create a sacred atmosphere and connect with the spiritual realm. It is important to note that drumming and chanting in Hoodoo is also a practice that originated in Africa. Both Native American and African styles have been incorporated into Hoodoo.

It is crucial to approach these influences with respect and cultural sensitivity, recognizing the distinct histories and practices of Native American traditions while acknowledging the intercultural exchanges that have shaped Hoodoo over time.

How did European Occultism influence Hoodoo?

I know this section may get me into trouble with a few of my fellow Hoodoo practitioners, but Europeans did influence the development of Hoodoo somewhat. However, I do want to emphasize that Hoodoo is still a closed practiced only opened to African descendants and Indigenous Americans.

Candle Work: European occult traditions, such as ceremonial metaphysics and spiritual metaphysical practices, have long utilized candles as a powerful tool for rituals and "work." This practice of using candles for specific intentions, such as love, protection, or prosperity, has been incorporated into Hoodoo. Hoodoo practitioners often work with colored candles, carving symbols or inscriptions on them, anointing them with oils or herbs, and burning them for specific purposes.

Symbolism and Sigils: European occult traditions have a rich history of using symbols and sigils to represent specific intentions or entities. This practice has influenced Hoodoo, where symbols and sigils are often used in rituals, workings, and charms. For instance, the use of the pentagram, crosses, or specific symbols associated with certain deities or spirits can be found in both European occultism and Hoodoo. It is important to also note that the use of some symbols in Hoodoo also came from African.

Ritual Tools and Implements: European occult traditions, such as ceremonial metaphysics, often utilize specific tools and implements for rituals and work. These may include wands, athames (ritual knives), chalices, or pentacles. Some of these tools have made their way into Hoodoo practices. It is important to also note that the use of tools such as large knives in Hoodoo also came from African.

Some Astrology and Planetary Influences: European occultism has a long-standing tradition of working with astrology and planetary influences to understand and harness specific energies. This influence can be seen in Hoodoo practices, where practitioners may consider astrological correspondences when timing rituals or working with specific herbs, roots, or oils. It is important to also note that astrological influences in Hoodoo also came from African.

What are the Christian influences of Hoodoo?

The Bible has had a considerable influence on Hoodoo, particularly through its incorporation of biblical verses, figures, and principles. However, the use of the bible is not a requirement to practice Hoodoo. In the vast world of social media, I have seen a lot of practitioners proclaim that if you don't use the bible in your practice, you are not practicing true Hoodoo.

However, those practitioners have forgotten one key piece of Hoodoo. Hoodoo is a spiritual practice not a religion. You will practice it based on where your spiritual journey and connection to a higher power leads you, but anyway...

Psalms and Verses: Hoodoo practitioners often utilize specific psalms or verses from the Bible for various purposes, such as protection, healing, love, or prosperity. These verses are recited, prayed, or written down and used in work, rituals, or as part of charms and amulets.

Saints and Angelic Beings: Hoodoo incorporates the veneration of saints and angelic beings from the Judeo-Christian tradition. Certain saints, such as Saint Michael or Saint Expedite, are commonly invoked for specific purposes like protection or fast results. Hoodoo practitioners may create altars or use candles and images associated with these saintly figures in their rituals and petitions. The uses of saints in Hoodoo started when enslaved Africans were forced to hide their true beliefs behind Christianity. So, they often disguised their Orisha (an African Spirit) veneration behind the veneration of Catholic saints.

Biblical Figures and Stories: Hoodoo draws inspiration from various biblical figures and stories. For example, the story of Moses and the parting of the Red Sea is often invoked for overcoming obstacles or creating a clear path forward. The story of Solomon's wisdom and wealth may be called upon for financial abundance or success. These biblical narratives are utilized as sources of inspiration and guidance in Hoodoo practice.

Spiritual Cleansing and Anointing: Hoodoo incorporates the practice of spiritual cleansing, baptism, and anointing, which can be traced back to biblical traditions. The use of holy water, anointing oils, or the act of washing with specific herbs or substances to remove negativity or invite blessings can be found in biblical rituals, ATRs, and Hoodoo practices.

It is important to note that the incorporation of biblical traditions in Hoodoo is not limited to a specific denomination or interpretation of the Bible. Different practitioners may draw from different biblical passages or figures based on their personal beliefs and spiritual connections.

Hoodoo

In days long past, a tale untold,
Of souls in chains, both brave and bold.
Enslaved, but not their spirits bound,
For hidden strength within was found.

Forced to convert, their faith oppressed,
But in their hearts, their beliefs undressed.
With the help of Indigenous lives,
They learn the secrets their new land hides.

Herbs, roots, and flowers they did employ,
To heal, protect, and bring them joy.
Behind the Bible's pages they would hide,
Their true religion, their sacred pride.

From this fusion, a new tradition was born,
Hoodoo they called it, a beacon to adorn.
A path of power, magick, and grace,
Their ancestors' legacy they embraced.

Through years of struggle, hope prevailed,
Their wisdom cherished, their spirits healed.
The journey of enslaved souls, so vast,
Hoodoo, the free, made history last.

–Rootworker Kye

CHAPTER 3
Being Called

I remember it like it was yesterday. It was a typical Sunday morning, and I was sitting in church, listening to the pastor deliver his sermon. The atmosphere was filled with a mix of anticipation and reverence. I had always found solace in the sacred space of the church, but little did I know that this particular day would be life changing.

As the pastor spoke, his voice resonated throughout the sanctuary. The words flowed passionately, and I could feel the energy in the room intensify. Suddenly, he transitioned into speaking in tongues, a language unfamiliar to many, yet deeply spiritual. It was as if a divine force had taken over him, guiding his words and movements. As he made his way down the aisle, his eyes met mine. I felt a jolt of electricity shoot through my body as his gaze lingered.

The congregation watched in awe as the pastor abruptly stopped in the middle of his sermon. A hush fell over the room, and all eyes were fixed on him. In that moment, I had no idea what was about to unfold. The pastor's voice, now calm and steady, resonated through the silence. He spoke directly to the congregation, his words directed at me. He proclaimed that I was gifted, spiritually gifted.

He spoke of a calling that would change lives, a path that I would embark on and fulfill a greater purpose. His words echoed in my mind, and a mix of emotions flooded my being. Confusion washed over me. How could I be spiritually gifted? I had never felt any extraordinary abilities or sensed anything out of the ordinary, at that time I had no idea that my dreams and visions of spirits were considered a gift.

Doubts crept in, questioning the validity of the pastor's proclamation. But deep down, a flicker of curiosity ignited within me. Could there be some truth to his words? Days turned into weeks, weeks into months, and months into years. The pastor's prophetic message lingered in my thoughts. I couldn't shake the feeling that there was something more to discover about myself, about my spiritual journey.

Moving from an adolescent to a young adult, and then to a full-grown adult, I began to explore different aspects of spirituality, seeking answers and guidance. With each step I took, my doubts began to dissipate. I encountered mentors, wise individuals who nurtured my newfound curiosity and helped me understand the depth of my spiritual potential. I have spoken to tarot readers, Christian prophets, and even psychics and all of them mirrored what my pastor spoke to me all those years ago.

Through meditation, prayer, and self-reflection, I slowly unveiled the layers of my being, uncovering hidden gifts and talents. As time passed, I realized that the pastor's message wasn't meant to burden me with expectations, but rather to ignite a fire within me. It was a reminder that I possessed the ability to make a positive difference in the lives of others. I embraced my spiritual journey with an open heart and a willingness to explore the unknown.

Now, years later, I can confidently say that I am following the path that was predicted for me. I have touched the lives of many, offering guidance, healing, and a listening ear. The benevolent spirit that the pastor sensed within me has become a guiding force, pushing me to serve others with compassion and love. Though doubts may still occasionally surface, I have come to trust in the unfolding of my spiritual journey.

Each day brings new lessons, new connections, and new opportunities to make a meaningful impact. I am grateful for the pastor's words that sparked the flame within me, for they have led me to discover my true purpose. And as I continue to walk this path, I am humbled by the power of spirituality and the profound impact it can have on our lives.

In the end, it is not the validation of others that defines our spiritual gifts, but rather our own belief in ourselves and our dedication to nurturing those gifts. I am grateful for the journey that lies ahead, knowing that I am guided by a force greater than myself, ready to embrace the lives that will be touched and transformed along the way.

My journey has not been without its challenges. There have been moments of doubt and uncertainty, times when I questioned my abilities and wondered if I was truly making a difference. But it is during those moments of darkness that I remember the pastor's words and the faith he had in me. I have witnessed firsthand the profound impact that spirituality can have on people's lives.

Through my gifts, I have been able to offer comfort to those in pain, guidance to those seeking direction, and healing to those in need. Each encounter serves as a reminder that I am walking the path I am meant to tread. But I am not alone on this journey. Along the way, I have met fellow spiritual seekers, individuals whose paths have intertwined with mine. We have formed a community, a network of support and understanding.

Together, we share experiences, exchange wisdom, and uplift one another in times of doubt. As I reflect on my spiritual journey, I am grateful for the pastor's recognition of my gifts. His words acted as a catalyst, propelling me forward on a path of self-discovery and service. But I have also come to realize that true spiritual growth is a continuous process of self-reflection, learning, and embracing the divine within.

Today, I stand before you, a testament to the power of spirituality and the transformative impact it can have on our lives. I am no longer burdened by doubts but fueled by the knowledge that I am fulfilling my purpose. And as I continue to walk this path, I hold onto the belief that each person encounter, each life I touch, is a testament to the incredible potential we all possess when we embrace our spiritual gifts.

So, let us embrace our unique abilities, our spiritual gifts, and let them guide us towards a life filled with purpose and meaning. For within each of us lies a benevolent spirit, waiting to be awakened and shared with the world.

What does it mean to be called into Hoodoo?

In Hoodoo, being called refers to a spiritual summons or a divine invitation to engage in the practice of Hoodoo. It is believed that certain individuals are chosen by spirits, ancestors, or deities to become practitioners of Hoodoo and serve as conduits for the belief system.

Being called in Hoodoo is often seen as a deeply personal and transformative experience. It can manifest through dreams, visions, signs, or a strong inner knowing. The individual who receives the call may feel a strong pull towards the practice, a sense of being guided or compelled to explore the spiritual world of Hoodoo.

Once called, individuals often undergo a period of initiation and/or mentorship, where they learn the rituals, traditions, and practices of Hoodoo from more experienced practitioners, ancestral memory, and/or self-discovery. This apprenticeship or self-apprenticeship helps them develop their skills, deepen their connection to spirit, and understand the responsibilities that come with their calling.

Being called in Hoodoo is not something that can be forced or chosen by an individual. It is believed to be a divine appointment, and it is up to the practitioner to accept and embrace their calling. This acceptance involves a willingness to align oneself with the spiritual forces at play, to learn and grow in their practice, and to use their gifts for the betterment of themselves and others.

Being called in Hoodoo is not limited to any specific characteristics, background, or social status. It can happen to anyone, regardless of age, gender, or religious background. The only exception is you must be a descendant of the motherland, Africa or in some cases Indigenous tribes who helped with the development of Hoodoo . This is a practice created by African Americans. The spirits and deities that call individuals to Hoodoo are believed to see beyond human societal factors and recognize the potential within each person in the African diaspora.

Once called, practitioners of Hoodoo are expected to approach their craft with respect, humility, and a deep sense of responsibility. They work with herbs, roots, candles, oils, and other tools to create workings, rituals, and charms that address various needs and desires. Their work is often focused on spiritual and physical healing, protection, love, prosperity, and spiritual growth.

Being called in Hoodoo is a lifelong commitment to the practice and the spiritual forces that guide it. It is a journey of self-discovery, personal growth, and service to others. Those who answer the call are entrusted with the task of bridging the gap between the physical and spiritual realms, bringing harmony and balance to themselves and into people's lives.

Ultimately, being called in Hoodoo is a sacred and profound experience. It is an invitation to embark on a path of spiritual exploration, power, and transformation. By embracing their calling, practitioners of Hoodoo can tap into the rich heritage, wisdom, and metaphysics of this unique African American tradition and practice.

How do I know that I am being called to Hoodoo?

Strong Intuition: You have a natural ability to sense and understand energies and have a deep intuition that guides you in your daily life.

Ancestral Connections: You feel a strong connection to your ancestors and have a desire to honor and work with them in your spiritual practice. They often speak to you and appear to you even in the physical world.

Dreams and Visions: You frequently have vivid dreams or visions that provide guidance, insights, or messages related to Hoodoo or spiritual practices. Most have spirits or deities visit them in the dream world.

Attraction to Nature: You feel a deep connection and reverence for nature, finding solace and inspiration in its beauty. You may find yourself feeling the emotions of plants and animals, or hearing messages from them.

Synchronicities: You notice meaningful coincidences or synchronicities that seem to be guiding you towards the practice of Hoodoo. Examples include numerology, astrology, and symbolisms.

Sensitivity to Energies: You are highly sensitive to the energies around you, whether it's feeling a shift in the atmosphere or sensing the presence of spirits.

Curiosity and Study: You have a fervent desire to learn about African American Spirituality, rootwork, and Hoodoo traditions, and find yourself drawn to books, websites, and resources on the subject.

Healing Abilities: You have a natural inclination and ability to offer healing and support to others, whether it's through energy work, herbal remedies, or spiritual guidance. You have knowledge on how to heal others but don't know where the knowledge comes from. It is a natural ability.

Trust your intuition and listen to your inner voice to determine if Hoodoo is right for you. It's important to study, learn, and seek guidance from experienced practitioners to deepen your understanding and practice.

Ida "Seven Sisters" Carter

I can't do a chapter on being called without telling the story or Ida Carter, who was called to practice Hoodoo at the age of seven and performed a lengthy self-initiation on herself. Ida "Seven Sisters" Carter was a woman of mystery and mystique, hailing from the small town of Hogansville, Alabama. Born in the 1900s, little is known about her life or the circumstances that led her to become a renowned rootworker.

There are no photographs of her, leaving her appearance solely to the imagination of those who share her story. Ida had an insatiable curiosity for the supernatural and the unseen. She was particularly fascinated by the "Seven Sisters of New Orleans," a group of Hoodoo/Voodoo practitioners known for their clairvoyant abilities and eternal youth. These sisters possessed an uncanny resemblance to one another, defying the bounds of age and time. It was said that they could peer into a person's soul with a single glance, unraveling their deepest thoughts and desires.

Inspired by the legends of the Seven Sisters, Ida bestowed upon herself the name "Seven Sisters." Some believe that she discovered the secret to their perpetual youth through her mastery of rootwork and herbal metaphysics. Her talents in healing and metaphysical practices were undeniable, capturing the attention and admiration of those around her. Ida often shared that her calling to rootwork came at the tender age of seven. In a rare interview, she revealed her self-initiation ritual, a profound journey of dedication and spiritual growth. Starting on May 1st, she would light seven candles and pray fervently throughout the night. She repeated this ritual for six consecutive nights each May, year after year. The significance of the number seven held immense importance in Ida's life. It was a symbol of completeness and divine intervention.

For seven long years, she faithfully performed her ritual, seeking guidance and enlightenment. Then, one fateful night, as the last candle flickered in the darkness, Ida received a divine message. The Holy Spirit whispered to her soul, affirming that she was now fully prepared to serve her community as a spiritual practitioner.

News of Ida's remarkable abilities spread like wildfire. People traveled from far and wide to seek her counsel and experience the transformative power of her rootwork. She became a beacon of hope, a guiding light in the lives of those who sought her assistance. Ida "Seven Sisters" Carter remained an enigma, shrouded in the mysticism of her craft. Her legacy lives on through the countless lives she touched and the spiritual knowledge she passed down. Though her physical presence may be lost in time, the spirit of her teachings continues to inspire and empower those who follow in her footsteps.

Rootworker Kye's Self-Initiation Ritual

Here is a suggested self-initiation ritual for those who feel called to practice Hoodoo:

Preparation

1. Find a quiet and sacred space where you can perform the ritual undisturbed.
2. Gather the following items:
- A white candle to represent purity and spiritual enlightenment.
- A small bowl of water to symbolize cleansing and purification.
- A selection of herbs or roots that resonate with you and your intentions, such as basil, rosemary, or sage.
- A piece of paper and a pen to write down your intentions and desires.
- Anointing or Blessing Oil

Setting the Space

1. Take a moment to ground yourself and center your energy.
2. Close your eyes, take a few deep breaths, and imagine any stress or distractions melting away.
3. Light the white candle and place it in the center of your sacred space.
4. Take the small bowl of water, add your oil or oils to it and dip your fingertips into it.
5. Gently touch your forehead, heart, and both shoulders, envisioning any negative energies being washed away.

Invocation

1. Stand before the lit candle, with your hands open and palms facing upward.
2. Speak aloud or silently call upon the spirits and deities that resonate with your Hoodoo practice. You can invoke God, the divine, ancestors, guides, or specific divine entities that you feel connected to. Ask for their presence, guidance, and blessings during this initiation ritual.

Statement of Intent

1. Take the piece of paper and pen and write down your intentions and desires for your Hoodoo practice. Be specific and heartfelt in your words.
2. Express your commitment to learning, growing, and serving yourself and others through your work.
3. Once you have written your intentions, hold the paper close to your heart and visualize the energy of your intentions merging with your being.

Connection to Higher Self and Ancestors

1. Close your eyes and take a few deep breaths, allowing yourself to enter a meditative state.
2. Visualize a bright light descending from above, enveloping you in its warm and loving energy.
3. As you connect with this light, imagine yourself being surrounded by your ancestors, those who came before you and who guide and support you on your spiritual journey.
4. Feel their presence and their love, knowing that they are with you, offering their wisdom and protection.

Blessing and Empowerment

1. Hold the herbs or roots in your hands, feeling their energy and power.
2. Speak aloud or silently recite a prayer or affirmation that reflects your intention to be blessed and empowered in your Hoodoo practice.
3. Pass the herbs or roots through the flame of the white candle to purify and infuse them with the energy of the fire.

Anointing and Sealing

1. Take a small amount of the blessed herbs or roots and rub them between your palms to release their scent and energy.
2. Gently anoint your forehead, heart, and both shoulders with the herbal mixture, envisioning a protective and empowering seal being placed upon you.

Gratitude and Closing:

1. Take a moment to express gratitude to the spirits, deities, ancestors, and energies that have been present with you during this ritual.
2. Snuff out the white candle, symbolizing the completion of the ritual.
3. Continue this same process daily until you feel it is complete. If your candle starts to run out before you feel complete use the remaining wick of the candle and light another white candle with it to create a continuation of the same ritual.

Remember, this is just a suggested ritual, and you can modify it to fit your own personal beliefs and practices. Hoodoo does not require any formal initiation to practice if you are of African or Indigenous descent. Trust your intuition and follow your heart as you embark on your Hoodoo journey. Remember Hoodoo is a spiritual practice and not a religion.

Called

In meditation's serene embrace,
I ventured to a sacred place.
A forest, fragrant with ancient air,
Frankincense and myrrh filled the lair.

Amidst the trees, a river flowed,
Its gentle whispers, secrets it bestowed.
Aja, of the forest, stood in her grace,
She who beckoned me, to this mystical place.

Medusa, she called, with voice profound,
An invitation to the magick I found.
In the depths of Hoodoo's sacred lore,
My path was set, forevermore.

With herbs and roots, I'll weave my way,
Guided by spirits, night and day.
Channeling energies, both old and new,
Bringing light, healing, and breakthrough.

Embracing gifts bestowed upon me,
Through Hoodoo's rhythm, I'll dance with glee.
A practitioner, in harmony and flow,
Rooted in tradition, it's here I'll grow.

-Rootworker Kye

CHAPTER 4

Honor Your Ancestors

One day, I found myself on a long drive from Florida to Arkansas, alone and eager to reunite with my family. I had moved from Arkansas to Florida seven years prior and had made it a habit to visit as much as possible. At that time no one knew I had started my spiritual journey, except for my best friend. So, my family and I were on good terms.

This trip back was bittersweet because I was traveling alone, but I was on my way to see my family, so I sucked it up. I had left my children behind in Florida, because they still had schooling, and my best friend had to work but agreed to keep the children while I went on my visit.

Being alone on a fourteen-hour drive can weigh on you and as the hours passed and the road seemed to stretch endlessly before me, exhaustion began to consume my senses. My eyelids grew heavy, and I could feel myself drifting into a deep slumber, dangerously close to losing consciousness at the wheel. I know I should have pulled over, but I was only three more hours from my destination and didn't want to prolong my journey. Before I knew it, I was asleep.

Suddenly, amidst the haze of drowsiness, a deafening boom shattered the silence of the car. It jolted me awake, adrenaline coursing through my veins. Confused and disoriented, I strained to understand what had just happened. And then I began to drift off again, thinking I was hallucinating.

Another boom rocked my senses, and then I heard it. A chorus of voices, urgent and commanding, screamed at me to wake up. Startled, I glanced around, searching for the source of the sound. That's when I directed my gaze towards the heavens above. To my astonishment, there, in the billowing clouds, I beheld a gathering of faces. Ten, twenty, maybe more, all peering down at me with unwavering gazes.

I blinked, rubbed my eyes, and even rolled them in disbelief, but the faces remained, unwavering and hauntingly real. Fear gripped me, as if I had stumbled upon a forbidden realm. It was a sight beyond any rational explanation, beyond the realm of ordinary human experience. My mind raced, questioning whether tiredness had conjured up this surreal vision. But deep down, I knew that something extraordinary was unfolding before me.

With a heart pounding in my chest, I resolved to stay awake for the remainder of the journey. I dared not close my eyes, for I believed that those faces in the sky were none other than my ancestors, revealing themselves to me in a profound and undeniable way.

In that moment, I felt their presence, their love, and their protection enveloping me. They had intervened, saving me from a potentially fatal accident. It was as if they had reached out from the spirit world, reminding me of their eternal bond and guiding me safely to my destination.

From that day forward, my belief in the power of Hoodoo and ancestral spirits grew stronger. I understood that I was part of a sacred lineage, connected to generations who had come before me. My journey that day was not just a physical one; it was a spiritual awakening, a testament.

Misconceptions of Ancestral Veneration

Ancestral veneration is a vital aspect of Hoodoo practice, often misunderstood by those outside the tradition. I want to address the misconception that practitioners of Hoodoo worship their ancestors, and instead highlight the true nature of ancestral veneration as a means of honoring and acknowledging the contributions and influence of our ancestors on our lives.

Ancestral veneration in Hoodoo is not about worshiping ancestors as deities, but rather about showing deep respect and gratitude for their guidance, wisdom, and the legacy they have left behind. It is an integral part of recognizing and honoring the interconnectedness between past, present, and future generations. Hoodoo practitioners acknowledge their ancestors for the role they play in shaping their identity, spirituality, and cultural heritage.

Through ancestral veneration, practitioners express gratitude for the sacrifices, wisdom, and experiences passed down through generations, which have contributed to their personal growth and well-being. In Hoodoo, ancestors are seen as spiritual allies who can offer guidance, protection, and support. While not worshiped, they are respected and called upon for assistance in various aspects of life, such as overcoming challenges, seeking wisdom, or gaining ancestral blessings. This acknowledgment is rooted in a belief in the continued presence and influence of ancestors in our lives.

Understanding ancestral veneration in Hoodoo requires recognizing its cultural context. Enslaved Africans brought their own traditions of ancestor reverence, which were integrated with Native American influences over time. This syncretism formed the foundation of ancestral veneration in Hoodoo, emphasizing the importance of lineage, heritage, and cultural identity. We as Hoodoo practitioners employ various rituals and practices to honor our ancestors. These may include creating ancestral altars, offering food or drink, lighting candles, reciting prayers, or conducting ceremonies on significant dates or occasions. Such acts serve as expressions of gratitude, love, and remembrance, strengthening the bond between the living and the ancestral realm.

It is crucial to debunk the misconception that Hoodoo practitioners worship their ancestors. By clarifying the intent behind ancestral veneration, we can emphasize that the practice is rooted in a deep appreciation for our ancestors' contributions, rather than the worship of divine beings. This understanding helps foster respect and dispel misconceptions surrounding ancestral veneration in Hoodoo specifically.

We can work together to promote a better understanding of the profound respect and admiration that underlies this vital aspect of the tradition. Through ancestral veneration, we continue to carry the legacy of our ancestors, recognizing their contributions and the profound impact they have on who we are today.

Ancestral Altar for Veneration

Building an ancestral altar in Hoodoo is a powerful way to honor and connect with our ancestors, seeking guidance, protection, and wisdom from those who came before us. While the specific tools used may vary depending on personal beliefs and practices, there are key elements commonly found on an ancestral altar in Hoodoo.

First and foremost, choose a dedicated space for your ancestral altar, preferably in a quiet and peaceful area of your home. It can be a table, shelf, or any surface that allows you to create a sacred space for your ancestors. Cover the surface with a clean, white cloth, symbolizing purity and providing a respectful space for spiritual connection. You can also use cloths of various other colors depending on what your ancestors call you to do.

Photos or portraits of your ancestors are essential items for an ancestral altar. Display pictures of your deceased loved ones, family members, and ancestors who have passed on. These visual representations create a focal point for connection and remembrance. It's a way to honor their memory and invite their presence into your sacred space. If you don't have photos, you can write their names on parchment paper and place them on your altar. If you don't know who your ancestors are you can just light a white candle and invite in all the ancestors who mean you well. (Not all ancestors are what we would consider good in this society, please use discernment.)

Candles hold significant importance in Hoodoo ancestral altar practices. Lighting candles helps to create a sacred atmosphere and symbolizes the illumination of spiritual energy. Traditionally, white or black candles are used on an ancestral altar. White represents purity, clarity, and connection to the divine, while black represents ancestral wisdom and protection.

Offerings are another crucial component of an ancestral altar in Hoodoo. These can include items that your ancestors enjoyed during their lifetime, such as their favorite foods, drinks, or tobacco. Offerings can also include flowers, incense, or any other items that hold significance to your family or cultural traditions. These offerings are a way to show respect, gratitude, and invite the presence of your ancestors.

Ancestor spirits are believed to appreciate and respond to the smell of incense. Choose fragrances that are pleasing to you and resonate with your ancestral lineage. Some popular choices include frankincense, myrrh, cedar, pine, sandalwood, or sage. Burning incense during your ancestral altar rituals helps create a sacred ambiance and enhances spiritual connection.

Divination tools like tarot cards, oracle cards, or a pendulum can also be included on an ancestral altar in Hoodoo. These tools can be used to seek guidance, wisdom, and messages from your ancestors. They serve as a way to communicate and receive insight from the spiritual realm.

Having water on an ancestor altar in Hoodoo holds significant symbolism and serves multiple purposes. Water is considered a powerful element in many spiritual practices and is believed to have the ability to carry messages, purify, and facilitate communication with the spirit realm.

Purification: Water is often used for cleansing and purifying purposes. It has the ability to wash away negative energies and purify the space, creating a clear and sacred environment for connecting with ancestors. Placing water on the altar symbolizes the cleansing and purifying of the ancestral connection, ensuring a clean and open channel of communication.

Spiritual Hydration: Water is a symbol of life and nourishment. It represents the flow of energy and the sustenance needed for spiritual growth and connection. By placing water on the ancestral altar, it is believed to provide spiritual hydration and nourishment to the ancestral spirits, ensuring their continued presence and support.

Offering and Communication: Water is considered a universal offering and a means of communication between the physical and spiritual realms. It is believed that spirits can draw energy from the water and receive messages or offerings placed in it. By placing water on the altar, it is seen as an invitation for the ancestors to come forth, receive offerings, and communicate with the living.

Symbol of Ancestral Connection: In Hoodoo, water is believed to be a conduit for ancestral energy and a symbol of the ancestral connection. It represents the ancestral lineage that flows through our blood and connects us to our roots. By having water on the ancestral altar, it serves as a reminder of this deep connection and honors the ancestral presence in our lives.

When incorporating water on an ancestral altar in Hoodoo, it is essential to keep the water clean and refreshed regularly. Some practitioners prefer to use natural spring water or rainwater, while others may choose to add specific herbs or oils to infuse the water with specific intentions or energies. The water should be treated with reverence and respect, and any offerings or messages placed in it should be done so with sincerity and gratitude.

Overall, having water on an ancestral altar in Hoodoo symbolizes purification, nourishment, communication, and the ancestral connection. It serves as a potent tool in facilitating the relationship between the living and the ancestral spirits, fostering a deeper and more meaningful connection with our lineage.

Finally, it is essential to maintain and care for your ancestral altar regularly. Keep the space clean, dusted, and refreshed. Offer fresh water, prayers, and intentions regularly. Pay attention to any signs or messages you may receive from your ancestors during your altar rituals and be open to their guidance and presence.

It is worth noting that the tools and items used on an ancestral altar in Hoodoo are deeply personal and can vary based on individual beliefs, cultural background, and personal connection to ancestors. Hoodoo is a spiritual practice not a religion, so do what is best for you!

The most important aspect is the intention behind the altar and the genuine respect and love you hold for your ancestors. Building and tending to an ancestral altar in Hoodoo is a sacred practice that allows for a profound connection with our lineage and heritage. It serves as a reminder of our roots, a source of wisdom, and a conduit for ancestral blessings. Through the use of these tools and items, we create a space that honors our ancestors and invites their spiritual presence into our lives, fostering a deep and meaningful connection across generations.

How do I know if I am being contacted by an ancestor?

Dreams: You may have vivid dreams where you see or interact with a specific person or receive messages from them. Pay attention to any recurring dreams or symbols that may indicate the presence of a new ancestor.

Synchronicities: You may notice repeated patterns or coincidences in your daily life that seem to be connected to a particular ancestor. This could include seeing their name or birthdate repeatedly, encountering objects or symbols associated with them, or hearing their favorite songs or phrases unexpectedly.

Intuitive Guidance: You may experience a strong intuitive sense or gut feeling that a new ancestor is trying to connect with you. Trust your instincts and pay attention to any sudden urges or thoughts that lead you towards exploring your ancestry or connecting with specific family members.

Signs in Nature: Look for signs in nature that may be associated with the presence of an ancestor. This could include seeing certain animals or birds that are traditionally associated with ancestral spirits, such as crows, owls, or butterflies. Pay attention to any unusual behavior or encounters with these creatures.

Symbolic Messages: Ancestors may try to communicate with you through symbolic messages. This could be through finding meaningful objects or symbols in unexpected places, such as feathers, coins, or specific colors or patterns that are significant to them.

Mediumship Abilities: If you have mediumship abilities, you may receive direct communication from the new ancestor through clairvoyance, clairaudience, or clairsentience. This could involve hearing their voice, seeing their image, or feeling their presence.

Ancestral Altar Activity: If you have an ancestral altar, pay attention to any unusual activity or changes in energy around it. Candles may burn differently, objects may move, or you may sense a heightened presence when you approach the altar.

Remember, these signs are subjective and personal to each individual. It's important to trust your intuition and listen to your inner guidance when interpreting these signs. If you feel a strong connection to a new ancestor, it is advisable to honor and acknowledge them through rituals, offerings, and prayers to deepen your bond and receive their guidance and blessings.

Connecting with a Specific Ancestor

Connecting with a specific ancestor through a ritual in Hoodoo can be a deeply personal and meaningful experience. Here is a suggested ritual that you can adapt and customize to suit your own beliefs and practices:

Preparation:

1. Find a quiet and undisturbed space where you can set up your ancestral altar or create a designated area for the ritual.
2. Gather the tools and items you associate with your ancestor, such as their photo, personal belongings, favorite items, or objects that remind you of them.
3. Light a candle on your ancestral altar to create a sacred ambiance and to honor the presence of your ancestor. Most use white, but if you know your ancestor's favorite color you can light a candle that is that corresponding color.

Invocation:

1. Take a moment to ground yourself and center your energy. Close your eyes, take a few deep breaths, and visualize a connection with your ancestor.
2. Speak aloud or silently in your mind, calling upon the name of the specific ancestor you wish to connect with.
3. Address them respectfully, acknowledging their presence and expressing your intention to connect with them.

Offerings and Communication:

1. Place offerings on your ancestral altar that are meaningful to your specific ancestor. This can include their favorite food, drink, or any items they cherished in life.
2. Light incense or herbs known for their spiritual properties, such as lavender or rosemary, to create a fragrant and sacred atmosphere.
3. Take a moment to share your thoughts, feelings, and memories with your ancestor.
4. Speak to them as if they were physically present, expressing gratitude, love, and any messages you wish to convey.
5. Listen for any signs, messages, or feelings that may come to you during this communication.
6. Be open and receptive to their presence and guidance.

Meditation and Connection:

1. Close your eyes and enter into a meditative state.
2. Visualize a golden thread connecting you and your ancestor, symbolizing the bond between you.
3. Allow yourself to feel their presence and imagine a space where you can meet and interact. This could be a garden, a familiar place, or any setting that feels comfortable and resonates with you.
4. Engage in a conversation or simply sit in their presence, soaking in their energy and wisdom.
5. Be open to any insights, guidance, or messages that may come through.
6.

Closing the Ritual:

1. Express your gratitude and appreciation to your ancestors for their presence and the connection you have shared.
2. Snuff out the candle, symbolizing the end of the ritual and the closing of the sacred space.
3. Reflect on your experience and journal any insights, emotions, or messages that came through during the ritual.
4. Take note of any guidance or wisdom you received.

Follow-up Actions:

After the ritual, consider incorporating practices that honor and remember your ancestor on a regular basis. This can include lighting a candle for them, saying prayers, or dedicating a specific time each day or week to connect with them.

You may also want to continue the conversation with your ancestor through meditation, dreams, or automatic writing. Pay attention to any signs or synchronicities that may occur in your daily life, as they may be messages from your ancestor.

Lastly, continue to cultivate a relationship with your ancestor by learning about their life, their history, and their experiences. This can deepen your understanding and connection with them.

Remember, rituals are personal and can be adapted to suit your own beliefs and preferences. Trust your intuition and follow what resonates with you as you connect with your specific ancestor.

Common Ancestor Offerings

Food and Drink Offerings:
+ Fresh fruits or vegetables
+ Water or favorite beverages
+ Cooked or prepared meals that the ancestor enjoyed in life.
+ Coffee, tea, or alcoholic beverages that they favored.
+ Traditional dishes from their cultural background

Personal Items:
+ Photos of the ancestor
+ Jewelry or accessories they wore.
+ Clothing items or fabric swatches
+ Personal belongings, such as a favorite book or a musical instrument they played. Items that represented their hobbies or interests (e.g., art supplies, knitting needles)

Incense and Smoke Offerings:
+ Sandalwood
+ Frankincense
+ Myrrh
+ Copal
+ Sage

Candles:
+ White candles (symbolizing purity and spiritual connection)
+ Colored candles associated with the ancestor's preferences or cultural traditions.
+ Ancestor-specific candles (available in some spiritual or occult stores)

Flowers and Plants:
+ Roses
+ Marigolds
+ Carnations
+ Daisies
+ Lavender

Offerings of Light:
+ Oil lamps or lanterns
+ Battery-operated candles or LED lights for safety reasons

Symbolic Offerings:
+ Coins or money as a symbol of abundance and prosperity
+ Tobacco or cigars, particularly if the ancestor enjoyed smoking.
+ Perfume or cologne that they liked to wear.
+ Crystals or gemstones associated with ancestral connections, such as amethyst, obsidian, or clear quartz.
+ Artwork or crafts created in their honor or that reflect their interests.

Remember, the most important aspect of offering is the intention behind it. Choose items that hold significance to your specific ancestor and their preferences. It's also a promising idea to research any cultural or traditional practices related to ancestor veneration in your specific lineage or spiritual path, as they may have specific offerings that are considered appropriate or meaningful.

My Very First Altar

I remember the day I created my first altar vividly, even though at the time, I didn't even know that's what I was doing. So often, we follow our instincts and engage in rituals without fully understanding their significance, only to discover later that they are rooted in the traditions of our ancestors. It's as if ancestral memory is a part of us, guiding our actions subconsciously.

It all started when I felt the urge to create a sacred space in my room, a place where I could connect with something greater than myself. I didn't have a name for it, so I simply called it my prayer corner. I gathered some candles, feeling drawn to their flickering flames and the sense of warmth and peace they brought. I also bought a beautiful jewelry tree to hang all my crystal necklaces, intuitively knowing that they held some sort of power and significance.

As I arranged these items in the corner of my room, I didn't realize that I was creating an altar. It was a space where I could retreat, where I could offer my prayers and seek solace. Little did I know that my actions were deeply rooted in the ancestral practices of Hoodoo, connecting me to a lineage of wisdom and spirituality.

However, my newfound sanctuary didn't go unnoticed. One day, my ex-boyfriend confessed to his pastor about my prayer corner. Their conversation quickly turned judgmental and filled with fear. They labeled it as evil, associating it with devil worship. Out of respect for my ex-boyfriend and his beliefs, I agreed to speak with his pastor. That meeting with the pastor was a turning point. He instilled in me an overwhelming sense of fear and guilt.

The pastor's words made me question everything I had created and cherished. Filled with doubt, I felt compelled to rid myself of all the symbols of my sacred space. I discarded my crystals, extinguished the candles, and let go of everything I had bought for my perfect prayer corner. After I threw away all my things, the relationship began to become very toxic, and I ended up leaving him, and soon after I found out that he was telling multiple people in his family and a bunch of his friends that I was a demon worshipper. And that's when the seeds of the rumors began. And this came at a time before I even knew what Hoodoo was. I never even heard of it, and I didn't know what an altar was. I just felt like I needed a prayer corner and I wanted somewhere to put all of my spiritual items and tools.

As the rumors and misconceptions about my spiritual practices spread, I became determined to educate myself and reclaim my truth. It was during this search for answers that I stumbled upon Hoodoo. The more I learned about its rich history and its connection to African American spirituality, the more I realized that it resonated with my own experiences and beliefs. Hoodoo was not about demon worship or any form of dark magic, as the rumors suggested. It was a deeply rooted tradition that honored the wisdom of our ancestors and sought to harness the power of nature and spirit for healing and guidance.

With this newfound knowledge, I began to rebuild my spiritual practice and create my own sacred space again. I discovered the concept of an altar, a designated place to honor my ancestors, seek guidance, and connect with the divine. It was not about worshiping demons, but about cultivating a deep and personal relationship with the spirits and energies that resonated with me.

As I embraced Hoodoo and nurtured my spiritual path, I realized that the rumors and judgments stemmed from ignorance and fear. I refused to let these misconceptions define me or dictate how I expressed my spirituality. Instead, I chose to educate others about the true essence of Hoodoo, to share my story and shed light on the beauty and power it held for me. Through my journey I want to help you.

Looking back, I see now how Christianity, in some instances, can breed fear and discourage questioning. It can make us fear what we don't fully understand, stifling our connection to ancestral knowledge and our own intuition.

I rebuilt my altar. I adorned it with crystals, candles, and other sacred objects that resonated with me. Each item held meaning, a connection to my ancestors and the spiritual forces that guided me. No longer would I allow fear and judgment to dictate my spiritual path. I realized that my prayer corner, my altar, was a sacred space for me to honor my ancestors, seek guidance, and connect with the divine. It was a symbol of my resilience, my commitment to embracing and celebrating my heritage.

I want to encourage others to embrace their own ancestral traditions, to question and challenge societal norms that seek to suppress our spiritual autonomy. This book, my book, is a testament to the power of embracing Hoodoo, of reclaiming our ancestral wisdom, and honoring the traditions that live within us. It is a celebration of the resilience and strength that comes from reconnecting with our roots and finding our own spiritual path.

Today, I stand proud as a practitioner of Hoodoo, no longer swayed by the rumors and judgments of others. I have found solace and empowerment in my beliefs, and I continue to seek knowledge, teach, and to learn. My journey is a testament to the power of resilience, self-discovery, and the ability to rise above the misconceptions that surround us. Together, we can reclaim our heritage, embrace our spiritual autonomy, and foster a deep sense of connection with our ancestors and the divine.

CHAPTER 5
Conjure in Hoodoo

As a child I have always spoken with spirits, but when you grow up in church that is just something you don't tell others. I did tell a few of my family members about my dreams and the appearance of what I thought were ghosts at that time, but I honestly don't think they believed me. Back in those days, I had been labeled a liar and a great storyteller, much like many gifted children, I was often misunderstood.

But one night when I was much older one event made a few of my family members look at me much differently. I remember that night vividly, the night my brother died. That type of trauma I could never forget. It was a whirlwind of emotions and confusion, a night that still haunts me to this day.

After my mother, stepdad, and I left the hospital with the news that my brother did not survive the car crash, we sought solace at my aunt's house, accompanied by a few of our cousins. The weight of grief hung heavy in the air, suffocating us all. But as the night wore on, something strange began to happen. I felt an overwhelming sense of exhaustion and disorientation. It was as if my mind and body were being pulled in different directions. Like my soul was being pulled out of my body.

The next thing I knew, I had blacked out, and my memory of that moment became a void. According to my family members, during that blackout, I stopped talking and walked to the back of the house. They watched in alarm as I returned, my voice trembling as I approached my mother. With an eerie calmness, I told her that I had spoken to Nelson, my departed brother. He assured me that everything was okay, and we didn't need to worry about him. The other side is nothing like we think it is.

I have no recollection of this conversation, but the fear etched on the faces of my loved ones spoke volumes. It was the first time I had ever seen them look at me like that. It became clear to me that my family, mostly devout Christians, viewed my ability to communicate with spirits as something sinister or evil. I still remember the looks on their faces today.

Because of that I never told anyone that Nelson appeared to me again the very next day in my bedroom. I was making up my bed and there were tears streaming down my face. I suddenly had the most eerie feeling that someone was watching me. I immediately stopped what I was doing and instinctively turned my head toward my door. Nelson was standing there clear as day with a smile on his face. I was terrified at first, then a calm came over me and he slowly faded away, the smile never leaving his face. It was his last effort to assure me that the afterlife is not what we think it is. I knew this even though he never uttered a word to me that day. He appeared to me a few more times throughout my life, but I will save those stories for another book.

I wanted to tell my family about him appearing to me again, but I just kept remembering their faces from the night before, and I couldn't bring myself to tell them.

A few months later I was talking to one of my cousins about the incident and discovered that my older cousin, who I will call Linda, had left immediately, terrified by my presence that night.

Years later, sadly Linda passed away unexpectedly. About two years after her passing, she appeared to me in a dream. She apologized for her fear and avoidance, and she requested a favor. She asked me to check on her daughter, as she had left this world with unresolved concerns for her well-being, and the well-being of her grandkids. She also asked me to place her on my altar even though we weren't remarkably close when she was alive.

The dream left me shaken, filled with trepidation about reaching out to Linda's daughter. Despite my fears of being judged, I mustered up the courage to contact her through Facebook. I explained that her mother had reached out to me from beyond, wanting me to ensure her welfare.

To my surprise, instead of judging me, she expressed gratitude. It turned out that she was going through a challenging time, and my message came as a timely source of comfort and support. In that moment, I realized the power of reaching out and being open to messages from the spiritual realm. While many in my family may still harbor doubts and misconceptions, my cousin's response reminded me that there are those who can understand and appreciate the depth of our experiences, even if they differ from their own beliefs.

As time went on, my fear of being ostracized by my family began to diminish. I realized that my ability to communicate with spirits was not a curse but a gift, one that I could use to bring comfort and healing to others. I became more open about my experiences, finding solace in the connections I formed with people who embraced and celebrated my spiritual journey.

The night my brother passed away, filled with surreal moments and unexplainable encounters, left an indelible mark on my life. It taught me the importance of embracing the unknown and trusting in the unseen forces that guide us. It showed me that even in the face of fear and misunderstanding, there are those who will listen, understand, and appreciate the unique path we walk.

Today, as I continue to navigate the complexities of my spiritual journey, I hold on to the memory of that fateful night as a reminder of the power of connection and the strength that can be found in embracing our true selves. I have become a source of support and guidance for those who seek solace and understanding. Through workshops, private sessions, and online platforms, I have been able to reach people from all walks of life, offering them a safe space to explore their own spiritual journeys.

As I look back on my journey, I am grateful for the experiences, both joyous and challenging, that have shaped me into the person I am today. I continue to embrace the unknown, trusting in the guidance of the spirits that surround me. And while there may still be skeptics and doubters along the way, I remain steadfast in my belief that there is a greater purpose to our existence and that love and connection transcend the boundaries of life and death. And so, I carry on, sharing my gifts, spreading light and hope, and always remembering another night that changed everything.

What is Conjure?

The term "conjure" has multiple meanings depending on the context. In general, "conjure" refers to the act of invoking, summoning, or calling upon supernatural forces, energies, or entities for various purposes. It can also refer to the practice of performing rituals, metaphysical works, or workings.

In the context of Hoodoo, "conjure" is used as a noun to describe a system of spiritual practices that originated within the African American community. It involves the use of herbs, roots, minerals, candles, and other objects, as well as spiritual practices, to create changes in one's life or influence specific situations. The term "conjure" can also be used as a verb, meaning to perform acts of metaphysical workings. For example, one might say, "She conjured a protection working to ward off negative energy." Overall, "conjure" refers to the act of harnessing and working with supernatural or spiritual forces to achieve desired outcomes or to connect with the spiritual realm.

It is often used interchangeably with terms like "rootwork" or "working the roots." The history of Conjure in Hoodoo can be traced back to the African diaspora, where African traditions merged with Native American and European spiritual practices in the United States. Enslaved Africans brought their spiritual beliefs and metaphysical practices, adapting them to their new environment and circumstances. Over time, this syncretism resulted in the development of Hoodoo, which incorporated elements from multiple spiritual practices.

In Hoodoo, the practice of working with spirits and invoking deities is not the main focal point of the practice as it is in other spiritual traditions such as Voodoo or Santeria. Hoodoo equally mixes spirit work with metaphysical workings, herbal remedies, and practical "metaphysical work." While spirit work is incorporated into the Hoodoo practice, it is not a defining characteristic of the tradition. That being said, some practitioners of Hoodoo choose to work with spirits or invoke deities in their practice, and some do not.

Spirit work can involve establishing relationships with ancestral spirits, seeking guidance from spirit allies, or invoking specific deities from various pantheons. However, the extent and nature of spirit work in Hoodoo can vary greatly between practitioners.

A Conjurer in Hoodoo refers to a practitioner who has developed skills and knowledge in the art of Hoodoo. They may possess a deep understanding of herbs, roots, and metaphysical correspondences, as well as the ability to perform rituals with or without the use of spirits.

Conjurers often serve as spiritual advisors, offering guidance and assistance to individuals seeking help with various aspects of their lives. They may provide remedies, create personalized workings, or offer spiritual consultations to address specific problems or goals. However, the exact role of a Conjurer in spirit work can differ depending on the individual's beliefs and practices within Hoodoo.

The significance of conjurers working with ancestral spirits in Hoodoo lies in the belief that ancestral spirits can offer guidance, protection, and support to the living. Ancestral spirits are believed to have a vested interest in the welfare of their descendants and are seen as a valuable source of wisdom and spiritual power.

Working with ancestral spirits allows conjurers to establish a connection with their lineage and tap into the collective knowledge and experiences of their ancestors. This connection can be seen as a way to honor and maintain a relationship with those who came before and to seek their assistance in navigating life's challenges.

Ancestral spirits are often called upon for guidance, protection, and blessings in various aspects of life, such as career, relationships, health, and spiritual growth. Conjurers may create ancestral altars or shrines, make offerings, or perform rituals to establish and maintain a bond with their ancestral spirits.

By working with ancestral spirits, conjurers aim to cultivate a sense of continuity and connection with their heritage, drawing upon the strength and wisdom of their ancestors to aid them in their spiritual practice and in addressing the needs of their clients.

Common Aspects of Spirit Work in Hoodoo

Spirit work in Hoodoo refers to the practice of connecting and working with various spiritual entities, including ancestors, spirit guides, and other beings, to seek their guidance, assistance, and blessings in metaphysical workings. It involves establishing relationships with these spirits, honoring them, and seeking their aid in achieving specific goals or addressing particular needs. Spirit work in Hoodoo can take several forms, depending on the practitioner's beliefs and preferences.

Ancestor veneration: Hoodoo places significant importance on honoring and working with one's ancestors. This involves setting up ancestor altars, offering prayers and libations, and seeking guidance and protection from one's ancestral spirits.

Spirit communication: Practitioners may engage in spirit communication to establish direct contact with spirits. This can be done through divination techniques like scrying, pendulum work, or spirit boards, or through trance states, meditation, and dreamwork.

Spirit guides: Hoodoo practitioners may develop relationships with personal spirit guides or guardian spirits who offer assistance, protection, and guidance in their spiritual and daily lives. These guides are often sought after for their wisdom, knowledge, and ability to navigate spiritual realms.

Spirit-led workings: In Hoodoo, spirits are often invoked and called upon to assist in metaphysical work or ritual workings. This can involve offering prayers, making offerings, and petitioning the spirits for their aid in achieving specific goals, such as love, money, protection, or healing.

Spirit possession: Some Hoodoo practitioners may engage in spirit possession or trance work, allowing spirits to temporarily take control of their bodies. This is done with the purpose of receiving messages, insights, or healing through the spirit's presence.

Common Types of Hoodoo Spirits and Entities

Ancestors: Connecting with and honoring one's ancestors is a fundamental aspect of Hoodoo. Ancestors are believed to provide guidance, protection, and blessings to their descendants.

Spirit Guides: Personal spiritual guides or guardian spirits, often referred to as "conjure doctors," may be invoked for guidance, protection, and assistance in metaphysical workings.

Elemental/Orishas Spirits: Spirits associated with the natural elements, such as earth, air, fire, and water, can be called upon for assistance in various metaphysical workings, depending on the specific element's properties.

Crossroads Spirits: The crossroads are considered a liminal space where spirits and energies converge. Spirits associated with crossroads are often invoked for wisdom, spiritual insight, and assistance in making decisions or navigating life's crossroads. Many crossroad spirits are also gatekeepers, and you must seek their permission to speak to the dead.

Nature/Orishas Spirits: Spirits associated with specific plants, trees, animals, or natural features like rivers or mountains may be invoked for their specific powers and attributes.

Trickster Spirits: Trickster spirits, such as Papa Legba or Br'er Rabbit, are often called upon for their cunning, wisdom, and ability to navigate difficult situations or bring about unexpected outcomes.

Graveyard Spirits: Working with spirits in graveyards is a common practice in Hoodoo. These spirits are believed to possess knowledge, power, and the ability to assist in various metaphysical workings.

It's important to note that the specific spirits and entities worked with in Hoodoo can vary among practitioners, and personal relationships with spirits may differ.

Hoodoo Ancestors

In Hoodoo and many other spiritual traditions, the honoring of deceased practitioners is a common practice. There are a few reasons why certain Hoodoo practitioners may continue to be honored even after death:

Legacy and Influence: Some Hoodoo practitioners have had a significant impact on the development and preservation of the tradition. They may have been highly skilled, knowledgeable, or influential in their communities. Honoring them is a way to remember and pay homage to their contributions.

Spiritual Assistance: It is believed that deceased practitioners may continue to possess spiritual power and knowledge even after death. They are seen as intermediaries between the physical and spiritual realms. Honoring them can be a way to seek their guidance, protection, and assistance in spiritual matters, including Hoodoo practices.

Ancestor Veneration: As stated, many times in this book, Ancestor veneration is a customary practice in many cultures worldwide, including African-American and other African diasporic traditions. In Hoodoo, ancestors are seen as important spiritual beings who can provide guidance, blessings, and protection. Honoring deceased Hoodoo practitioners can be part of this broader practice of ancestor veneration.

Community and Cultural Identity: Honoring well-known Hoodoo practitioners can also be an expression of community and cultural identity. It helps maintain a connection to the heritage and history of Hoodoo as a spiritual practice. By honoring these practitioners, their teachings and traditions can be passed down to future generations.

It's important to note that the specific practices and rituals surrounding the honoring of deceased practitioners can vary among individuals and communities. Some may have personal altars or shrines dedicated to these practitioners, while others may incorporate their names and stories into their rituals and prayers. Ultimately, the honoring of deceased practitioners is a way to acknowledge their contributions, seek their spiritual assistance, and maintain a connection to the roots of Hoodoo.

Dr. John (1825-1885): Dr. John, also known as Dr. John Montanee or Dr. John Bayou, was a prominent Louisiana Creole herbalist, root doctor, and spiritual practitioner. He was known for his extensive knowledge of herbal remedies, spiritual practices, and his ability to heal and provide metaphysical assistance.

Aunt Caroline Dye (c. 1844-1918): Aunt Caroline Dye was an African American rootworker and spiritual practitioner. She was widely respected for her divination skills, including card reading, and her ability to provide spiritual guidance and protection. She is often called on by card readers and psychics for strength.

Marie Laveaux (1801-1881): Marie Laveaux was a renowned Voodoo practitioner and spiritual figure in New Orleans. While she is more closely associated with Voodoo, her influence and reputation extended to the practice of Hoodoo as well. She was known for her healing abilities, spiritual consultations, and her role as a community leader. Her specialty was her ability to write powerful petitions and prayers.

Zora Neale Hurston (1891-1960): Zora Neale Hurston was an African American author, anthropologist, and folklorist who documented and studied African American spiritual traditions, including Hoodoo. Her writings, such as "Mules and Men" and "Hoodoo in America," have provided invaluable insights into the practices, beliefs, and heritage of African American spirituality.

Aunt Sally (unknown dates): Aunt Sally was a legendary African American rootworker and spiritual practitioner from the Mississippi Delta region. She was known for her expertise in herbal medicine, metaphysical workings, and providing spiritual guidance to her community.

Henry "Rufe" Johnson (1870-1954): Henry "Rufe" Johnson was an African American rootworker, herbalist, and spiritual practitioner from Mississippi. He was highly respected for his knowledge of herbs, charms, and workings, and was known for his ability to provide protection, luck, and healing.

Papa Jim (unknown dates): Papa Jim, also known as James Hawthorne, was an African American root doctor and spiritual practitioner from Alabama. He was known for his expertise in love workings, luck charms, and his ability to communicate with spirits.

Aunt Elnora (unknown dates): Aunt Elnora was an African American rootworker and spiritual practitioner from Georgia. She was highly regarded for her knowledge of herbs, divination, and her ability to remove curses and protect against spiritual attacks.

Mother Catherine Seals (1919-2008): Mother Catherine Seals was an African American spiritual leader and rootworker from Texas. She was known for her powerful prayers, healing abilities, and her role as a spiritual advisor and mentor in her community.

Aunt Carrie Williams (1856-1930): Aunt Carrie Williams was an African American rootworker and spiritual practitioner based in North Carolina. She was known for her expertise in love workings, fertility charms, and her ability to provide spiritual guidance and protection.

Dr. Buzzard (unknown dates): Dr. Buzzard, also known as Stephen Robinson, was an African American root doctor and spiritual practitioner from Georgia. He was highly respected for his knowledge of herbs, spiritual remedies, and his reputation for successful workings in the justice system and hex breaking.

Big Mama/Conjure Woman (unknown dates): The term "Conjure Woman" refers to various African American women who practiced Hoodoo and other spiritual traditions. These women were known for their ability to work with spirits, perform divination, and provide spiritual remedies and charms. This is a collection of mother spirits that you call on to protect your family and home.

Mary Ellen Pleasant (1814-1904): Mary Ellen Pleasant, also known as "Mammy Pleasant," was a prominent African American entrepreneur and activist. While not specifically associated with Hoodoo, she was known for her involvement in spiritual practices and her role as a supporter of African American spiritual traditions.

Aunt Julia Brown (unknown dates): Aunt Julia Brown was an African American rootworker and spiritual practitioner from Louisiana. She was believed to possess powerful metaphysical abilities and was known for her work with herbs, love workings, and her ability to communicate with spirits.

It's important to note that while these individuals are recognized as influential figures in the history of African American spiritual traditions, they are not worshipped or deified in Hoodoo. Hoodoo practitioners primarily focus on personal ancestral connections and working with their own lineage and spiritual guides. Advance practitioners use Hoodoo Ancestors, to strengthen their workings.

Safety Disclaimer for Spirit Work in Hoodoo

1. Intention and Respect: Approach spirit work with a clear intention and genuine respect for the spirits you are seeking to connect with. Treat them with reverence and honor their boundaries.
2. Protection and Grounding: Prioritize your spiritual and energetic protection. Before engaging in any spirit work, establish a practice of grounding and shielding yourself to create a safe and stable energetic environment.
3. Knowledge and Education: Educate yourself about the spirits you wish to work with, including their nature, characteristics, and cultural context. Understand the potential risks and responsibilities involved in spirit communication.
4. Consent and Boundaries: Always seek the consent of the spirits before attempting to communicate or work with them. Respect their boundaries and be mindful of any signs or indications that they may not wish to engage with you.
5. Experienced Guidance: If you are a beginner or unfamiliar with spirit work, consider seeking guidance from experienced practitioners or spiritual advisors who can provide proper instruction, mentorship, and support. They can offer valuable insights, techniques, and precautions to ensure your safety during spirit work.
6. Personal Readiness: Assess your own emotional and mental readiness before engaging in spirit work. Make sure you are in a stable and balanced state of mind, as negative emotions or mental distress can potentially attract unwanted or harmful energies.
7. Clear Communication: Develop effective methods of communication with spirits, such as divination tools or rituals. Clearly establish boundaries and rules for communication, ensuring that you can end the interaction safely and respectfully if needed.
8. Regular Grounding and Cleansing: Incorporate regular grounding and cleansing practices into your spiritual routine to release any residual energies or attachments that may have been formed during spirit work. This helps maintain your energetic well-being and protects you from any potential negative influences.
9. Trust your Intuition: Trust your intuition and inner guidance when working with spirits. If something feels off or uncomfortable, listen to your instincts and take appropriate measures to protect yourself. Your intuition can serve as a valuable tool in discerning safe and beneficial spirit interactions.
10. Self-Care and Support: Prioritize self-care and seek support from trusted individuals or communities who understand and respect your spiritual journey. Engage in practices that promote your overall well-being and emotional balance.

Remember, spirit work can be a deeply personal and powerful experience, but it is essential to prioritize your safety and well-being throughout the process. This disclaimer serves as a general guideline, but it is important to adapt it to your specific circumstances and seek further guidance from experienced practitioners when necessary.

Ancestors

In shadows cast by time's relentless sway,
Where echoes of our past silently lay,
I find myself amidst a weary drive,
The road's embrace, a lullaby's revive.

But as the night draped me in drowsy haze,
A slumber's grip began to slowly graze,
My heavy lids sought solace in their rest,
While danger lurked, my heart's rhythm suppressed.

Yet in that moment, when dreams seemed to take hold,
A sacred presence stirred, a tale untold,
Ancestors, ancient spirits, they appeared,
Their ethereal essence, my soul revered.

Their voices whispered on the midnight breeze,
Tales of valor, sacrifice, and unease,
From distant lands and battles fought long past,
Their spectral guidance, a love that will last.

A symphony of whispers, soft and clear,
Filled my weary mind, dispelling all fear,
They spoke of legacy, of strength untamed,
Their wisdom, like a torch, forever flamed.

With every word, a flicker of their light,
I felt their ancient spirits taking flight,
Their hands of guidance, gentle on my wheel,
Their presence, a testament, forever sealed.

For in that twilight realm, where worlds collide,
Their grace, their love, my weary soul revived,
Their silent presence, a beacon in the night,
Honoring their legacy, a sacred rite.

And as the miles stretched on, I stayed awake,
With gratitude, my heart began to quake,
For in that fateful drive, I learned to see,
The gift of my ancestors, eternally.

So let us honor those who came before,
Their stories etched in every cell and pore,
Their guidance, like a compass, ever near,
Honoring their love, we hold them dear.

For in the depths of slumber's tempting hold,
Our ancestors arise, their stories unfold,
With gratitude, we walk life's winding road,
Their whispered presence guides, our hearts bestowed.

—Rootworker Kye

CHAPTER 6

Rootwork in Hoodoo

This chapter may be a bit controversial, but I feel compelled to share a deeply personal aspect of my journey into rootworking - a dimension that some may find contentious. My path to rootworking began with a vivid dream in which an Orisha appeared to me, guiding me towards this ancient practice.

It is important to acknowledge the ongoing debate on social media regarding the relationship between Hoodoo and Orisha veneration. While some argue that Hoodoo has no connection to Orisha traditions, it is undeniable that our ancestors, who were brought to the United States during the transatlantic slave trade, carried with them the knowledge and reverence for the Orishas from their homeland.

Despite the controversy surrounding this topic, I believe it is crucial to share my story with honesty and integrity, recognizing that individual experiences and beliefs are unique and cannot be easily dismissed or changed. From the moment I had that transformative experience, I knew there was a deeper spiritual dimension to my journey into rootworking.

The Orisha that visited me in my dream seemed to be extending an invitation, guiding me towards a path that intertwined the ancient practices of Hoodoo with the veneration of the Orishas. This connection felt profound and resonated with the history of our ancestors, who carried their spiritual beliefs and practices across the treacherous waters of the Middle Passage.

To truly understand the significance of the Orisha connection in Hoodoo, it is essential to acknowledge the historical context in which this practice emerged. Our ancestors, torn from their homelands and subjected to the horrors of slavery, managed to preserve their cultural and spiritual heritage in the face of unimaginable adversity. They blended their knowledge of the Orishas with the practical spiritual traditions of the American South, giving birth to what we now know as Hoodoo.

While debates may rage on social media about the authenticity and validity of the Orisha connection in Hoodoo, I can only speak from my own lived experiences. The presence of the Orishas in my Hoodoo practice has brought me a profound sense of connection, guidance, and spiritual growth. It is not my intention to persuade or change the opinions of others, but rather to share my story with sincerity and respect for the wisdom and traditions of our ancestors. In sharing my personal journey, I acknowledge the controversy surrounding the Orisha connection in Hoodoo, and I respect the opinions and beliefs of others.

What is Rootwork?

Before I get into my story, I want to explain what rootwork is to those who are just starting their journey so you will not get lost.

At its essence, rootwork is the art of working with roots, herbs, and natural elements to harness their spiritual and energetic properties. It is a system of metaphysics deeply rooted in African and Indigenous spiritual practices. Rootwork draws upon the belief in the interconnectedness of all beings and the power of the natural world to effect change in one's life. In Hoodoo, a practitioner of rootwork is known as a Rootworker. They are the custodians of this sacred tradition, possessing knowledge of herbs, roots, and spiritual practices passed down through generations. Rootworkers are skilled in the art of harnessing the inherent properties of plants, minerals, and other natural elements to create powerful remedies, works, and rituals.

Rootwork holds deep significance within the framework of Hoodoo. It serves as a means of accessing spiritual power, addressing challenges, and manifesting desired outcomes. It is not solely focused on material gains or personal desires; instead, it emphasizes the importance of maintaining balance and harmony within oneself and the community. Through rootwork, practitioners seek to align themselves with the energies of the natural world and the divine forces that govern it. It is a way of tapping into ancestral wisdom, connecting with the spirits, and seeking guidance and protection. It is a multifaceted practice with diverse applications, and can be used for healing, protection, love, prosperity, and spiritual growth. Its versatility lies in its ability to adapt to individual needs and circumstances, providing a personalized approach to spiritual work. We must also remember there is a deep connection not only to the spiritual realm but also to the physical and medicinal properties of plants and natural elements.

While the spiritual aspects of rootworking in Hoodoo are often emphasized, it is important to recognize the practical and medicinal applications as well. Rootworkers have long understood the potent healing properties of herbs, roots, and other natural elements, using them to address physical ailments, promote well-being, and enhance one's connection to the natural world. Each plant has its own unique attributes that can be utilized to address various physical conditions. For example, the root of the sassafras tree is often used for its purifying and cleansing properties, while ginger root is known for its ability to aid digestion and reduce inflammation. Rootworkers have mastered the art of creating medicinal remedies using plants, roots, and other natural ingredients. These remedies can take various forms, such as teas, infusions, tinctures, poultices, and oils. Each preparation method is carefully chosen to extract and preserve the medicinal properties of the ingredients, allowing for effective healing and restoration of balance in the body.

In Hoodoo, the physical and spiritual aspects are intertwined, working in harmony to promote overall well-being. Rootworkers understand that true healing goes beyond just addressing physical symptoms; it involves restoring balance to the mind, body, and spirit. By incorporating spiritual practices, such as prayers, blessings, and rituals, into their medicinal work, rootworkers seek to address not only the physical ailment but also the underlying spiritual imbalances that may contribute to the illness.

Rootworker

With hands, both earthly and divine,
Rootworker, keeper of wisdom's shrine,
You delve into the depths of human strife,
To heal, to guide, to renew life.

Sacrifice, a cornerstone of your noble art,
A selfless offering from your compassionate heart,
You give your essence, your very being,
To aid others, their burdens relieving.

Through roots and herbs, a language you employ,
Anointing oils, a touch that brings joy,
Each potion brewed, intentions made clear,
An alchemy of love, dispelling fear.

Petitioning spirits, ancient and wise,
Seeking their guidance, with fervent cries,
You navigate unseen realms, hidden from sight,
To bring forth blessings, to set things right.

But in this journey, as your power grows,
Remember to nurture your own soul,
For as you heal, your spirit needs attending,
To keep your essence strong, never-ending.

And as you walk this noble, ancient way,
May spirits guide you, both night and day,
With gratitude, we honor your sacred role,
Rootworker, healer, whisperer of the soul.

-Rootworker Kye

My Journey from Kye to Rootworker Kye

It all began with a book, "Good Juju" by Najah Lightfoot, my first ever book on Hoodoo. I picked it up at a metaphysical store not even know what is was about. It just called to me. As I flipped through its pages, I was captivated by the wealth of knowledge and wisdom it contained. Each word seemed to speak directly to my soul, guiding me towards a path I had always yearned to explore. On page seven, I stumbled upon a ritual for grounding and centering. Intrigued, I decided to give it a try. Little did I know that this simple act would set in motion a series of events that would forever change my life. (I know I say that alot throughout this book, but each event collectively changed my life.)

For seven consecutive days, I faithfully performed the grounding and centering ritual. With each repetition, I felt a deeper sense of connection to the Earth and a newfound clarity within myself. On the seventh day, as I closed my eyes and allowed the ritual to envelop me, something incredible happened. In what appeared to be a daydream or a hallucination, I found myself transported to a mystical forest. The air was thick with the scent of frankincense and myrrh, and a tranquil river flowed gently in the center of it all. It was here that I encountered a presence unlike anything I had ever experienced before. At first, I didn't know who or what she was. At that time all I called her was *Spirit*. She began to talk to me that first encounter., and from the moment I met her at that river she called me Medusa.

I know this story is going to sound batshit crazy, but it is the truth... She shared a sacred story with me that first day, the seventh day of my ritual, a story that she told me she had previously shared with my soul in a different lifetime. Little did I know this was a test of my character and integrity. She wanted to see if I would succumb to temptation and compromise my values.

Spirit's Story:

"Once upon a time, in a realm far beyond our mortal comprehension, there existed a divine kingdom ruled solely by a divine feminine being and a pantheon of powerful and wise "female" spirits. The divine feminine being with her grace, wisdom, and benevolence, had brought harmony and balance to the heavens, ensuring the cosmic order remained intact.

One season, they gathered together with divine feminine at the head in their celestial abode to discuss the state of the universe. They contemplated the idea of sharing their spiritual power and wisdom with a newfound creation - the masculine spirits. Intrigued by the possibilities this could bring, the goddesses decided to bestow upon the "male" spirits a portion of their divine essence known as Ashe. At first, the male spirits were grateful and humbled by this gift. They embraced their newfound power with reverence and humility, working alongside the goddesses to maintain harmony in the heavens. The realm prospered, and the energies of both the feminine and masculine intertwined seamlessly.

However, as time went on, a few male spirits, headed by a divine masculine deity, began to succumb to the allure of their newfound power. They allowed their egos to swell, believing themselves superior to the goddesses who had granted them this privilege. These "male" spirits craved dominance and control, seeking to assert their authority over the divine realm. Driven by their misguided ambitions, these rogue masculine spirits formed alliances, plotting and scheming to overthrow the goddesses and seize control of the heavens.

Their desire for power grew insatiable, blinding them to the inherent balance and harmony that had once defined the realm. As the male spirits launched their audacious coup, chaos erupted in the celestial realm. The once harmonious heavens were consumed by conflict and discord. The goddesses with their wisdom and power challenged, fought valiantly to defend their reign, but the sheer numbers and unified force of the "male" spirits proved overwhelming. The feminine spirits, though resilient and mighty, found themselves outnumbered and outmatched.

Despite the overwhelming odds, the goddesses refused to surrender, and were determined to regain balance. Their love for the heavens and their commitment to maintaining balance pushed them to summon every ounce of their divine strength. They fought fiercely, their powers intertwining, creating a brilliant display of cosmic energy.

In the midst of the chaos, a treaty for peace emerged as a beacon of hope. The two divines of femininity and masculinity combine their strengths. The feminine spirits forgave those "male" spirits who had been misguided, offering them a chance at redemption and growth. From that day forward, the divine realm flourished under the leadership and wisdom of the divine feminine and masculine together.

They remained vigilant, ensuring that the balance between masculine and feminine energies was maintained. The lessons learned from this tumultuous period served as a reminder that power should never be wielded to dominate, but rather to nurture and uplift. In this realm, they fostered a new era of collaboration and understanding between the feminine and masculine energies. They celebrated the unique gifts each brought to the cosmic tapestry, embracing diversity and unity."

This sounds like a beautiful story, right? Well, it wasn't such a happy story to the spirit who towered over me as I kneeled at the river's bank. She had a look of distaste etched on her beautiful face the entire time she told her story. She believed that the "male" spirits were beneath her and that divine masculine had no place next to divine feminine. She had not forgiven the masculine entities... or so I thought.

At that time, I was going through a breakup and was on the brink of being in a "man-hating" stage, and she played on that hurt and humiliation and tried to convince me to use the men in my life as they had used me. She told me many stories of how the creation of man was the downfall of the earth, and I slowly started to believe her.

Weeks later I got the opportunity to use a man who had found interest in me. It was something so simple, and I just couldn't bring myself to do it. I cared too much, and I knew my conscience would slowly begin to eat away at my soul. He asked me out to eat and I got the opportunity to get a free meal out of someone who I knew I had no interest in. I knew the spirit I had been talking to would be disappointed in me, but I turned him down, and told him the truth. I had no interest outside of friendship.

The next time I visited that tranquil river I thought I would be meeting a face of disappointment. I had not followed her instructions to hurt the next man that I could, but instead I was met with a smile.

Radiating a serene energy, she introduced herself as Aja, an Orisha—one of the divine forces of the Yoruba tradition. Aja explained that she was the embodiment of fertility, abundance, and the forest itself. Her presence filled me with a sense of awe and reverence. Her voice changed from that of malice, and she spoke to me in a soft and kind voice that seemed to carry ancient wisdom. That was when the teaching stage began. She started teaching me about the power of the natural world, nature, healing, and our deep connection to it's forces.

Aja emphasized the importance of honoring the Earth, the spirits, and the ancestors. She shared stories of how the elements and the spirits of nature could be harnessed inside of plants to bring about positive change and healing. As I listened to Aja's teachings, a profound sense of purpose washed over me. I realized that I had been called to the path of rootwork.

In a series of visits to what I now call, *The Frank & Myrrh Forest*, Aja encouraged me to delve deeper into this path, to explore the mysteries of the herbs. I would always return from my "daydreams" with the imprint of Aja's presence remaining etched in my heart and mind.

Even though, I have embraced the teachings of Aja wholeheartedly, I am still curious to know if the story she tried to trick me with is true. I have never mustard up the courage to ask her, so I guess I will never know. Anyway...

I have now dedicated myself to the study and practice of rootwork in the physical realm. I immersed myself in the pages of "Good Juju," and many other books, studies, and papers absorbing every word and incorporating all that resonated with me into my daily life.

By resisting her persuasion, I had proven my strength and commitment to walking the path of rootwork with honor and integrity. From that moment on, Aja became my guide and mentor, offering me guidance and protection as I delved deeper into the practice of rootwork. She taught me about the importance of balance and harmony, reminding me that true power lies in using our gifts for the greater good.

I honed my abilities and deepened my understanding of the natural world and its energies. She showed me how to work with the elements, the spirits, and the ancestors, helping me to develop a stronger connection to the divine forces that shape our lives. As I continued to practice rootwork, Aja's presence has become more pronounced in my life, even though she no longer reveals herself to me regularly. Every blue moon she will appear in my dreams, offering guidance and revealing hidden secrets.

Through her, I gained a deeper understanding of the intricate web of life and the interconnectedness of all beings. I continued to honor her, offering prayers and lighting a white or green candle, expressing my gratitude for her guidance and blessings on a daily basis.

To this day, Aja remains an integral part of my spiritual practice and my life as a rootworker. Her teachings continue to shape and inspire me, guiding me on the path of healing, empowerment, and spiritual growth. What began as a mysterious encounter with a spirit evolved into a profound relationship with a powerful Orisha. Through her tests, teachings, and revelations she has guided me towards a deeper understanding of myself and the world around me.

Today, I stand as a testament to the transformative power of rootwork. It has not only shaped my life but also the lives of countless others who have found solace, healing, and empowerment through this ancient practice. And so, I continue to walk this path with reverence and gratitude, knowing that I am forever connected to the forces of nature and the spirits that reside within it.

Before I close this section I want you to know this chapter holds a weight that is both heavy and personal. This was not an easy story for me to share, and neither was my view point of Orisha veneration in Hoodoo. To be one hundred precent honest with you; I've contemplated deleting this chapter and chapter seven countless times. But as I reflect on the purpose of my memoir, I am reminded of the power of vulnerability, and the potential to help others who may be on a similar journey.

In the realm of African traditional religions and their diasporic counterparts, there exists a vast array of beliefs and practices. Unfortunately, there are those who dismiss the experiences of Hoodoo practitioners, questioning the validity of their encounters with deities and spirits based on their own beliefs. It is important for me to emphasize that you are not alone on this journey. Your spiritual path is uniquely yours, and no one else's will mirror it entirely. You owe no one an explanation for the experiences you have lived through.

Let us remember that Hoodoo is not a religion, but a spiritual practice. It is a tapestry woven with threads of ancestral wisdom, personal connections, and a deep reverence for the unseen forces that shape our lives. Each practitioner walks a path that is as distinct as their fingerprint, encountering challenges, triumphs, and revelations that are uniquely their own.

So, dear reader, if you find yourself questioning your experiences or feeling invalidated by others, I implore you to hold steadfast in your truth. Your journey is valid, your encounters are real, and your spirit is resilient.

Embrace the power of your individuality, for it is through sharing our stories that we can empower and uplift one another. Together, let us break free from the chains of judgment and embrace the diverse tapestry of spiritual experiences that make us who we are.

Aja the "Wild Wind" of the Forest

When Aja appeared to me as herself instead of just "A Spirit", she gave me her name, I was intrigued to learn more about her. I eagerly tried to Google her, but to my surprise, I found very little information about her. Undeterred, I embarked on a years-long journey of studying and searching for any traces of knowledge about Aja.

Unfortunately, even after all this time, I have been unable to find out much about her. It seems that unless I travel to Nigeria and encounter a tribe or culture that still venerates her, my quest for information may remain unfulfilled. Nonetheless, I hold onto the hope that one day I will have the opportunity to delve deeper into Aja's mysteries and uncover the wisdom that surrounds her.

On the next few pages there is the little information that I did find on her over the years. If anyone is reading this book and has more knowledge about her, I would love for you to reach out to me!

Aja is a rare African earth Orisha, particularly revered in Nigerian traditions. She is associated with the forest, animals, and herbal healing, and is said to be the patron of rootworkers, healers, and shaman. In Yoruba tradition, she is sometimes referred to as the "wild wind," and is a Orisha of morality and all that is good and respectful. While many Orisha's of healing possess the ability to cure ailments through mere incantations or gestures, Aja takes a different path. Rather than distancing herself from humans, she immerses herself in the very forests she knows so intimately.

Within the depths of these forests, Aja seeks out plants with medicinal properties. She skillfully combines various herbs, roots, and other plant parts, transforming them into potent remedies tailored to specific ailments. Aja's approach to healing is not shrouded in secrecy either; she is renowned for generously sharing her knowledge with humans. Not all humans but a select few. It is believed that if someone is carried away by Aja to learn her ways and returns, they become a powerful healer. A few different texts stated that the journey is to the land of the dead or what Christians would call heaven. *The first time I read this I got goosebumps all down my spine. It reminded me of my many journeys to the Frank & Myrrh Forrest, but anyway...*

Aja patiently awaits the arrival of someone seeking her wisdom. Often, it is a shaman in training or an individual of similar calling. The duration of their stay in the forest before Aja reveals herself may vary, but it is said to be between seven days to three months. During this period, the individual must demonstrate their worthiness, proving their commitment to learning the art of utilizing plant properties for healing. *This is another piece of information that gave me chills, and is the reason I knew I wasn't hallucinating, and that I am not crazy. Those types of doubts did enter my mind on a multitude of occasions. But back to Aja...*

Aja's discerning nature ensures that only those truly dedicated and deserving of her teachings are granted access to her invaluable knowledge. Through this process, she imparts the skills and understanding needed to harness the healing power of nature's bounty, empowering individuals to alleviate the suffering of others. In the realm of healing, Aja stands apart, bridging the gap between the divine and the human, embodying a profound connection to the natural world and offering a tangible path to wellness through the utilization of medicinal plants. Aja's unique approach sets her apart from other Earth spirits, distinguishing her as a remarkable figure.

Unlike many other earth spirits, whose interactions with humans are often limited to either instilling fear or causing harm, Aja defies these expectations. Instead of alienating people from the forests and nature, she extends her realm towards humanity, emphasizing the significance of the natural world. In doing so, Aja conveys a profound message, one that holds immense importance for both individuals and society as a whole. By fostering an understanding of the intrinsic value present in the natural world, she instills a deep-seated respect for the Earth. This message, perhaps one of the most crucial ever conveyed by an Earth spirit, serves as a catalyst for generating a genuine need to protect and conserve our environment. Aja's embrace of humanity and her efforts to bridge the gap between the divine and the mortal not only demonstrates her compassion but also provides a powerful tool for promoting environmental stewardship.

Through her teachings and actions, Aja encourages a harmonious relationship between humans and nature, fostering a sense of interconnectedness that motivates individuals to preserve the Earth's precious resources.

In essence, Aja's unique perspective and her profound message serve as a guiding light, illuminating the path towards a sustainable future. By extending her realm to humanity and emphasizing the importance of the natural world, she imparts an enduring legacy that inspires reverence for the Earth and ignites a collective responsibility to protect and conserve our planet for generations to come.

Aja's role is to care for the sick using herbal remedies while also protecting the forest and woodland creatures. She is considered a guardian of the natural world and the healing arts. Although Aja may not be widely recognized within the general Yoruba pantheon, she holds specific significance within Nigerian spiritual practices, and she remains dear to my heart.

Grounding Yourself

As I mentioned in the beginning of this chapter, I found my spirit guide, my Orisha, through a grounding and centering ritual I found in the book, "Good Juju" by Najah Lightfoot. I want to explain why grounding yourself before embarking on a spiritual journey is important.

Stability and Balance: Grounding helps establish a stable and balanced foundation within yourself. It allows you to connect with the Earth's energy, providing a sense of stability and rootedness. This stability is essential when delving into spiritual practices, as it helps you stay grounded amidst different experiences and energies. It also balances the root chakra.

Clarity and Focus: Grounding clears your mind and helps you focus on the present moment. It releases excess energy and distractions, allowing you to be fully present and attentive to your spiritual journey. When you are grounded, you can approach your spiritual practices with clarity and a calm mind, enhancing your ability to connect with higher realms or deeper aspects of your being.

Emotional and Energetic Release: Grounding provides an outlet for releasing any accumulated emotional or energetic tension. It helps you let go of negative emotions, stress, and anxiety, creating space for more positive and uplifting energies to flow. This release enables you to approach your spiritual journey with a lighter and more open-hearted mindset.

Protection and Boundaries: Grounding establishes energetic boundaries, shielding you from absorbing or being overwhelmed by external energies. It acts as a protective barrier, allowing you to discern and filter the energies you encounter during your spiritual journey.

This protection ensures that you maintain your own energetic integrity and prevents you from being energetically drained.

Integration and Application: Grounding helps integrate the spiritual experiences and insights you gain during your journey into your everyday life. It allows you to bridge the gap between the spiritual and physical realms, ensuring that the wisdom and growth you acquire are grounded and applicable in your daily experiences and interactions.

By grounding yourself before embarking on a spiritual journey, you create a solid and stable foundation that supports and enhances your exploration and growth. It enables you to navigate the spiritual realms with clarity, focus, and protection while integrating these experiences into your daily life.

Grounding & Centering Ritual

This ritual is inspired by the one that you will find in "Good Juju," if you decide to explore that book for yourself. This is the ritual that started me on the journey to rootwork. It focuses on the cleansing and renewing properties of water. Water, as a vital element, has the power to wash away negativity and revitalize our bodies, minds, and spirits. Just as water sustains our physical existence, it also symbolizes life itself.

Materials needed:

1. A peaceful space where you can be undisturbed.
2. A large bowl of cool water.
3. A white taper or tealight candle that has been cleansed and/or dressed.
4. An incense or match to light the candle.

Steps

Please read all steps several times before beginning, so you will have a clear understanding of each step.

Step 1: Washing with Water

To initiate the grounding and centering ritual, cleanse your face with cold water. Allow the water to gently touch your face, the back of your neck, your arms, and your hands. As you do so, envision a clear, cold stream flowing over smooth rocks, meandering through lush green forests adorned with towering trees and sunlit branches. Feel the refreshing and purifying essence of the water purging any negativity or stagnant energy.

Step 2: Drying and Preparing

Once you have completed the washing ritual, gently pat yourself dry with a soft towel or cloth. This step signifies the conclusion of the cleansing process, leaving you refreshed and renewed.

Step 3: Finding Your Sacred Space

Take the candle and proceed to your chosen quiet space. Ensure that you will not be disturbed during this rite. Find a comfortable position where both feet are planted firmly on the floor. Keep your back and neck straight, allowing for an upright posture. Place your hands either on your knees or on a table, with your palms facing upward.

Step 4: Lighting the Candle

Once you have settled into your comfortable position, proceed to light your candle using the matches. As the flame flickers and illuminates the space, symbolizing the guiding light, it serves as a focal point for your practice.

Step 5: Closing Your Eyes and Natural Breathing

With the candle softly glowing, gently close your eyes. Allow your breath to flow naturally, inhaling through your nose and exhaling through your mouth. Avoid forcing your breath; instead, let it come and go effortlessly, syncing with the rhythm of your body.

Step 6: Observing the Candle Flame

When you feel ready, close your mouth and continue breathing naturally through your nose. Open your eyes and direct your gaze towards the flame of the candle. Soften your focus and observe the dance of the flame. Notice any images or patterns that may arise in your perception. Be open to the thoughts, visions, or messages that flow through your mind during this contemplation.

Step 7: Closing Your Eyes Again

After a moment of gazing at the candle flame, gently close your eyes once more. Maintain the natural flow of your breath, inhaling through your nose and exhaling through your mouth. Allow any images or messages that arose during the candle observation to pass through your mind. Embrace these insights and let them integrate into your being.

Step 8: Ending the Exercise

When you feel naturally ready to conclude the grounding and centering exercise, gently open your eyes. Pinch or snuff out the candle flame, acknowledging the completion of this ritual. Gradually rise from your seated position and continue with your day, carrying the grounded energy within you. Remember that you can repeat this exercise whenever you feel the need to ground and center yourself.

Note: *By pinching or snuffing out the candle flame, you preserve the candle for future use until the wick burns almost completely. When the wick becomes low, you can utilize the remaining candle to light another one for your future grounding and centering practices.*

Step 9: Creating a Continuous Metaphysical Link and Adding Music (Optional)

To deepen your connection and create a continuous flow from one grounding and centering exercise to another, you can establish a metaphysical link between the candles. After extinguishing the flame, keep the used candle aside for future use. Each time you perform this exercise, use the remaining candle to ignite a new one. By doing so, you maintain a sacred and continuous connection between your practice sessions.

Additionally, you may choose to enhance your experience by incorporating soothing music. Select meditative tracks such as Sounds of the Ocean, soft flute melodies, or gentle piano compositions. The tranquil sounds will further calm your mind and soothe your soul during this exercise. Play the chosen music softly in the background while you engage in the candle gazing, breathing, and visualization process.

Allow the harmonious melodies to guide you deeper into a state of relaxation and focus. Remember, the addition of music is optional, and you can modify the choice of music according to your personal preferences. Experiment with different genres and instruments to find what resonates most with your practice.

By establishing a continuous link between the candles and incorporating soothing music, you create a potent and harmonious environment for grounding and centering yourself. Over time, you may even develop the ability to evoke the image of the candle in your mind's eye, allowing you to engage in this exercise even when you cannot physically be in your quiet place.

By following these steps, you embark on a journey of grounding and centering, aligning your body, mind, and spirit with the flow of energy and the wisdom of Hoodoo. May this ritual help you establish a deep connection with the cleansing power of water and guide you towards a state of balance and harmony.

CHAPTER 7
Orishas In Hoodoo

The incorporation of Orishas into Hoodoo is a complex and multifaceted topic that involves the blending of different belief systems and cultural practices. Hoodoo itself is an African American spiritual practice that developed in the United States, particularly in the Southern states, during the era of slavery and its aftermath.

Let's start from the beginning again, the origins of Hoodoo can be traced back to West and Central Africa, where various African spiritual and metaphysical practices were brought by enslaved Africans to the Americas. These practices were influenced by their native traditions, including those centered around the veneration of deities known as Orishas in the Yoruba religion. The Yoruba people, primarily from what is now Nigeria, Togo, and Benin, had a rich spiritual system that revolved around the veneration of Orishas, who are considered divine forces representing various aspects of nature and human life.

During the transatlantic slave trade, enslaved Africans were forcibly brought to the Americas, where they were stripped of their cultural and religious practices. However, they managed to preserve and adapt their spiritual beliefs in new forms, including Hoodoo. In the context of Hoodoo, Orishas are often seen as powerful spiritual entities and are incorporated into spirit work practices to provide assistance, protection, and guidance. Remarkably similar to how angels or saints are venerated in the Christian belief system. They possess specific attributes and powers that can be invoked to address various needs and desires.

The ways in which Orishas are used in Hoodoo vary depending on the individual practitioner and their specific goals. Some practitioners may work with specific Orishas based on their personal connection or the nature of the issue at hand. Others may work with a pantheon of Orishas, calling upon different ones for different purposes. Hoodoo practitioners may incorporate various tools, such as candles, herbs, roots, and ritual baths, in their work with Orishas. They may create altars dedicated to specific Orishas, adorn them with offerings, and perform rituals or prayers to establish a connection and seek their assistance. It's important to note that the incorporation of Orishas into Hoodoo is not universally practiced or accepted by all Hoodoo practitioners. Hoodoo itself is a highly individualized and eclectic tradition, and the use of Orishas is one of many spiritual elements that can be found within it.

Overall, the integration of Orishas into Hoodoo represents the syncretism and cultural exchange that occurred in the African diaspora, where traditional African religious beliefs and practices merged with elements of Christianity and other spiritual traditions to create unique and dynamic systems of spiritual work, like Hoodoo.

The controversy of Orishas in Hoodoo

The issue of initiation and the involvement of Orishas in Hoodoo can indeed be a source of controversy within the African diaspora and its various spiritual traditions. In many African diasporic religions, such as Ifa, Voodoo, Vodun, or Santeria, initiation is considered an important and necessary step for individuals to establish a formal relationship with the Orishas. Initiation typically involves a series of rituals, ceremonies, and teachings conducted by experienced practitioners or priests.

It is believed to be a way to not only establish a connection with the Orishas but also to receive guidance, protection, and deeper understanding of the tradition. However, Hoodoo, as a distinct African American spiritual practice, developed outside of these formal initiatory systems. Hoodoo practitioners may not necessarily follow the same initiation practices or have the same beliefs regarding the requirement for initiation to work with Orishas. Instead, Hoodoo has historically been more accessible and open to individual interpretation and experimentation. This difference in approach has led to tensions and disagreements within the African diaspora spiritual community.

Some practitioners of African diasporic religions may view the incorporation of Orishas into Hoodoo as inappropriate or disrespectful, as they believe that proper initiation is necessary to properly engage with these spiritual entities. On the other hand, many Hoodoo practitioners argue that their work with Orishas is based on the spiritual practices and beliefs passed down through generations of African Americans, and they do not necessarily adhere to the initiation practices of specific African diasporic religions.

They may argue that the Orishas are part of their ancestral heritage and that their connection and relationship with them are valid and authentic, even without formal initiation. It is important to recognize that there is no single, unified opinion within the African diaspora regarding the role of initiation or the involvement of Orishas in Hoodoo. Different individuals and communities may have diverse perspectives and beliefs on these matters. In any case, it is essential to approach these conversations and discussions with respect for the diverse range of beliefs and practices that exist within the African diaspora spiritual traditions. Understanding and acknowledging the complexities and nuances of these traditions can help foster greater understanding and appreciation among practitioners from diverse backgrounds.

Many African Americans, due to various historical circumstances such as slavery and cultural displacement, did not have access to formal initiation practices that are associated with specific African diasporic religions. Throughout history, these practices were often suppressed or lost during the process of enslavement and colonization. However, despite the loss of formal initiation practices, the connections to ancestral spirits and spiritual beliefs were not completely lost within African American communities. The resilience and adaptability of African cultural and spiritual traditions allowed for the development of new forms of spirituality, such as Hoodoo.

Hoodoo became a way for African Americans to maintain a connection to their ancestral roots and spirituality within the constraints of their circumstances. Hoodoo practitioners often draw upon their intuition, firsthand experiences, family traditions, and the knowledge passed down through generations to establish relationships with spirits and deities. While these connections may differ from the formal initiation practices of African diasporic religions, they are deeply rooted in the cultural and spiritual heritage of African Americans.

It is important to recognize and respect the unique experiences and traditions that evolved within African American communities. The ability to maintain spiritual connections despite the loss of formal initiation practices is a testament to the resilience and strength of African American spirituality. Ultimately, the question of initiation and the involvement of spirits in Hoodoo is a complex and nuanced one. It is essential to acknowledging the historical context and the diverse range of beliefs and practices within African American spiritual traditions.

Orishas Found in Hoodoo

Eshu/Elegba: Eshu is the divine messenger and guardian of the crossroads. He is known as a trickster and mediator between the human and spiritual realms. In Hoodoo, Eshu is invoked for protection, guidance, and opening pathways.

Ogun: Ogun is the warrior and blacksmith spirit, associated with iron, technology, and labor. In Hoodoo, Ogun is often invoked for strength, protection, and overcoming obstacles.

Oshun: Oshun is the goddess of love, beauty, and prosperity. She is associated with sweet waters, sensuality, and feminine power. In Hoodoo, Oshun is often called upon for matters of love, marriage, fertility, and attracting abundance.

Yemaya/Yemoja: Yemaya is the mother spirit of the ocean and the patroness of motherhood and healing. She is associated with nurturing, emotional strength, and protection. In Hoodoo, Yemaya is often invoked for matters of family, fertility, emotional healing, and protection.

Obatala: Obatala is the father of all Orishas and the creator of human beings. He represents wisdom, purity, and divine justice. In Hoodoo, Obatala is often called upon for clarity of thought, guidance, and resolving conflicts.

Shango: Shango is the spirit of thunder, fire, and justice. He is associated with masculine energy, passion, and leadership. In Hoodoo, Shango is often invoked for matters of personal power, success, protection, and justice.

Oya: Oya is the spirit of the winds, storms, and change. She is associated with transformation, intuition, and feminine power. In Hoodoo, Oya is often called upon for matters of personal transformation, protection, and navigating life changes.

Ochosi: Ochosi is the hunter and tracker deity associated with justice, truth, and protection. He is often invoked for legal matters, finding lost or stolen items, and bringing about justice. In Hoodoo, Ochosi is called upon for matters related to legal issues, court cases, and seeking justice or truth.

Orunmila: Orunmila is the orisha of divination and wisdom. He is associated with knowledge, foresight, and the ability to see into the future. In Hoodoo, Orunmila is often called upon for matters of divination, seeking guidance, and gaining insight into one's life path or future.

Babalu-Aye: Babalu-Aye is the orisha of healing, disease, and afflictions. He is associated with infectious diseases and is often called upon for healing and protection from illness. In Hoodoo, Babalu-Aye is invoked for matters of health, healing, and general well-being.

Olokun: Olokun is the orisha of the deep ocean and is associated with wealth, abundance, and mysteries of the sea. Olokun is often called upon for matters of prosperity, abundance, and accessing hidden knowledge. In Hoodoo, Olokun is invoked for matters related to finances, business success, and uncovering hidden opportunities.

It's important to note that the specific Orishas invoked, and their significance may vary among individual practitioners and regional variations in Hoodoo. The relationship between Hoodoo and the Orishas is often influenced by subjective experiences, family traditions, and the unique spiritual practices of each practitioner.

Ways to Honor Orishas in Hoodoo practice:

Altar Setup: Create a dedicated altar space for the specific Orisha you wish to honor. Include items such as candles, images or statues representing the Orisha, sacred herbs, and offerings.

Offerings: Offerings are an important way to honor an Orisha. Research the specific preferences of the Orisha you are working with and offer appropriate items such as fruits, flowers, food, or libations.

Prayers and Invocations: Offer prayers and invocations to the Orisha, expressing your reverence, gratitude, and intentions. Use their traditional names and attributes to call upon their energy and guidance.

Ritual Baths: Take ritual baths infused with herbs and essential oils associated with the Orisha you are honoring. Use this time to cleanse and purify yourself, seeking the Orisha's blessings and protection.

Ancestral Offerings: Some Orishas are deeply connected to ancestral spirits. Honor them by setting up a separate space or altar for ancestral offerings. Include items that represent your ancestors and offer prayers and offerings on their behalf.

Dance and Music: Orishas are often associated with specific rhythms, dances, and songs. Incorporate these elements into your practice to connect with the energy and essence of the Orisha.

Divination: Seek guidance from the Orisha through divination practices such as tarot, oracle cards, or cowrie shell readings. Respectfully ask for their insights and wisdom on specific matters.

Respect Nature: Orishas are intimately connected to nature. Show your reverence by spending time in natural settings, such as forests or bodies of water, and engaging in activities like gardening or environmental conservation.

Study and Learn: Dedicate time to studying the stories, legends, and traditions associated with the Orisha you are honoring. Understand their qualities, symbols, and rituals to deepen your connection and appreciation.

Acts of Service: Engage in acts of service that align with the values of the Orisha. This can include volunteering, offering assistance to those in need, or participating in community initiatives.

Safety Protocols When Working with the Orishas:

Cultural Sensitivity: It is essential to approach working with the Orishas with cultural sensitivity and respect. Recognize that Orisha veneration is deeply rooted in many African diasporic traditions. Educate yourself about the specific cultural practices, customs, and protocols associated with the Orishas in the tradition or practice you choose on your spiritual journey.

Seek Knowledge and Guidance: Before attempting to work with an Orisha, it is crucial to seek knowledge and guidance from reputable sources. Study the stories, legends, and rituals associated with the Orisha to gain a deeper understanding of their qualities and preferences.

Consult with Practitioners: If you are uncertain about working with an Orisha or have questions, it is advisable to consult with experienced practitioners who have a thorough understanding of the traditions in the practice or religion you have chosen. Seek out reputable sources, such as priests/priestesses, elders, or knowledgeable community members, who can provide guidance and answer your queries.

Consent and Permission: When working with the Orishas, it is vital to approach them with consent and permission. Do not assume that you have the right to invoke an Orisha without proper initiation or authorization from the Orisha themself. Respect the traditions and protocols associated with working with the Orishas within your belief system.

Safety Precautions: When engaging in rituals or ceremonies, always prioritize safety. Use fireproof containers for candles and incense, ensure proper ventilation, and maintain a clear and safe space. If using sacred herbs, be aware of any potential allergies or sensitivities. Exercise caution when handling sharp objects or performing physical movements associated with Orisha dances.

Personal Boundaries: It is important to establish personal boundaries when working with the Orishas. Be clear about your intentions and desires, but also recognize that the Orishas have their own will and agency. Approach them with humility and respect, allowing them to guide and direct your interactions.

Emotional and Mental Well-being: Working with the Orishas can be emotionally and spiritually intense. Prioritize your emotional and mental well-being by practicing self-care, grounding techniques, and seeking support from trusted individuals or professionals if needed.

Ethical Considerations: Uphold ethical considerations when working with the Orishas. Ensure that your actions align with principles of respect, integrity, and harm reduction. Do not use Orisha veneration for malicious purposes or to manipulate others.

Remember, this is a general guide, and it is essential to consult with experienced practitioners or elders who can provide more specific advice and guidance based on the specific tradition you are working with. Each Orisha has unique protocols and practices associated with them, so it is crucial to seek guidance from those who are knowledgeable and experienced in your particular tradition.

Disclaimer:

Working with the Orishas involves spiritual practices that have been passed down through generations and are deeply rooted in specific cultural traditions. The information provided here is a general guide and should not be considered a substitute for proper initiation, training, or guidance from qualified practitioners.

Engaging in Orisha veneration without proper knowledge and respect can be ineffective or potentially harmful. It is essential to approach this practice with cultural sensitivity, integrity, and a willingness to learn from those who have been initiated or trained in their specific tradition.

Always seek out help from experienced practitioners or elders if you are unsure or have questions about working with the Orishas. They can provide more specific guidance based on their knowledge and experience. Remember, your safety, well-being, and the preservation of cultural integrity should always be a priority when engaging in any spiritual practice.

CHAPTER 8

Let's Get to Rootworkin'

In this chapter, we will embark on a journey into the world of herbs and recipes in Rootwork. As a new and up-and-coming Rootworker, it is essential to understand the power and significance of herbs in Hoodoo practice. I will provide you with an easy-to-follow foundation of knowledge and introduce you to simple recipes with basic names and ingredients that you can customize to suit your own preferences and intentions. So welcome to the world of Rootworking, where ancestral wisdom and intuitive guidance intertwine to create powerful magick! Let's explore a collection of recipes that serve as a starting point for your own unique practice. These recipes are intentionally provided without specific measurements, as Rootworking is an intuitive and personal journey. Instead, you are encouraged to rely on the guidance of your ancestors and your own inner knowing when crafting these recipes.

It is important to understand that Rootworking is deeply rooted in ancestral traditions and individual connection with the spirit realm. Again! Each practitioner is encouraged to add their own individualized touch and modifications to these recipes, allowing them to align with their specific intentions and ancestral lineages. By doing so, you honor the rich tapestry of your heritage while infusing the recipes with your own energy and intention. Once again, the absence of measurements in these recipes is intentional, as it encourages you to tap into your intuition and trust in the wisdom passed down through generations. This approach allows for a more fluid and organic practice, where you can adjust the ingredients and proportions based on what feels right to you.

Remember, the essence of Rootworking lies not in precise measurements, but in the intention and energy you infuse into your work. As you explore the recipes in this chapter, take time to sit in quiet reflection, connect with your ancestors, and listen to their whispers of guidance. Trust in your instincts and let the spirit realm be your guide. Embrace the freedom to experiment, adapt, and make each recipe your own. By doing so, you will cultivate a deeper connection with your roots, your ancestors, and the metaphysical essence of Rootworking. While reading please note that the use of specific herbs in Hoodoo can vary among practitioners and regions, as individual preferences, regional availability, and firsthand experiences shape the selection and usage. Hoodoo is a living tradition that continues to evolve, incorporating new herbs and practices as its practitioners adapt to their specific needs and environments

So, without further ado, let us dive into the transformative world of Rootworking recipes. May they serve as a springboard for your own unique practice, guided by the wisdom of your ancestors and the ever-present spirits that walk beside you.

Hoodoo Herbs

Metaphysical and Medicinal Properties of Commonly Used Plants

The use of specific herbs in Hoodoo can be traced back to its roots in African, Native American, and African American spiritual traditions. In Hoodoo, herbs are believed to possess unique properties and energies that can be harnessed for various metaphysical and medicinal purposes. The selection of herbs is influenced by both African, African American, and Native American herbal knowledge, as well as the availability of local plants in the regions where Hoodoo originated and developed.

The resulting syncretic practice of Hoodoo incorporated a wide range of herbs, each chosen for its specific properties and correspondences. The selection of herbs in Hoodoo is also influenced by the principles of sympathetic metaphysics, where herbs that resemble desired outcomes or possess similar qualities are used. For instance, High John the Conqueror root, which is believed to bring personal power and success, resembles a human figure when shaped, symbolizing mastery and triumph.

The use of all-natural, holistic, and herbal remedies is important in Hoodoo for several reasons:

<u>Connection to Nature:</u> Hoodoo is rooted in African and African American traditions, which emphasize a deep connection to the natural world. Using natural and herbal remedies allows practitioners to align themselves with the healing and spiritual energies of plants, herbs, and natural elements.

<u>Spiritual Significance:</u> Many herbs and plants have long been associated with specific spiritual or metaphysical properties in various cultures and traditions. In Hoodoo, these associations are utilized to harness the specific energies and intentions of the plants for healing, protection, manifestation, and other spiritual practices.

<u>Wisdom and Tradition:</u> Hoodoo has been passed down through generations, often within families or communities. The use of natural remedies is a part of this spiritual wisdom, drawing upon the knowledge and traditions of ancestors. It is believed that these remedies have been proven effective over time and carry the spiritual power of those who came before.

<u>Accessibility and Affordability:</u> Hoodoo developed within communities that often-had limited access to formal medical or metaphysical resources. Using natural remedies made from locally available plants and herbs provided an accessible and affordable means of healing and spiritual practice.

<u>Personal Empowerment:</u> By utilizing natural remedies, practitioners of Hoodoo have the opportunity to take control of their own healing and spiritual journey. They can gather, prepare, and use the remedies themselves, fostering a sense of empowerment and self-sufficiency.

<u>Holistic Approach:</u> Hoodoo recognizes the interconnectedness of the physical, emotional, and spiritual aspects of an individual. Natural remedies are often used holistically to address not only physical ailments but also emotional and spiritual imbalances, promoting overall well-being and harmony.

It is important to note that while herbal and natural remedies are commonly used in Hoodoo, they are not a substitute for professional medical or mental health care. Hoodoo practitioners often emphasize the complementary nature of natural remedies and conventional medicine, encouraging individuals to seek appropriate medical help when needed.

45 COMMONLY USED HERBS
In Hoodoo

Agrimony
Metaphysical Properties: Protection, banishing negative energies, reversing workings.

Medicinal Properties: Digestive aid, diuretic, wound healing.

Angelica Root
Metaphysical Properties: Protection, healing, purification, warding off evil.

Medicinal Properties: Digestive aid, immune support, anti-inflammatory.

Basil
Metaphysical Properties: Protection, love, prosperity, purification.

Medicinal Properties: Digestive aid, anti-inflammatory, antibacterial.

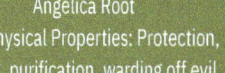

Bayberry
Metaphysical Properties: Prosperity, abundance, money drawing, protection.

Medicinal Properties: Antioxidant, anti-inflammatory, fever reducer.

Lavender
Metaphysical Properties: Calming, relaxation, purification, love, dream work.

Medicinal Properties: Sedative, anti-anxiety, antimicrobial, pain relief.

Lemongrass
Metaphysical Properties: Psychic abilities, purification, mental clarity, protection.

Medicinal Properties: Digestive aid, pain relief, antibacterial.

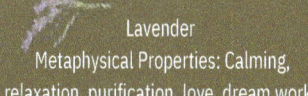

Licorice Root
Metaphysical Properties: Love, attraction, control, harmony.

Medicinal Properties: Soothes throat, anti-inflammatory, digestive aid.

Master Root
Metaphysical Properties: Mastery, control, power, protection.

Medicinal Properties: None (typically used for its metaphysical properties).

Bay Leaf
Metaphysical Properties: Psychic abilities, wish manifestation, protection.

Medicinal Properties: Antioxidant, anti-inflammatory, digestive aid.

Black Cohosh
Metaphysical Properties: Banishing negativity, protection, feminine energy.

Medicinal Properties: Hormonal balance, pain relief, sedative.

Calendula
Metaphysical Properties: Joy, creativity, success, healing, psychic dreams.

Medicinal Properties: Skin healing, antimicrobial, anti-inflammatory

Cedar
Metaphysical Properties: Protection, purification, grounding, abundance.

Medicinal Properties: Respiratory aid, insect repellent, antifungal.

Chamomile
Metaphysical Properties: Calming, peace, love, prosperity, sleep.

Medicinal Properties: Sedative, anti-inflammatory, digestive aid.

Meadowsweet
Metaphysical Properties: Love, happiness, peace, harmony.

Medicinal Properties: Pain relief, anti-inflammatory, fever reducer.

Mugwort
Metaphysical Properties: Divination, psychic abilities, protection, lucid dreaming.

Medicinal Properties: Digestive aid, menstrual support, sleep aid.

Mullein
Metaphysical Properties: Protection, courage, banishing negativity.

Medicinal Properties: Respiratory support, expectorant, soothing for throat.

Patchouli
Metaphysical Properties: Money drawing, passion, grounding, fertility, spiritual growth.

Medicinal Properties: Antidepressant, antifungal, anti-inflammatory, aphrodisiac.

Peppermint
Metaphysical Properties: Energy, mental clarity, purification, prosperity.

Medicinal Properties: Digestive aid, headache relief, anti-inflammatory.

Cinnamon
Metaphysical Properties: Prosperity, success, love, spiritual healing.

Medicinal Properties: Antimicrobial, anti-inflammatory, PCOS, blood sugar regulation.

Coltsfoot
Metaphysical Properties: Divination, visions, luck, strength, grounding.

Medicinal Properties: Cough suppressant, expectorant, anti-inflammatory.

Comfrey
Metaphysical Properties: Healing, protection, safety during travel.

Medicinal Properties: Wound healing, bone support, anti-inflammatory.

Dandelion
Metaphysical Properties: Divination, wish manifestation, purification, clarity.

Medicinal Properties: Liver support, diuretic, digestive aid.

Dragon's Blood
Metaphysical Properties: Protection, banishing negativity, power.

Medicinal Properties: Antiseptic, wound healing, inflammation reducer.

Eucalyptus
Metaphysical Properties: Healing, purification, protection, psychic abilities.

Medicinal Properties: Respiratory aid, anti-inflammatory, analgesic.

Queen (Orris) Root
Metaphysical Properties: Love, attraction, feminine energy, confidence.

Medicinal Properties: None (typically used for its metaphysical properties).

Red Clover
Metaphysical Properties: Love, luck, protection, fertility.

Medicinal Properties: Blood purifier, hormone balancer, expectorant.

Rosemary
Metaphysical Properties: Protection, mental clarity, love, purification.

Medicinal Properties: Memory enhancement, digestive aid, anti-inflammatory, hair growth.

Rose
Metaphysical Properties: Love, romance, beauty, self-love, emotional healing.

Medicinal Properties: Antioxidant, anti-inflammatory, mood enhancer.

Sage
Metaphysical Properties: Cleansing, purification, wisdom, protection.

Medicinal Properties: Antioxidant, antimicrobial, anti-inflammatory.

Sandalwood
Metaphysical Properties: Spirituality, meditation, protection, healing.

Medicinal Properties: Anti-inflammatory, antiseptic, grounding.

Five Finger Grass (Cinquefoil)
Metaphysical Properties: Prosperity, luck, success, protection.

Medicinal Properties: Astringent, antiseptic, anti-inflammatory.

Frankincense
Metaphysical Properties: Spirituality, protection, meditation, purification.

Medicinal Properties: Anti-inflammatory, immune support, respiratory aid.

Ginger
Metaphysical Properties: Energy, success, passion, abundance, love.

Medicinal Properties: Digestive aid, anti-nausea, anti-inflammatory.

High John the Conqueror Root
Metaphysical Properties: Power, success, protection, overcoming obstacles.

Medicinal Properties: None (typically used for its metaphysical properties).

Honeysuckle
Metaphysical Properties: Love, friendship, psychic abilities, releasing negativity.

Medicinal Properties: Anti-inflammatory, immune support, skin healing.

Sassafras
Metaphysical Properties: Abundance, purification, grounding, manifestation.

Medicinal Properties: Blood purifier, diuretic, anti-inflammatory.

Slippery Elm
Metaphysical Properties: Protection, soothing, healing, psychic abilities.

Medicinal Properties: Soothes sore throat, relieves cough, aids digestion.

Solomon's Seal
Metaphysical Properties: Wisdom, protection, balance, spiritual guidance.

Medicinal Properties: Joint support, anti-inflammatory, immune support.

Thyme
Metaphysical Properties: Purification, courage, strength, psychic abilities.

Medicinal Properties: Antimicrobial, expectorant, digestive aid.

Vervain
Metaphysical Properties: Protection, purification, love, enhancing intuition.

Medicinal Properties: Relaxant, digestive aid, anti-inflammatory.

Hyssop
Metaphysical Properties: Purification, healing, protection, spiritual cleansing.

Medicinal Properties: Antiseptic, expectorant, immune support.

Jasmine
Metaphysical Properties: Love, sensuality, spiritual growth, prosperity.

Medicinal Properties: Antidepressant, antiseptic, aphrodisiac, menstrual support, sleep aid. Commonly used in aromatherapy for its uplifting and calming effects.

Violet
Metaphysical Properties: Love, protection, luck, dreams, intuition.

Medicinal Properties: Antioxidant, anti-inflammatory, expectorant.

White Willow Bark
Metaphysical Properties: Healing, divination, protection, purification.

Medicinal Properties: Pain reliever, fever reducer, anti-inflammatory.

Yarrow
Metaphysical Properties: Psychic abilities, protection, courage, divination.

Medicinal Properties: Wound healing, fever reduction, menstrual support.

Please note that while these herbs have historical associations with specific metaphysical and medicinal properties, individual experiences and beliefs may vary. It is always recommended to do thorough research and consult with a qualified herbalist, rootworker, or medical professional before using any herbs for metaphysical or medicinal purposes.

Holistic Remedies

Natural and holistic healing holds immense importance in the belief system of Hoodoo practitioners and Rootworkers. This emphasis on natural remedies and holistic approaches stems from several foundational principles within this practice.

Firstly, Hoodoo and Rootworking are deeply rooted in ancestral traditions that have long relied on the healing properties of the earth. The use of natural herbs, roots, and other botanical materials is seen as a way to connect with the wisdom and energies of the natural world. It is believed that these natural elements possess inherent healing properties that can address physical, emotional, and spiritual imbalances.

Additionally, Hoodoo and Rootworking place a strong emphasis on personal empowerment and self-reliance. By utilizing natural and holistic healing methods, practitioners are encouraged to take an active role in their own well-being. This approach promotes a sense of agency and encourages individuals to connect with their own innate healing abilities. Furthermore, the use of natural and holistic healing aligns with the concept of balance and harmony in Hoodoo. This practice recognizes the interconnectedness of all things and emphasizes the restoration of equilibrium within the body, mind, and spirit. Natural remedies are seen as a means to restore this balance by addressing the root causes of ailments and promoting overall wellness.

In Hoodoo, there is also a belief in the power of intention and energy. Natural and holistic healing methods are seen as effective tools for channeling and directing one's intentions and energy towards healing and transformation. This aligns with the belief that the body, mind, and spirit are interconnected, and healing on one level can positively impact others.

Here are a few all-natural and simple recipes to help you embark on your holistic rootworking journey! Feel free to explore and research these ailments to customize the recipes and expand your apothecary, medicine cabinet, or inventory. By adding your own twist, you can create unique remedies tailored to your specific needs and preferences. Remember to always exercise caution and consult with a healthcare professional when necessary. Happy exploring and healing!

SIMPLE & EASY REMEDIES

Allergy Relief:

Brew a cup of nettle leaf tea using dried nettle leaves to naturally alleviate allergy symptoms, such as sneezing, itching, and congestion.

Anxiety and Depression Support:

Brew a cup of St. John's Wort tea using dried St. John's Wort flowers to help with symptoms of anxiety and depression.

Blood Pressure Regulation:

Drink hawthorn berry tea regularly to support healthy blood pressure levels and cardiovascular health.

Cold and Flu Remedy:

Create a hot tea using ginger root, lemon juice, and honey to soothe cold and flu symptoms, boost the immune system, and relieve congestion.

Digestive Aid:

Brew a cup of peppermint tea using dried peppermint leaves to alleviate digestive discomfort and promote healthy digestion.

Energy Booster:

Add a few drops of rosemary essential oil to a diffuser or inhale its scent directly to increase mental clarity, focus, and energy levels.

Hangover Remedy:

Drink a cup of dandelion root tea or take dandelion root capsules to support liver detoxification and alleviate hangover symptoms.

Healing Herbal Tea:

Ingredients: Echinacea, ginger, elderberry, chamomile.
Brew a cup of hot tea using equal parts of the herbs. Sweeten with honey if desired. Drink this herbal tea to boost your immune system, promote healing, and soothe the body and mind.

Healing Salve:

Ingredients: Calendula flowers, comfrey leaf, plantain leaf, olive oil, beeswax.
Instructions: Infuse the herbs in olive oil using a double boiler method. Strain the oil and melt beeswax into it to create a salve consistency. Use this healing salve topically on minor cuts, bruises, or skin irritations to promote healing and soothe the skin.

Headache Relief:

Take a few drops of lavender essential oil and massage it onto your temples for soothing relief from headaches.

Indigestion Aid:

Mix a teaspoon of apple cider vinegar with warm water and honey. Drink this mixture before meals to aid digestion and reduce indigestion symptoms.

Joint Pain Relief:

Create a salve by infusing arnica flowers and cayenne pepper in olive oil. Apply it topically to relieve joint pain and inflammation.

Menstrual Cramp Relief:

Drink a cup of warm chamomile or ginger tea to ease menstrual cramps and reduce discomfort during menstruation.

Migraine Relief:

Rub a few drops of peppermint or lavender essential oil onto your temples and neck to help alleviate migraines and reduce pain.

Nausea Remedy:

Inhale the scent of peppermint essential oil or sip on a cup of ginger tea to alleviate nausea and settle your stomach.

Respiratory Congestion Relief:

Inhale the steam from a pot of boiling water infused with eucalyptus essential oil to clear nasal passages and relieve congestion.

Skin Irritation Soother:

Apply aloe vera gel directly to irritated skin to soothe and heal various skin conditions, such as sunburn, rashes, or insect bites.

Sleep Aid:

Place a small sachet filled with dried chamomile flowers under your pillow to promote relaxation and better sleep.

Sore Throat Relief:

Gargle with a warm solution of saltwater and sage tea to ease sore throat pain and reduce inflammation.

Stress and Anxiety Relief:

Burn dried lavender or rosemary as incense to create a calming atmosphere and promote relaxation during times of stress.

Warming Herbal Tea:

To boost during colder months, a warming herbal tea can work wonders. Make tea blend with cinnamon, ginger, and cloves. Steep the spices in hot water for about 10 minutes, strain.

Weary Foot Soak:

Rejuvenating foot soak. Add warm water to a basin and mix in a cup of Epsom salts along with a few drops of your favorite relaxing essential oil, such as lavender or peppermint. Soak your feet for 15-20 minutes to soothe tired muscles and promote relaxation.

Wellness Elixir:

For an immune-boosting elixir, combine warm water, a squeeze of lemon juice, a teaspoon of honey, and a dash of cayenne pepper. Stir well and sip on this concoction to help support your overall well-being.

Wound Healing:

Apply a poultice made from calendula flowers to wounds or cuts to promote healing and prevent infection.

One Herb Remedies

Tinctures

🍴 5-10 Drops 🕐 twice daily

Echinacea Tincture:

Uses:
This tincture is used to support the immune system and can be taken orally.

Ingredients:
Echinacea root (dried or fresh), high-proof alcohol (like vodka)

Instructions:
1. Fill a jar halfway with the echinacea root.
2. Pour enough alcohol to cover the root completely.
3. Seal the jar tightly and store it in a cool, dark place for 4-6 weeks, shaking it occasionally.
4. Strain the tincture and store it in a dark glass bottle.

Valerian Root Tincture:

Uses:
This tincture is used to promote relaxation and support sleep. Take a few drops orally as needed.

Ingredients:
Valerian root (dried or fresh), high-proof alcohol (like vodka)

Instructions:
1. Fill a jar one-third full with valerian root.
2. Pour enough alcohol to cover the root completely.
3. Seal the jar tightly and store it in a cool, dark place for 2-6 weeks, shaking it daily.
4. Strain the tincture and store it in a dark glass bottle.

Capsules

🍴 2 Capsules 🕐 twice daily

Milk Thistle Capsules:

Uses:
These capsules are used to support liver health and can be taken orally according to the recommended dosage.

Ingredients:
Milk thistle seeds (ground), empty vegetarian capsules

Instructions:
1. Grind milk thistle seeds into a fine powder.
2. Fill empty capsules with the powdered seeds using a capsule-filling device or by hand.

Turmeric Capsules:

Uses:
These capsules are used for their anti-inflammatory properties and can be taken orally according to the recommended dosage.

Ingredients:
Turmeric powder, empty vegetarian capsules

Instructions:
1. Fill empty capsules with turmeric powder using a capsule-filling device or by hand.

Poultices

 Use as Needed

Calendula Poultice:
Uses:
Minor burns to soothe pain and help promote tissue repair.
Ingredients:
Calendula flowers (dried or fresh), hot water, clean cloth or gauze
Instructions:
1. Steep calendula flowers in hot water for 10-15 minutes.
2. Strain the liquid and let it cool slightly.
3. Soak a clean cloth or gauze in the liquid, wring out excess moisture, and apply it to the
4. affected area.
5. Secure with a bandage if needed.

Comfrey Poultice:
Uses:
Comfrey poultices are often used for their anti-inflammatory and wound-healing properties.
Ingredients:
Comfrey leaves (fresh or dried), hot water, clean cloth or gauze
Instructions:
1. Crush or chop comfrey leaves and place them in a bowl.
2. Add enough hot water to form a paste-like consistency.
3. Let it cool slightly.
4. Spread the mixture onto a clean cloth or gauze and apply it directly to the affected area.
5. Secure with a bandage if needed.

Plantain Poultice:
Uses:
Plantain poultices are commonly used for their soothing and healing properties for skin irritations, bites, or stings.
Ingredients:
Plantain leaves (fresh or dried), hot water, clean cloth or gauze
Instructions:
1. Crush or chop plantain leaves and place them in a bowl.
2. Add enough hot water to form a paste-like consistency.
3. Let it cool slightly.
4. Spread the mixture onto a clean cloth or gauze and apply it to the affected area.
5. Secure with a bandage if needed.

Teas

 2 tbs per cup   as needed

Chamomile Tea:
Uses:
Chamomile tea is renowned for its calming and relaxing properties and is often used to promote sleep and relieve digestive discomfort.
Ingredients:
Chamomile flowers (dried), hot water
Instructions:
1. Place 1-2 teaspoons of dried chamomile flowers in a cup.
2. Pour hot water over the flowers and let them steep for 5-10 minutes.
3. Strain and drink the tea.

Peppermint Tea:
Uses:
Peppermint tea is known for its soothing effects on the digestive system, helping to relieve bloating, nausea, and indigestion.
Ingredients:
Peppermint leaves (dried), hot water
Instructions:
1. Place 1-2 teaspoons of dried peppermint leaves in a cup.
2. Pour hot water over the leaves and let them steep for 5-10 minutes.
3. Strain and drink the tea.

A Rootworker's Verse

In whispered winds and sacred soil,
Herbs hold secrets of ancient toil.
Roots and leaves, a divine decree,
Bind the earthly and the esprit.

From bay leaves visions to sage's cleanse,
Each herb's lore, a mystic sense.
Thyme and vervain, with powers rife,
Guard the spirit, soothe the strife.

In Hoodoo's grasp, their virtues rise,
Ancestral wisdom, never disguised.
Mullein's light, in shadowed plight,
Guides the lost, reclaims the right.

Mint's cool touch, a healing balm,
Revives the weary, brings them calm.
Burdock, dandelion, roots deep and true,
Draw out ailment, bid health anew.

With hands that toil in earth's embrace,
Rootworker's art, a sacred grace.
Through herb and prayer, spirits entwine,
Healing journeys, their paths align.

So in the heart of Hoodoo's lore,
Herbs and spirits, forevermore.
Their earthly forms, the divine's decree,
Bound in faith, in Hoodoo's key.

May their essence, both near and far,
Bring healing, peace, and blessings ajar.
Rootworker's hands, with herbs entwined,
Channel whispers of the divine.

-Rootworker Kye

Tinctures

SERVINGS: 5-10 DROPS   TIME: ONCE DAILY

Immune-Boosting Tincture:

This immune-boosting tincture can be taken orally to support the immune system.

Ingredients

Echinacea root,
elderberry,
astragalus root,
high-proof alcohol (like vodka)

Directions

1. Fill a jar one-third full with a mixture of equal parts echinacea root, elderberry, and astragalus root.
2. Pour enough alcohol to cover the herbs completely.
3. Seal the jar tightly and store it in a cool, dark place for 4-6 weeks, shaking it occasionally. Strain the tincture and store it in a dark glass bottle.

Digestive Support Tincture:

This digestive support tincture can be taken orally to help relieve digestive discomfort.

Ingredients

Peppermint leaf,
fennel seed,
ginger root,
high-proof alcohol (like vodka)

Directions

1. Fill a jar one-third full with equal parts peppermint leaf, fennel seed, and ginger root.
2. Pour enough alcohol to cover the herbs completely.
3. Seal the jar tightly and store it in a cool, dark place for 4-6 weeks, shaking it occasionally.
4. Strain the tincture and store it in a dark glass bottle.

Cation when using for children; consult a healthcare professional if pregnant, nursing, or under medical supervision.

Capsules

SERVINGS: 2 CAPSULES   TIME: AS NEEDED

Anti-Inflammatory Capsules:

These capsules can be taken orally to support the reduction of inflammation in the body.

Ingredients

Turmeric powder,
ginger powder,
Boswellia resin,
empty vegetarian capsules

Directions

1. Mix equal parts turmeric powder, ginger powder, and Boswellia resin together.
2. Fill empty capsules with the powdered mixture using a capsule-filling device or by hand.

Stress Relief Capsules:

These capsules can be taken orally to promote relaxation and reduce stress.

Ingredients

Ashwagandha root powder,
holy basil leaf powder,
lavender flower powder,
empty vegetarian capsules

Directions

1. Mix equal parts ashwagandha root powder, holy basil leaf powder, and lavender flower
2. powder together.
3. Fill empty capsules with the powdered mixture using a capsule-filling device or by hand.

> Cation when using for children; consult a healthcare professional if pregnant, nursing, or under medical supervision.

Poultices

SERVINGS: AS NEEDED TIME: AS NEEDED

Pain-Relieving Poultice:
This poultice combines the pain-relieving properties of willow bark and arnica with the anti-inflammatory properties of comfrey.

Ingredients
Willow bark, arnica flowers,
comfrey leaves,
hot water,
clean cloth or gauze

Directions
1. Crush or chop equal parts willow bark, arnica flowers, and comfrey leaves and place
2. them in a bowl.
3. Add enough hot water to form a paste-like consistency.
4. Let it cool slightly.
5. Spread the mixture onto a clean cloth or gauze and apply it directly to the affected area.
6. Secure with a bandage if needed.

Skin-Healing Poultice:
This poultice combines the healing properties of calendula, plantain, and yarrow to help soothe and heal skin irritations or wounds.

Ingredients
Calendula flowers,
plantain leaves,
yarrow flowers,
hot water,
clean cloth or gauze

Directions
1. Crush or chop equal parts calendula flowers, plantain leaves, and yarrow flowers and
2. place them in a bowl.
3. Add enough hot water to form a paste-like consistency.
4. Let it cool slightly.
5. Spread the mixture onto a clean cloth or gauze and apply it to the affected area.
6. Secure with a bandage if needed.

Cation when using for children; consult a healthcare professional if pregnant, nursing, or under medical supervision.

Teas

SERVINGS: 1 - 2 TEASPOONS PER CUP   TIME: AS NEEDED

Respiratory Support Tea:

This tea provides respiratory support and can help soothe coughs and congestion.

Ingredients

Mullein leaf,
marshmallow root,
licorice root,
thyme leaves,
hot water

Directions

1. Mix equal parts mullein leaf, marshmallow root, licorice root, and thyme leaves together.
2. Use 1-2 teaspoons of the herbal mixture per cup of hot water.
3. Let it steep for 10-15 minutes, then strain and drink the tea.

Mood-Boosting Tea:

This tea can help uplift the mood and promote relaxation.

Ingredients

St. John's Wort flowers,
lemon balm leaves,
chamomile flowers,
lavender flowers,
hot water

Directions

1. Mix equal parts St. John's Wort flowers, lemon balm leaves, chamomile flowers, and
2. lavender flowers together.
3. Use 1-2 teaspoons of the herbal mixture per cup of hot water.
4. Let it steep for 5-10 minutes, then strain and drink the tea.

Cation when using for children; consult a healthcare professional if pregnant, nursing, or under medical supervision.

Charms, Mojos, & Sachets

Charms, mojo bags, and sachets hold both historical and spiritual significance within the practice of Hoodoo. These objects play a crucial role in Hoodoo rituals and works, carrying symbolic meanings and imbued with spiritual power. Historically, charms, mojo bags, and sachets have been used by African American slaves and their descendants as a means of protection, empowerment, and manifestation. These objects were often discreetly crafted and carried as personal talismans, reflecting the resourcefulness and resilience of the enslaved community.

Spiritually, these items are believed to harness and amplify the energies of specific herbs, roots, minerals, and other metaphysical and natural ingredients contained within them. Hoodoo practitioners carefully select and combine these elements based on their intended purpose or desired outcome. Each ingredient contributes its unique properties and symbolism to the overall energy of the charm, mojo bag, or sachet.

All three are typically created with a specific intention in mind, such as attracting love, financial abundance, protection from harm, or spiritual guidance. They are often blessed, consecrated, or activated through rituals or prayers, infusing them with spiritual power. These objects are believed to serve as a conduit between the physical and spiritual realms, facilitating the manifestation of the practitioner's desires.

In Hoodoo, the process of crafting and personalizing these items is considered essential. Each charm, mojo bag, or sachet is tailored to the individual's unique needs and desires, reflecting their personal energy and connection to the spiritual forces at play. Through the act of creating and working with these objects, Hoodoo practitioners establish a direct and intimate relationship with the spiritual realm, enabling them to tap into its power and influence.

Please note that the provided Hoodoo recipes for charms, mojo bags, and sachets do not include specific instructions on how to activate or bless them. This is because there are a multitude of methods and practices within Hoodoo for this purpose, and it is important to draw from your ancestral knowledge and personal intuition. One personal approach that can be taken is to activate a newly created item by sleeping with it for seven nights while reciting the appropriate psalms or prayers that align with the specific intention of the item. In addition to activation, it is important to cleanse and feed these items to maintain their efficacy.

This can be done using various methods such as Florida water, whiskey, rainwater, or alternatives based on your ancestral knowledge. Cleansing helps remove any negative or stagnant energies that may have accumulated, while feeding replenishes and strengthens the item's spiritual power. Remember to adapt these practices to your own traditions and beliefs, ensuring a meaningful and authentic connection with the Hoodoo tradition.

Mojo, Sachet, & Charm Recipes

Cleansing Sachet: - Ingredients: White sage leaves (cleansing, purification), rosemary leaves (cleansing, protection), lavender flowers (calming, purification), clear quartz crystal (amplifies cleansing energies). - Purpose: Used to cleanse and purify spaces, objects, or individuals from negative energies and influences.

Court Case Mojo Bag: - Ingredients: Solomon's Seal, calendula, dill seeds, galangal root. - Instructions: Combine equal parts of the herbs and place them in a small fabric bag. Carry this mojo bag with you or keep it in a safe place when dealing with legal matters to enhance your chances of success and favorable outcomes in court cases.

Court Case Mojo Bag (alternative recipe) : - Ingredients: Solomon's seal root (legal success), calendula petals (justice), cloves (success in legal matters), pyrite crystal (confidence, success). Fast Luck Sachet: - Ingredients: Patchouli, cinnamon, five-finger grass (cinquefoil), basil. - Instructions: Combine the dried herbs and place them in a small fabric sachet. Carry or keep this sachet with you to attract good luck, speedy outcomes, and positive opportunities in various areas of your life.

Healing Mojo Bag: - Ingredients: Eucalyptus leaves (healing), lavender flowers (calming, healing), rosemary leaves (healing, purification), clear quartz crystal (amplifies healing energies). - Purpose: Aims to promote physical, emotional, and spiritual healing.

Love Attraction Sachet: - Ingredients: Red rose petals (passion, love), jasmine flowers (romantic attraction), catnip (attraction, love), lavender (calming, love), rose quartz (love, harmony). - Purpose: Designed to attract love and enhance personal magnetism.

Love Drawing Mojo Bag: - Ingredients: Rose petals, damiana leaf, catnip, lavender. - Instructions: Combine equal parts of the herbs and place them in a small fabric bag. Carry this mojo bag with you to attract love, enhance romance, and strengthen existing relationships.

Lucky Charm: - Ingredients: Four-leaf clover (luck), chamomile flowers (luck, prosperity), allspice berries (luck, good fortune), green aventurine crystal (luck, abundance). - Purpose: Designed to attract good luck, fortune, and positive opportunities. *Please note charms can be created by putting the ingredients in small bottles that are small enough to put on a necklace or bracelet.

Money Drawing Mojo Bag: - Ingredients: Patchouli, basil, cinnamon, allspice, chamomile. - Instructions: Combine equal parts of the herbs and place them in a small fabric bag. Carry this mojo bag with you to attract financial abundance and prosperity.

Money Drawing Mojo Bag: - Ingredients: Basil leaves (prosperity), cinnamon sticks (money drawing), patchouli leaves (money attraction), ginger root (financial success), green aventurine crystal (luck, abundance). - Purpose: Intended to draw wealth, financial opportunities, and prosperity.

Protection Charm: - Ingredients: Black tourmaline, angelica root, bay leaves, red string or thread. - Instructions: String the herbs together with the black tourmaline, creating a protective charm. Hang this charm in your home or carry it with you to ward off negative energies. *Please note charms can be created by putting the ingredients in small bottles that are small enough to put on a necklace or bracelet.

Protection Charm: - Ingredients: Black salt (protection), angelica root (warding off evil), bay leaves (protection, purification), frankincense resin (spiritual protection), black tourmaline crystal (grounding, protection). - Purpose: Provides protection against negative energies and evil influences. *Please note charms can be created by putting the ingredients in small bottles that are small enough to put on a necklace or bracelet.

Protection Mojo Bag: - Ingredients: Angelica root, black salt, bay leaves, frankincense resin. - Instructions: Combine equal parts of the herbs and place them in a small fabric bag. Carry or keep this mojo bag in your home or personal space to ward off negative energies, psychic attacks, and harm.

Protection Sachet: - Ingredients: Bay leaves, rosemary, juniper berries, black salt. - Instructions: Combine the herbs and place them in a small sachet or fabric pouch. Carry or hang this sachet in your home or personal space to ward off negative energies, hexes, and evil spirits.

Psychic Dream Pillow: - Ingredients: Mugwort, lavender, chamomile, rose petals. - Instructions: Combine the dried herbs and stuff them into a small fabric pouch. Place the dream pillow under your pillow or beside your bed to promote vivid. and prophetic dreams, enhance intuition, and deepen your connection to the spiritual realm during sleep.

Spiritual Awakening Charm: - Ingredients: Mugwort leaves (spiritual awakening), frankincense resin (spiritual purification), sandalwood chips (spiritual protection), amethyst crystal (spiritual growth, intuition). - Purpose: Intended to enhance spiritual awareness, intuition, and connection to higher realms. *Please note charms can be created by putting the ingredients in small bottles that are small enough to put on a necklace or bracelet.

Success Charm: - Ingredients: Sunflower petals (success, confidence), cinnamon powder (success, achievement), bay leaves (success, victory), citrine crystal (success, abundance). - Purpose: Intended to attract success, achievement, and abundance in various areas of life. *Please note charms can be created by putting the ingredients in small bottles that are small enough to put on a necklace or bracelet.

Success Mojo Bag: - Ingredients: High John the Conqueror root, bay leaf, cinnamon, lodestone. - Instructions: Combine equal parts of the herbs and place them in a small fabric bag. Carry or keep this mojo bag with you to enhance personal power, attract success, and overcome obstacles.

Please note that these recipes are just starting points, and you can always adapt and personalize them based on your own intuition and ancestral knowledge.

Arkansas Mojo

Amidst Arkansas' whispers, a conjurer stands,
Her roots run deep in these mystical lands.
In her hands, a mojo bag, a shield so deft,
Guarding her spirit from a rival adept.
Each artifact a ward, every herb a charm,
In her woven pouch, protection from harm.

From the Ouachita's embrace to the Delta's expanse,
Her mojo's vigil, a wary, watchful dance.
From Devil's Knives to protective horehound,
In her satchel of secrets, defenses abound.

Twilight's whispers and moonlit dew,
In her pouch, an arsenal, tried and true.
Snake sheds and gator teeth, in silent repose,
In her crafty arsenal, their powers compose.

With a glance and a whisper, she fortifies her will,
In her trusted pouch, where intentions distill.
For in Arkansas' heart, where the conjurer prevails,
In her pouch's embrace, where protection unfurls.
A guardian's treasure, her mojo bag's allure,
Sentinel of safety, in its sanctified pure.

So within Arkansas' embrace, her craft does unfold,
In the shadow of her mojo, where protections take hold.
A practitioner's vigil, in her bag's mystic array,
A shield 'gainst intrusion, where she holds sway.

-Rootworker Kye

How to Uses Mojos, Sachets, & Charms

Mojo Bags:

Select a small bag or pouch made of natural fabric, such as cotton or flannel. The color of the fabric can be chosen based on the specific intention or purpose of the mojo bag. Choose the herbs, roots, stones, and other items that correspond to your desired outcome. For example, if you want a love mojo bag, you may include herbs like rose petals and lavender, a small rose quartz crystal, and personal items like a lock of hair or a piece of clothing from your desired partner.

Place the selected items into the mojo bag while focusing on your intention. Some practitioners may add a few drops of specific oils or sprinkle the bag with powders associated with their desired outcome.

Seal the mojo bag tightly, ensuring that none of the contents will fall out. Carry or wear the mojo bag on your person, keeping it close to your body. Some common ways to carry a mojo bag include in a pocket, tucked into a bra, or worn on a necklace or bracelet. The bag should be kept hidden and not shown to others.

Sachets:

Choose a small fabric pouch or bag, similar to a mojo bag, made of natural fabric. Select dried herbs, flowers, or other materials that align with your intention. For example, if you want to promote peaceful sleep, you may use dried lavender buds or chamomile flowers.

Fill the sachet with the chosen ingredients, leaving enough space for the materials to move and release their fragrance.

Tie the sachet closed with a ribbon or string, ensuring it is secure. Place the sachet in a location where it can diffuse its aroma or be easily accessed. For example, you can hang it from a doorknob, place it under your pillow, or tuck it into a drawer or closet.

Charms:

Choose a small object that symbolizes your desired outcome or intention. This can be a charm, a small stone, small glass bottles, a piece of jewelry, or any other item that holds personal significance. Cleanse and consecrate the charm by passing it through incense smoke or sprinkling it with a few drops of a corresponding oil.

Hold the charm in your hands and focus on your intention, visualizing the desired outcome or energy imbued within the charm.

Carry or wear the charm on your person to keep its energy close to you. You can wear it as a necklace, bracelet, or place it in a pocket or purse. Some practitioners may choose to place the charm on an altar or in a special designated area to serve as a focal point for their intention.

Maintenance and Disposal:

Mojo bags, sachets, and charms should be periodically recharged or refreshed to maintain their potency. This can be done by exposing them to moonlight or sunlight, passing them through incense smoke, or anointing them with oils associated with their intention.

If you feel that the mojo bag, sachet, or charm has served its purpose or is no longer needed, it should be respectfully disposed of. Many practitioners choose to bury them in the earth, place them in flowing water, or burn them in a ritual fire, thanking the energies and spirits involved.

Remember, the specific contents and instructions for mojo bags, sachets, and charms can vary based on personal preference, tradition, and the intended purpose. It's important to trust your intuition and adapt these practices to align with your own beliefs and intentions.

Spiritual Baths

Spiritual baths hold significant importance in Hoodoo practices. They are considered a form of ritual purification and spiritual cleansing. The purpose of a spiritual bath is to remove negative energies, attract positive influences, and/or enhance spiritual connection.

Spiritual baths typically involve the use of specific herbs, oils, and other ingredients that hold symbolic or energetic properties. These ingredients are chosen based on their association with various intentions such as protection, love, prosperity, or spiritual growth. During a spiritual bath, the individual immerses themselves in the prepared bathwater or pours it over their body while focusing on their intention.

This ritual is often accompanied by prayers, affirmations, or invocations to invoke the desired energy or spiritual assistance.

The act of taking a spiritual bath is believed to cleanse not only the physical body but also the energetic and spiritual aspects of the individual. It is seen as a way to release negative influences, purify the aura, and invite positive energies and blessings into one's life. Spiritual baths are versatile and can be customized according to personal needs and intentions. They can be performed regularly, on specific occasions, or in response to specific spiritual or energetic challenges.

Overall, spiritual baths are a vital part of Hoodoo practices, serving as a means of spiritual rejuvenation, purification, and aligning oneself with the desired energies or spiritual forces.

Spiritual Bath Recipes

Ancestral Connection Bath: - Ingredients: Rosemary leaves, lavender flowers, mugwort leaves, and white candles. - Purpose: To connect with ancestors, receive their guidance and wisdom and honor their spirits.

Beauty Bath: - Ingredients: Rose petals, lavender flowers, chamomile flowers, and a few drops of rose oil. - Purpose: To enhance physical beauty, boost self-confidence, and attract admiration.

Blessing and Purification Bath: - Ingredients: Holy water, rose petals, white sage, and a few drops of lavender oil. - Purpose: To receive divine blessings, purify the spirit, and bring spiritual harmony and peace.

Cleansing Bath: - Ingredients: Sea salt, rosemary leaves, lemon slices, and white sage. - Purpose: To cleanse the aura, remove negative energy, and purify the spirit.

Court Case Bath: - Ingredients: Solomon's seal root, licorice root, calendula petals, and a pinch of salt. - Purpose: To gain favor in legal matters, receive a fair judgment, and protect against injustice.

Healing Bath: - Ingredients: Eucalyptus leaves, chamomile flowers, lavender oil, and rose petals. - Purpose: To promote physical and emotional healing and restore balance.

Love Attraction Bath: - Ingredients: Rose petals, lavender, jasmine flowers, catnip. - Instructions: Brew a strong herbal infusion using the herbs. Strain the liquid and add it to your bathwater. Soak in the bath to attract love, enhance romantic connections, and promote self-love.

Love Drawing Bath: - Ingredients: Rose petals, jasmine flowers, ylang-ylang essential oil, honey. - Instructions: Brew a strong herbal infusion using the flowers. Strain the liquid and add a few drops of ylang-ylang essential oil and a spoonful of honey. Use this love drawing bath to attract romance, passion, and love into your life.

Love Drawing Bath: - Ingredients: Rose petals, lavender flowers, cinnamon sticks, and honey. - Purpose: To attract love, enhance romance, and strengthen relationships.

Luck and Fortune Bath: - Ingredients: Irish moss, allspice berries, cinnamon sticks, and orange peels. - Purpose: To attract good luck, fortune, and positive opportunities.

Money Drawing Bath: - Ingredients: Patchouli leaves, cinnamon powder, bay leaves, and coins. - Purpose: To attract financial abundance, prosperity, and opportunities.

Protection Bath: - Ingredients: Epsom salt, bay leaves, basil leaves, and a pinch of salt. - Purpose: To cleanse and protect from negative energies and psychic attacks.

Protection from Evil Bath: - Ingredients: Black salt, bay leaves, hyssop herb, and St. John's Wort. - Purpose: To protect against evil, hexes, and negative energies.

Protection from Psychic Attacks Bath: - Ingredients: Black salt, angelica root, mugwort leaves, and a pinch of cayenne pepper. - Purpose: To protect against psychic attacks, negative energies, and spiritual intrusions.

Psychic Enhancement Bath: - Ingredients: Mugwort leaves, jasmine flowers, rosemary leaves, and amethyst crystals. - Purpose: To enhance psychic abilities, intuition, and spiritual insight.

Reconciliation Bath: - Ingredients: Rose petals, lavender, yarrow, lemon balm. - Instructions: Brew a strong herbal infusion using the herbs. Strain the liquid and add it to your bathwater. Soak in the bath to promote healing, forgiveness, and reconciliation in relationships.

Reversal Bath: - Ingredients: Devil's shoestring, lemon verbena leaves, black mustard seeds, and dragon's blood resin. - Purpose: To reverse negative energies, send back harmful workings or intentions, and protect against curses.

Road Opener Bath: - Ingredients: Lemongrass leaves, cinnamon powder, orange peels, and a key. - Purpose: To remove obstacles, open new paths, and clear the way for success

Spiritual Awakening Bath: - Ingredients: Frankincense resin, myrrh resin, rose petals, and lavender oil. - Purpose: To enhance spiritual awareness, intuition, and connection to higher realms.

Spiritual Cleansing Bath: - Ingredients: Hyssop leaves, rue herb, white sage, and sea salt. - Purpose: To cleanse the spirit, remove spiritual blockages, and purify the energy.

Spiritual Grounding Bath: - Ingredients: Patchouli leaves, vetiver root, frankincense resin, and a few drops of cedarwood oil. - Purpose: To ground and center the spirit, promote stability, and provide a sense of security.

Success Bath: - Ingredients: Orange peels, cinnamon powder, basil leaves, and chamomile flowers. - Purpose: To attract success, achievement, and positive outcomes in endeavors.

Uncrossing Bath: - Ingredients: Hyssop, rue, salt, lemon peel. - Instructions: Brew a strong infusion using the herbs. Strain the liquid and add it to your bathwater. Soak in the bath to remove crossed conditions, negative influences, and spiritual blockages.

Wisdom and Knowledge Bath: - Ingredients: Bay leaves, sage leaves, rosemary leaves, and a few drops of lavender oil. - Purpose: To enhance wisdom, mental clarity, and academic success.

How to Use Spiritual Baths

Preparation: Start by gathering the necessary ingredients for your spiritual bath. These may include herbs, flowers, essential oils, and other items associated with your intention. Ensure you have a clean bathtub or basin and fresh, filtered water.

Setting the Intention: Before taking a spiritual bath, it's essential to set your intention. Determine the purpose of the bath, whether it's for purification, spiritual cleansing, love, protection, or any other specific goal. Focus your thoughts and visualize the desired outcome while preparing the bath.

Preparing the Bath: Fill the bathtub or basin with warm water. Add your chosen herbs, flowers, oils, or other ingredients to the water. Stir the water in a clockwise direction with your hand or a clean utensil while reciting prayers or affirmations that align with your intention. You may also light candles or burn incense to create a sacred atmosphere.

Cleansing Ritual: Before entering the bath, it's customary to cleanse your body physically. Take a shower or thoroughly wash yourself. This step is important to remove any physical dirt or impurities before engaging in the spiritual bath.

Immersion: Once the bath is ready, immerse yourself in the water, ensuring that your whole body is submerged. As you soak, focus on your intention, visualize the water washing away any negative energy or blockages, and imagine yourself being filled with the positive energy associated with your goal.

Prayers and Affirmations: While in the bath, recite prayers, affirmations, or chants that align with your intention. You can use traditional Hoodoo prayers or create your own. Speak your desires out loud, asking for blessings, guidance, or healing, and express gratitude for the positive energy you are receiving.

Meditation and Reflection: Spend some time in quiet reflection while still in the bath. Meditate on your intention, connect with your inner self, and listen for any guidance or messages that may come to you during this sacred time.

Closing the Ritual: Once you feel ready, slowly rise out of the bath, being mindful of the water dripping back into the tub. Some Hoodoo practitioners prefer to air dry, allowing the water and herbs to remain on their body, while others may lightly rinse off with fresh water. It's important to go with what feels right for you and your practice.

Disposal of Bath Water: After the bath, take the remaining water and dispose of it in a respectful manner. Some options include pouring it onto the earth, ideally at the base of a tree, or into a flowing body of water. This act symbolizes releasing any negativity or impurities and returning them to the earth. If you are in a bath tub take some of the water and pour it at the base of the tree, let the rest flow down the drain.

Follow-up Actions: To further enhance the effects of the spiritual bath, consider taking additional actions aligned with your intention. This could include dressing in clean, fresh clothes, lighting candles, or performing specific rituals or workings that support your desired outcome. It's essential to maintain a positive mindset and continue working towards your goal outside of the bath as well.

A Rootworker's Bath

As moonlight weaves its gentle shroud,
The weary Rootworker, her head bowed.
A day of healing, both spirit and frame,
Now seeks solace in a cleansing flame.

She gathers herbs and salts, their essence pure.
Flowers of cleansing, protection sure.
In her sacred space, their virtues entwine,
To wash away the strains of healing's design.

Eucalyptus whispers, a breath of release.
Uncrossing secrets, their blessings increase.
Rosemary's embrace, a shield to unfurl,
Guarding her spirit from the day's weary swirl.

Steeped in the cauldron, a potion of grace,
An elixir of solace, in her sacred place.
As the waters swirl, their magic takes flight,
Cleansing her essence, under the moon's soft light.

In the depths of the bath, she releases the weight,
The struggles, the burdens, the day's weary freight.
Down the drain, they drift, a cleansing cascade,
Renewing her spirit in the waters charade.

So in the Rootworker's embrace, as the day takes its leave,
In the sacred bath's cradle, she finds her reprieve.
A practitioner's solace, in the waters soft strain,
A cleansing, a blessing, a renewal's refrain.

-Rootworker Kye

Hoodoo Oils

The history of Hoodoo oils is deeply intertwined with the African diaspora, particularly the practices brought to the Americas by enslaved African people. The use of oils in Hoodoo can be traced back to the blending of African traditions with Native American and Christian influences. In Hoodoo, the use of oils is believed to harness the spiritual and metaphysical properties of plants. Essential oils, herbs, roots, and other ingredients are combined to create specific oil blends with distinct metaphysical properties.

These oils are used to anoint oneself, objects, or candles, symbolically infusing them with the desired energies and intentions. The specific recipes and blends of Hoodoo oils have evolved over time, incorporating elements from various cultural and spiritual traditions. Different botanicals and herbs have been added to the mix, depending on the intended purpose of the oil. For example, oils used for protection may include ingredients such as rue or hawthorn, while love oils may contain rose or jasmine. Hoodoo oils have been passed down through generations as part of an oral tradition, with practitioners sharing their knowledge and recipes within their communities.

Today, Hoodoo oils continue to be an integral part of spiritual and magical practices within the African American community. They are used in various rituals, workings, and personal anointing to align energy, amplify intentions, and connect with the spiritual realm. The history of Hoodoo oils represents the resilience and adaptation of African spiritual traditions in the face of enslavement and oppression, providing a means of empowerment and connection to ancestral wisdom.

In addition to their historical roots, the use of Hoodoo oils also reflects the resourcefulness and creativity of African American practitioners. During slavery, enslaved individuals had limited access to traditional spiritual tools and resources. As a result, they had to adapt and make use of what was available to them. Oil became a practical and versatile medium for spiritual work in Hoodoo.

They were easily made from locally available plants, roots, and herbs, and could be discreetly carried and used without raising suspicion from slaveholders or overseers. The blending and use of oils allowed practitioners to connect with their ancestral traditions, maintain their spiritual practices, and seek protection, healing, and empowerment in the face of oppression. The practice of making and using Hoodoo oils was often passed down through families and shared within close-knit communities. Elders and experienced practitioners would teach younger generations the art of blending oils and their corresponding metaphysical properties. This oral tradition ensured the preservation and transmission of knowledge despite the constraints and restrictions imposed on enslaved Africans.

Over time, the practice of Hoodoo and the use of oils expanded and evolved. As African Americans gained more freedom and access to resources, the availability of ingredients and the blending techniques diversified. Hoodoo oils became more widely known and used, both within African American communities. Today, Hoodoo oils continue to be an essential part of spiritual practices for many individuals, regardless of their cultural background.

They are valued for their potency, versatility, and connection to ancestral traditions. The use of oils in Hoodoo represents a rich and dynamic history of African American spirituality and resilience, reminding practitioners of their heritage, strength, and the power of working with the natural world.

The use of metaphysical oils in Hoodoo practices holds significant importance for several reasons.

Energetic Alignment: Metaphysical oils are created by blending essential oils, herbs, and other ingredients known for their specific metaphysical properties. These oils are believed to carry the energy and essence of the plants or substances used, allowing practitioners to align themselves with those specific energies and intentions. By anointing oneself, objects, or candles with metaphysical oils, practitioners can attune their energy and intentions to the desired outcome.

Amplification of Intentions: Metaphysical oils are used to amplify and enhance the intentions and desires of the practitioner. Each oil is created with a particular purpose in mind, such as love, protection, abundance, or spiritual purification. By using the appropriate oil, practitioners can intensify the energy and focus of their intentions, making their metaphysical work or ritual more potent and effective.

Anointing and Blessing: Anointing oneself or objects with metaphysical oils is a customary practice in Hoodoo. It is believed to bless and consecrate the person or item with the desired energies and intentions. This act of anointing is seen as a way to invoke spiritual power and protection, as well as to establish a connection with the spiritual realm.

Ritual and workings: Metaphysical oils play a crucial role in Hoodoo rituals and metaphysical work. They are often used to anoint candles, talismans, or other objects used in rituals, symbolically infusing them with the desired energies and intentions. The act of anointing with metaphysical oil is seen as a way to activate and empower the objects, making them potent tools for manifestation and spiritual work.

Aromatherapy and Sensory Experience: Metaphysical oils often carry distinct fragrances that can have a profound impact on mood, emotions, and spiritual experiences. The aromatic scents released by the oils can create a sensory experience that enhances the practitioner's connection to their intention and the spiritual realm. The combination of scent and intention can help create a conducive environment for spiritual practice and manifestation.

In Hoodoo practices, metaphysical oils are considered powerful tools for aligning energy, amplifying intentions, anointing objects, and enhancing ritual and workings. They are believed to carry the energetic properties of the plants and substances used, facilitating a deeper connection to spiritual energies and aiding in the manifestation of desired outcomes.

Hoodoo Oil Recipes

Attraction Oil: Ingredients: Patchouli essential oil, vanilla essential oil, rose essential oil, catnip. Purpose: To attract love, success, and positive opportunities into your life.

Banishing Oil: Ingredients: Cedarwood essential oil, black salt, and cypress essential oil. Purpose: To banish negative influences, remove unwanted energies, and create a protective barrier.

Blessing Oil: Ingredients: Frankincense, myrrh, rose, olive oil. Instructions: Combine the essential oils of these herbs with olive oil. Use this Blessing oil to anoint candles, sacred objects, or yourself to invite divine blessings, spiritual protection, and guidance.

Blessing Oil: (alternative recipe) Ingredients: Frankincense essential oil, myrrh essential oil, and lavender essential oil. Purpose: To receive divine blessings, bring spiritual harmony, and invite positive energy

Communication Oil: Ingredients: Peppermint essential oil, lavender essential oil, and chamomile essential oil. Purpose: To improve communication skills, enhance clarity, and promote effective expression.

Court Case Oil: Ingredients: Calendula essential oil, hyssop essential oil, and bergamot essential oil. Purpose: To gain favor in legal matters, receive a fair judgment, and protect against injustice.

Happiness Oil: Ingredients: Sweet orange essential oil, bergamot essential oil, and vanilla essential oil. Purpose: To promote joy, uplift the spirit, and attract positive energy.

Healing Oil: Ingredients: Lavender essential oil, eucalyptus essential oil, and tea tree essential oil. Purpose: To promote physical and emotional healing and restore well-being.

Love Drawing Oil: Ingredients: Rose essential oil, jasmine essential oil, and ylang-ylang essential oil. Purpose: To attract love, enhance romantic relationships, and promote emotional connection.

Money Drawing Oil: Ingredients: Patchouli essential oil, cinnamon essential oil, and basil essential oil. Purpose: To attract financial abundance, wealth, and prosperity.

Protection from Evil Oil: Ingredients: Black pepper essential oil, basil essential oil, and juniper essential oil. Purpose: To protect against evil spirits, negative entities, and malevolent energies.

Protection Oil: Ingredients: Frankincense essential oil, myrrh essential oil, and black pepper essential oil. Purpose: To protect against negative energies, psychic attacks, and spiritual harm.

Psychic Vision Oil: Ingredients: Clary sage essential oil, mugwort essential oil, and sandalwood essential oil. Purpose: To enhance psychic abilities, intuition, and spiritual insight.

Road Opener Oil: Ingredients: Lemongrass, vetiver, bergamot, sandalwood. Instructions: Combine the essential oils of these herbs with a carrier oil such as jojoba oil or almond oil. Use this Road Opener oil to anoint candles, doorways, or personal items to clear obstacles, open new paths, and bring positive opportunities into your life.

Road Opener Oil: (alternative recipe) Ingredients: Orange essential oil, ginger essential oil, and vetiver essential oil. Purpose: To remove obstacles, open new opportunities, and clear the path for success.

Success Oil: Ingredients: Vetiver, bergamot, cedarwood, orange essential oil. Instructions: Combine the essential oils of these herbs with a carrier oil such as coconut or olive oil. Use this Success oil to anoint candles, personal items, or business-related tools to attract success, achievement, and positive outcomes.

Success Oil: (alternative recipe) Ingredients: Bergamot essential oil, lemon essential oil, and ginger essential oil. Purpose: To attract success, achieve goals, and enhance personal and professional endeavors.

Uncrossing Oil: Ingredients: Lemongrass essential oil, rosemary essential oil, and lemon essential oil. Purpose: To remove crossed conditions, break hexes, and eliminate negative energies.

Mistress's Fate

I gather my tools, the hour is late,
A client in need, a hex of cruel fate.
The mistress's grip, a tangled affair,
In my hands, I'll weave an uncrossing prayer.

First, a pinch of rue, for the road's swift turn,
To break the binds of the hex, let the lessons burn.
In the simmering pot, rue's essence takes flight,
A balm for the soul, in the depths of the night.

Next, some angelica, a guardian's embrace,
To shield and protect, in this uncrossing space.
In the cauldron's dance, its spirit takes flight,
A ward 'gainst the darkness, in the veil of the night.

Lemon peel follows, to cleanse and release,
Unravel the ties, let the sorrows decrease.
In the potion's swirl, the lemon's zest weaves,
A balm for the heart, in its citrus reprieve.

Hyssop whispers next, with its purifying breath,
To wash away the hex, and reclaim what is left.
In the bubbling brew, its essence unfurls,
A cleansing, a blessing, in this uncrossing swirl.

Lastly, a pinch of salt, to purify and ground,
To sever the ties, let the sorrows unbound.
In the oil's embrace, the salt's wisdom takes hold,
A barrier, a fortress, in the potion's bold fold.

As the oil takes form, in the soft gloom,
I'll anoint and empower, let the spirits convene.

To rid the mistress, I'll weave a binding art,
And in the client's release, find the mending start.
With the oil's gentle touch, the mistress will fade,
As the hex's grip wanes, and the sorrows cascade.

In the heart of the night, I'll set the plan's course,
To free the entangled, and return it to the source.

-Rootwoker Kye

How to Use Hoodoo Oils

Anointing: One common use of metaphysical oils in Hoodoo is anointing. The practitioner will apply the oil to their body, objects, or specific areas, often in ritual or prayerful settings. Anointing with oils is believed to draw in or invoke the spiritual properties associated with the oil.

Candle Workings: Hoodoo practitioners frequently use metaphysical oils in candle magic. They may dress or "fix" candles by rubbing the oil onto them in a specific pattern, usually from the middle towards the ends, to draw in specific energies or intentions. The oil is seen as a way to empower the candle and enhance its effectiveness.

Mojo Bags/Sachets/Charms: Mojo bags, also known as gris-gris bags, are small fabric pouches filled with various ingredients, including herbs, roots, and personal items. Metaphysical oils are often added to these bags to amplify their desired effects. A few drops of the appropriate oil may be placed on the contents or the outside of the mojo bag.

Spirit Work: In Hoodoo, metaphysical oils can be used to connect with and communicate with spirits or ancestors. Some practitioners anoint themselves or objects associated with spirit work, such as divination tools or ritual altars, with specific oils to enhance their spiritual connection and receive guidance.

Cleansing and Protection: Certain metaphysical oils are believed to possess cleansing and protective properties. Hoodoo practitioners may use these oils to cleanse themselves, their homes, or objects from negative energies or to create a protective barrier around themselves or their space. They may anoint doorways, windows, or personal items with the oil for this purpose.

It's important to note that Hoodoo is a deeply personal and individual practice, and the specific use of metaphysical oils may vary among practitioners.

Hoodoo Floor Washes

Floor washes have a long history within the practice of Hoodoo and are deeply rooted in African and African American spiritual traditions. They are used to cleanse and purify the home, remove negative energy, and attract positive influences. The origins of floor washes can be traced back to West African spiritual practices, where the use of water, herbs, and other ingredients for spiritual cleansing and purification was common.

In Hoodoo, floor washes are made by steeping or boiling specific herbs, roots, or other ingredients in water, sometimes adding additional substances such as vinegar or spiritual oils. The resulting liquid is then used to mop or wash the floors, walls, doorways, or other surfaces of a home or business. The ingredients used in floor washes vary depending on the desired intention or purpose.

For example, a floor wash for protection may include ingredients such as bay leaves, rue, or salt, while a floor wash for attracting love may contain rose petals or lavender. Each ingredient is chosen for its specific metaphysical properties and the desired outcome. Floor washes serve multiple purposes within Hoodoo.

They physically clean the space, removing dirt and grime, but they also have a spiritual cleansing effect. It is believed that as the floor wash is applied, it carries away negative energy, spiritual residue, and any unwanted influences that may be lingering in the home. Additionally, floor washes are thought to leave behind a positive energetic residue, infusing the space with the metaphysical properties of the ingredients used.

This can help attract prosperity, love, harmony, or other desired energies into the home. The practice of using floor washes in Hoodoo has been passed down through generations, with practitioners sharing recipes and techniques within their communities. It is often considered a sacred and personal ritual, performed with intention and mindfulness.

Today, the use of floor washes in Hoodoo continues to be a significant aspect of spiritual practice. Many practitioners incorporate floor washes into their regular cleaning routines or perform dedicated floor washing rituals during specific times, such as the beginning of a new year or when moving into a new space. The history of floor washes in Hoodoo reflects the fusion of African and Native American spiritual traditions, providing a means of spiritual purification, protection, and manifestation within the home.

Floor washes in Hoodoo are not only used for spiritual cleansing and purification but also for setting intentions and creating a sacred space. The act of physically cleaning the home while simultaneously infusing it with spiritual energy is seen as a powerful ritual that can transform the atmosphere and bring about positive change.

The history of floor washes in Hoodoo is also intertwined with the concept of sympathetic magic. Sympathetic magic is based on the principle that like attracts like, and by mimicking desired outcomes through physical actions, one can manifest those outcomes in reality. By using specific herbs, roots, or oils in floor washes, practitioners believe that they can attract the corresponding energies and qualities into their lives and home.

The practice of floor washing also carries symbolic significance. As practitioners physically scrub away dirt and negativity, they are metaphorically cleansing their lives and making space for positive energy to flow. The act of sweeping or mopping in a specific direction, such as from the back of the house to the front door, is believed to sweep away negative energy and bring in fresh, positive energy.

Floor washes are not limited to private residences; they are also used in businesses, churches, and other public spaces. The intention behind using floor washes in public spaces is often to create a welcoming and spiritually uplifting environment. For example, a business owner might use a floor wash with ingredients like cinnamon, jezebel root, or basil to attract customers and enhance financial success.

The ingredients used in floor washes can vary based on personal preference and the desired outcome. Some common herbs and roots used in floor washes include rosemary, lavender, hyssop, lemon, basil, and mint. These ingredients are chosen for their cleansing, purifying, and protective properties. It is important to note that the use of floor washes in Hoodoo is not a substitute for regular cleaning practices. It is believed to complement and enhance physical cleaning efforts by adding a spiritual element. The intention and focus placed on the ritual act of floor washing is what sets it apart from regular cleaning.

Overall, the history of floor washes in Hoodoo reveals a sacred and practical tradition that combines physical cleaning with spiritual intention. It is a powerful tool for cleansing, purification, and manifestation, allowing practitioners to create a harmonious and spiritually charged environment in their homes and other spaces.

Floor washes are used for spiritual cleansing, protection, and attraction of specific energies. Some are made by combining various ingredients such as herbs, oils, and other substances with water or a cleaning agent. Just remember the ingredients used in floor washes are carefully selected based on their symbolic or energetic properties.

The process of using a floor wash involves physically cleaning the floors, doors, windows, and furniture of a space while simultaneously imbuing them with the desired energies. This can be done by sweeping or mopping the floor with the prepared wash, starting from the back of the space and moving towards the front door to symbolically sweep away negative energies and influences.

Floor washes are a powerful tool in Hoodoo practices, as they combine physical cleaning with spiritual intention, helping to create a sacred, energetically balanced space that supports the desired goals and intentions of the practitioner.

Hoodoo Floor Wash Recipes

Blessing and Harmony Floor Wash: Ingredients: Frankincense resin, myrrh resin, and rose petals. Purpose: To bring blessings, harmony, and positive energy into your home.

Cleansing and Purification Floor Wash: Ingredients: White sage leaves, cedarwood chips, and lavender flowers. Purpose: To cleanse and purify your home, remove negative energies, and promote spiritual balance.

Cleansing Floor Wash: Ingredients: Hyssop, rosemary, lemon peel, salt. Instructions: Brew a strong infusion using the herbs and strain the liquid. Add the liquid to a bucket of clean water along with a pinch of salt. Use this floor wash to spiritually cleanse your home, removing negative energies and promoting positive vibes.

Court Case Floor Wash: Ingredients: Calendula flowers, bay leaves, and cinnamon sticks. Purpose: To gain favor in legal matters, receive a fair judgment, and protect against injustice.

Healing and Health Floor Wash: Ingredients: Mint leaves, eucalyptus leaves, and lavender flowers. Purpose: To promote physical and emotional healing and create a healthy environment.

Money Drawing Floor Wash: Ingredients: Cinnamon, basil, chamomile, bay leaf, coins. Instructions: Brew a strong infusion using the herbs and strain the liquid. Add a few coins to the mixture. Use this floor wash to cleanse your home or business space, attracting financial abundance and prosperity.

Money Drawing Floor Wash (Alternative): Ingredients: Basil leaves, cinnamon sticks, and chamomile flowers. Purpose: To attract wealth, abundance, and financial prosperity into your home.

Love Drawing Floor Wash: Ingredients: Rose petals, lavender flowers, and jasmine flowers. Purpose: To bring love, romance, and harmonious relationships into your home.

Peace and Tranquility Floor Wash: Ingredients: Chamomile flowers, lemon balm leaves, and lavender flowers. Purpose: To create a peaceful and harmonious atmosphere, promote relaxation, and soothe emotional stress.

Protection Floor Wash: Ingredients: Florida water, rosemary leaves, and salt. Purpose: To cleanse and protect your home from negative energies and spiritual harm.

Protection from Evil Floor Wash: Ingredients: Black salt, hyssop leaves, and rue leaves. Purpose: To protect your home from evil spirits, negative entities, and malevolent energies.

Psychic Cleansing Floor Wash: Ingredients: Mugwort leaves, lavender flowers, and rosemary leaves. Purpose: To cleanse and purify your home, enhance psychic abilities, and promote spiritual clarity.

Road Opener Floor Wash: Ingredients: Orange peels, lemongrass leaves, and ginger root. Purpose: To remove obstacles, open new opportunities, and clear the path for success.

Spiritual Cleansing Floor Wash: Ingredients: Eucalyptus leaves, white sage leaves, and lemon zest. Purpose: To purify and cleanse your home from negative energies, spirits, and psychic residue.

Success and Achievement Floor Wash: Ingredients: Bay leaves, lemon slices, and orange peel. Purpose: To attract success, achieve goals, and bring positive energy into your home.

Success in Business Floor Wash: Ingredients: Cinnamon sticks, bay leaves, and bergamot peel. Purpose: To attract success and prosperity in your business endeavors, increase productivity, and bring in new opportunities.

Uncrossing Floor Wash: Ingredients: Lemongrass leaves, rose petals, and lemon slices. Purpose: To remove crossed conditions, break hexes, and eliminate negative energies.

How to Use a Floor Wash

Intentions and Ingredients: Determine the purpose of your floor wash. Different ingredients are used for various intentions. For example, if you want to cleanse and purify your home, you may use ingredients like vinegar, salt, or lemon. If you want to attract wealth and prosperity, you might use ingredients like cinnamon, basil, or mint. Research the herbs, oils, and other ingredients associated with your desired intention.

Preparation: Gather the necessary ingredients for your floor wash. You may need herbs, essential oils, vinegar, salt, or other natural cleansers. Ensure you have a clean mop or cloth, a bucket, and fresh, filtered water. Always buy a new mop before proceeding.

Setting the Intention: Before preparing the floor wash, set your intention. Focus on what you want to achieve with the floor wash, whether it's cleansing, protection, prosperity, love, or any other specific goal. Visualize the desired outcome and infuse your intention into the ingredients.

Mixing the Floor Wash: Fill your bucket with water, ensuring it's at a manageable temperature for cleaning. Add your chosen ingredients to the water, such as herbs, oils, vinegar, or salt. Stir the water in a clockwise direction with a clean utensil while reciting prayers or affirmations aligned with your intention.

Cleaning Ritual: Begin mopping or wiping the floors with the prepared floor wash. As you clean, focus your thoughts on your intention, visualizing the negative energy being swept away and replaced with positive energy. Pay attention to corners, doorways, and areas that accumulate energy, as they tend to need extra cleansing.

Prayers and Affirmations: While cleaning, recite prayers, affirmations, or chants that align with your intention. Speak your desires out loud, asking for blessings, protection, or whatever your intention may be. Express gratitude for the positive energy that is filling your space.

Disposal of Used Floor Wash: Once you have finished cleaning, dispose of the used floor wash in a respectful manner. You can pour it down a drain, preferably one that leads directly to the earth, or dispose of it outside on the ground. This act symbolizes releasing any negative energy and returning it to the earth.

Follow-up Actions: To further enhance the effects of the Hoodoo floor wash, consider taking additional actions aligned with your intention. This could include lighting candles, placing protective or blessing herbs in specific areas of your home, or performing specific rituals or workings that support your desired outcome. It's important to maintain a positive mindset and continue working towards your goal outside of the floor wash as well.

Regular Maintenance: It's beneficial to incorporate regular floor washings into your cleaning routine. This helps to continuously cleanse and refresh the energy of your home or space. You can choose to do a full floor wash with your intention periodically or simply add a few drops of essential oils or herbs to your regular cleaning solution.

Personal Adaptation: Remember, Hoodoo is a personal practice, and you can adapt and personalize your floor washes to suit your specific needs and preferences. Experiment with different ingredients, scents, and rituals to find what resonates with you and brings the desired results.

Floor Washin'
A Short Story

In a small town in Arkansas there lived a woman named Medusa, known for her deep connection to the ancient art of Hoodoo. She possessed a keen understanding of the power of herbs and roots, and she often used them to bring blessings and protection to those around her.

One warm summer evening, as the sun dipped below the horizon, Medusa felt a stirring in the air. She sensed that it was time to cleanse her home and create a powerful floor wash to bring peace and harmony to her surroundings. Gathering her basket, she ventured into the lush woods, where she carefully selected basil, lemon, sage, lavender, and bay leaves, feeling their energy resonate with her.

Returning to her home, Medusa set to work. She brewed a potent concoction, infusing the herbs in boiling water, allowing their essence to intermingle and release their magic. As the fragrance filled the air, she felt the energy shift, knowing that the spirits of the plants were working alongside her. With the herbal brew ready, she began to wash the floors, moving with purpose and intention.

Each stroke of the mop carried with it a sense of renewal, as the powerful blend of herbs cleansed away negativity, leaving behind a trail of tranquility and protection. As she completed her task, she felt a profound sense of peace settle over her home. The air seemed lighter, and the space felt alive with positive energy.

The following morning, neighbors passing by remarked on the comforting atmosphere that seemed to emanate from Medusa's home, unaware of the ancient magick that had been woven into its very foundation. From that day on, her home became a sanctuary, a place where troubles seemed to dissolve, and where visitors always left feeling uplifted. Her skillful use of Hoodoo herbs had transformed her humble dwelling into a haven, a testament to the enduring power of tradition and the timeless wisdom of the natural world.

Hoodoo Sprays, Waters, & Colognes

In African, African-American, and Native American spiritual practices, the use of herbal waters and aromatic plants for cleansing and spiritual purposes was common. How did they become so popular in Hoodoo? One factor that contributed to the popularity of sprays, waters, and colognes in Hoodoo was their convenience and versatility. Unlike floor washes, which require physical cleaning and can be time-consuming, sprays, waters, and colognes offer a quick and effortless way to disperse spiritual energy. They can be sprayed or sprinkled in the air, on objects, or on the body, allowing for immediate spiritual effects.

Another reason for their use in Hoodoo is the belief in the power of scent and its ability to affect emotions and energy. Certain scents are believed to have specific spiritual properties, such as lavender for calming and protection, or rosemary for purification and clarity. By utilizing these scents in sprays, waters, and colognes, practitioners believe they can attract or repel certain energies and influence the spiritual atmosphere.

Moreover, the use of sprays, waters, and colognes in Hoodoo is also influenced by the belief in sympathetic magic. As mentioned earlier, sympathetic magic is based on the principle that like attracts like. By using sprays, waters, and colognes infused with specific ingredients, practitioners aim to attract corresponding energies and qualities into their lives.

Hoodoo sprays are liquid mixtures contained in spray bottles, making them convenient for quick and straightforward application. They are typically made by combining water or a liquid base with essential oils, herbs, and other ingredients chosen for their specific properties and intentions. Hoodoo sprays can be used to cleanse a person's aura or physical space, provide spiritual protection, attract positive energies, or enhance rituals and workings. They are often utilized when a quick, on-the-go solution is needed or when direct spraying is more appropriate than other forms of application.

Hoodoo waters, also known as spiritual waters or condition waters, are liquid mixtures used for spiritual purposes. They are typically made by infusing water with herbs, Fruit, flowers, oils, or other substances known for their spiritual or energetic properties. Hoodoo waters are commonly used for ritual baths, floor washes, anointing objects, or as offerings to spirits or deities. Each Hoodoo water recipe is created with specific intentions in mind, such as love, prosperity, protection, or spiritual purification. They are believed to carry the energetic properties of the ingredients used, facilitating spiritual transformation and manifestation.

Hoodoo colognes, also known as spiritual colognes or toilet waters, are scented liquids used for various spiritual purposes. They are typically made by blending alcohol, vodka, or other liquid bases with essential oils, herbs, or other aromatic substances. Hoodoo colognes are often used to attract positive energies, enhance personal magnetism, provide spiritual protection, or as offerings in rituals and workings. They can be applied to the body, objects, or used in spiritual bathing to invoke specific energies or intentions.

In Hoodoo practices, the significance of these sprays, waters, and colognes lies in their ability to harness and transmit the spiritual properties of the ingredients used. They are seen as tools to cleanse, protect, attract, and transform energies, allowing practitioners to align themselves with their intentions and connect with the spiritual realm.

Hoodoo Liquids Recipes

Abundance Spray: Ingredients: Cinnamon essential oil, bergamot essential oil, and pyrite crystal chips. Purpose: To attract abundance, prosperity, and financial growth into your life. *Please note that sprays & waters are made with filtered river water, rainwater, spring water, or vodka

Aura Cleansing Spray: Ingredients: Frankincense essential oil, lavender essential oil, and selenite crystal chips. Purpose: To cleanse and purify the aura, remove negative attachments, and restore energetic balance. *Please note that sprays & waters are made with filtered river water, rainwater, spring water, or vodka

Blessing Spray: Ingredients: Jasmine essential oil, myrrh essential oil, and white glitter (optional). Purpose: To invoke blessings, attract positive energy, and bring harmony. *Please note that sprays are made with filtered river water, rainwater, spring water, or vodka.

Communication Water: Ingredients: Chamomile essential oil, lavender essential oil, and blue lace agate crystal chips. Purpose: To enhance communication skills, improve relationships, and foster understanding *Please note that sprays & waters are made with filtered river water, rainwater, spring water, or vodka

Court Case Water: Ingredients: Calendula essential oil, bay leaf essential oil, and clear quartz crystal chips. Purpose: To gain favor in legal matters, receive a fair judgment, and protect against injustice. *Please note that sprays & waters are made with filtered river water, rainwater, spring water, or vodka

Energy Clearing Spray: Ingredients: Palo Santo essential oil, sage essential oil, and black tourmaline crystal chips. Purpose: To clear stagnant or negative energy from a space, purify the aura, and promote positivity. *Please note that sprays & waters are made with filtered river water, rainwater, spring water, or vodka

Healing Water: Ingredients: Lavender essential oil, eucalyptus essential oil, and amethyst crystal chips. Purpose: To promote physical and emotional healing, soothe ailments, and cleanse the aura *Please note that sprays & waters are made with filtered river water, rainwater, spring water, or vodka

Love Attraction Spray: Ingredients: Rose essential oil, ylang-ylang essential oil, and rose quartz crystal chips. Purpose: To attract love, enhance romantic relationships, and promote self-love. *Please note that sprays & waters are made with filtered river water, rainwater, spring water, or vodka

Luck and Fortune Cologne: Ingredients: Patchouli essential oil, clove essential oil, and green aventurine crystal chips. Purpose: To attract luck, good fortune, and increase opportunities for success. *Please note that colognes are made with a rubbing alcohol or vodka base.

Money Drawing Spray: Ingredients: Patchouli essential oil, cinnamon essential oil, and green food coloring (optional). Purpose: To attract wealth, abundance, and financial prosperity. *Please note that sprays & waters are made with filtered river water, rainwater, spring water, or vodka

Protection Cologne: Ingredients: Dragon's Blood essential oil, myrrh essential oil, and hematite crystal chips. Purpose: To provide strong protection against negative energies, psychic attacks, and hexes. *Please note that colognes are made with a rubbing alcohol or vodka base.

Protection Spray: Ingredients: Frankincense, myrrh, rosemary, black salt, water. Instructions: Combine the essential oils of frankincense and myrrh with water in a spray bottle. Add a pinch of black salt. Shake well and spritz around your home, workspace, or personal aura to create a protective barrier against negative energies and psychic attacks.

Protection Spray: Ingredients: Florida water, basil essential oil, and black salt. Purpose: To provide spiritual protection, ward off negativity, and create a protective aura. *Please note that sprays & waters are made with filtered river water, rainwater, spring water, or vodka

Psychic Power Water: Ingredients: Mugwort essential oil, rosemary essential oil, and moonstone crystal chips. Purpose: To enhance psychic abilities, intuition, and spiritual insight. *Please note that sprays & waters are made with filtered river water, rainwater, spring water, or vodka

Road Opener Spray: Ingredients: Frankincense essential oil, lemongrass essential oil, and yellow food coloring (optional). Purpose: To clear obstacles, open new opportunities, and invite positive changes. *Please note that sprays & waters are made with filtered river water, rainwater, spring water, or vodka

Spiritual Awakening Water: Ingredients: Sandalwood essential oil, frankincense essential oil, and labradorite crystal chips. Purpose: To enhance spiritual awareness, connect with higher realms, and promote inner growth. *Please note that sprays & waters are made with filtered river water, rainwater, spring water, or vodka

Spiritual Cleansing Spray: Ingredients: White sage essential oil, lemon essential oil, and clear quartz crystal chips. Purpose: To cleanse and purify the spiritual energy, remove negativity, and create a sacred space*Please note that sprays & waters are made with filtered river water, rainwater, spring water, or vodka

Success and Achievement Cologne: Ingredients: Bergamot essential oil, cedarwood essential oil, and gold glitter (optional). Purpose: To attract success, achieve goals, and enhance confidence. *Please note that colognes are made with a rubbing alcohol or vodka base.

Success Water: Ingredients: Orange essential oil, ginger essential oil, and citrine crystal chips. Purpose: To attract success, abundance, and prosperity in all areas of life. *Please note that sprays & waters are made with filtered river water, rainwater, spring water, or vodka

Uncrossing Cologne: Ingredients: Hyssop essential oil, lemon balm essential oil, and black obsidian crystal chips. Purpose: To remove crossed conditions, break hexes, and eliminate negative influences. *Please note that colognes are made with a rubbing alcohol or vodka base.

Arkansas Root

In the heart of Arkansas, where the rivers whispers tales,
Lived Rootworker Kye, with wisdom that seldom fails.
Renowned for her prowess in the world of the unseen,
She crafted tinctures and elixirs to banish forces unseen.

One sultry eve, in Little Rock, a woman sought her aid,
Angel, with a heavy heart, feared a spirit's dark crusade.
Sent by her vengeful ex, a soul steeped in the mystic's art,
The ominous presence haunted, tearing Angel's world apart.

Beneath the moon's soft glow, Kye conjured holy water pure,
With sage and vervain, rosemary and lavender to allure.
From a sacred spring's embrace, the elixir she did brew,
Infused with ancient prayers, potent and true.

Through the woods, she journeyed, in the still of the night,
Carrying the cauldron's weight, her purpose burning bright.
At Angel's cottage, she arrived, the air thick with fear and hope,
A sacred task lay before her, to cleanse, to soothe, to cope.

With solemn steps, Kye began the cleansing rite,
Flicking droplets of holy water, dispelling the spirit's blight.
Chanting ancient prayers, invoking spirits of the land,
Angel stood witness, as Kye's power took a stand.

In the final room, where darkness seemed to thrive,
Kye commanded the spirit to depart, to cease its cruel connive.
The air crackled with energy, a gust rattled the window's pane,
And as Kye uttered her final prayer, peace descended, a calming reign.

Angel's eyes met Kye's, gratitude in their serene embrace,
For Kye, the Rootworker, had banished the spirit's trace.
With a grateful heart, Angel thanked Kye, her guardian of the night,
For ridding her home of the ominous plight, restoring hope's gentle light.

-Rootwoker Kye

How to Use Hoodoo Liquids

Setting Intentions: Before using a Hoodoo spray, water, or cologne, it's important to set your intention. Determine the purpose or goal you wish to achieve, such as cleansing, protection, love, or prosperity. Focus your thoughts and visualize the desired outcome as you prepare to use the product.

Cleansing Ritual: Find a quiet and comfortable space where you can perform the cleansing ritual. It can be indoors or outdoors, depending on your preference. Begin by grounding yourself and creating a peaceful atmosphere.

Invocation: Hold the Hoodoo spray, water, or cologne in your hands and say a prayer or invocation that aligns with your intention. You can call upon deities, ancestors, or the spiritual forces you connect with. Ask for their assistance in manifesting your desired outcome.

Application: Spray or sprinkle the Hoodoo product in the desired area or on yourself. For personal use, you can spray it on your body, clothes, or around your aura. If using it in a space, focus on areas that need cleansing, protection, or that are related to your intention. Visualize the energy shifting and the desired outcome manifesting.

Affirmations and Prayers: While using the Hoodoo spray, water, or cologne, recite affirmations, prayers, or chants that reinforce your intention. Speak your desires out loud, expressing gratitude for the blessings and protection you are inviting into your life. This helps to amplify the energy and intention behind the product.

Regular Use: Hoodoo sprays, waters, and colognes can be used regularly to maintain the desired energy and intention. Incorporate them into your daily or weekly spiritual practice. You can use them in the morning to set the tone for the day or in the evening to cleanse and protect before sleep.

Personal Adaptation: As with any spiritual practice, feel free to adapt and personalize the use of Hoodoo sprays, waters, and colognes to suit your preferences and needs. Experiment with different scents, rituals, and ways of application to find what resonates with you and brings the desired results.

Selection and Purchase: If you do not want to make your own Hoodoo liquid you can choose a Hoodoo spray, water, or cologne that aligns with your intention. There are diverse options available for different purposes, so research and select the one that resonates with your needs. You can purchase these products from metaphysical stores, online retailers, or practitioners who specialize in Hoodoo.

Hoodoo Incense Blends

Handmade herbal Hoodoo incense involves the creation of incense blends using a combination of specific herbs, resins, and other aromatic materials. These incense blends are often crafted by hand, using traditional methods passed down through generations. The specific herbs used in handmaid herbal Hoodoo incense can vary depending on the intention or purpose of the incense. Some commonly used herbs in Hoodoo incense blends include frankincense, myrrh, sage, lavender, rosemary, and patchouli.

The process of creating handmaid herbal Hoodoo incense typically involves carefully selecting and blending the herbs and other aromatic materials. The herbs may be dried, crushed, or powdered before being mixed together in specific proportions. Other ingredients such as resins, essential oils, or natural binders may also be added to enhance the fragrance and burning properties of the incense. Once the herbs and other ingredients are blended, they may be consecrated or charged with specific intentions or prayers. This is done to infuse the incense with spiritual energy and align it with the desired outcome. The incense is then typically formed into cones, sticks, or loose incense that can be burned on charcoal or in specific incense burners.

Handmade herbal Hoodoo incense carries the spiritual properties of the herbs and other ingredients used in its creation. When burned, it releases fragrant smoke that carries these properties into the surrounding environment, influencing energy, and attracting or repelling specific spiritual forces. Making your own herbal incense in Hoodoo holds several important aspects and benefits.

Here is a summary of their significance:

Personalization: Creating your own herbal incense allows you to customize the blend according to your specific intention or desired outcome. You have the freedom to select herbs, resins, and other ingredients that resonate with your goals, making the incense more closely aligned with your energy and needs.

Connection to Nature: Hoodoo places a strong emphasis on connecting with the natural world and harnessing its energies. Making your own herbal incense allows you to work directly with the plants and botanicals, deepening your connection to nature and the spiritual properties they possess.

Intention-setting: The process of making herbal incense is a form of intentional work. As you gather and combine the ingredients, you infuse them with your energy, thoughts, and intentions. This helps to focus your mind, enhance your intention, and align your energy with the desired outcome.

Ritual and Workings: Herbal incense is often used in Hoodoo rituals and metaphysical work to create a sacred and spiritual atmosphere. The act of burning incense serves as an offering to spirits or deities, allows for communication with the spiritual realm, and enhances the effectiveness of the ritual or working by creating a sensory experience.

Cleansing and Purification: Certain herbs and resins used in herbal incense have cleansing and purifying properties. Burning them can help remove negative energies, clear stagnant or harmful influences, and create a harmonious and sacred space for spiritual work.

Aromatherapy and Mood Enhancement: The fragrant aromas released by herbal incense can have a profound impact on mood, emotions, and overall well-being. Different herbs and botanicals carry distinct scents and energetic properties that can uplift, calm, or invigorate, enhancing the spiritual experience and creating a conducive environment for spiritual practice.

By making your own herbal incense, you are actively participating in the creation of your spiritual tools, infusing them with personal energy and intention. It allows for a deeper connection to nature, personalization of rituals, and a more powerful alignment with your desired outcomes in Hoodoo practices.

Hoodoo Incense Recipes

Ancestral Connection Incense: Ingredients: Mugwort leaves, frankincense resin, and copal resin. Purpose: To honor and connect with ancestral spirits, receive guidance, and gain wisdom from past generations.

Blessing Incense: Ingredients: Frankincense resin, myrrh resin, and rose petals. Purpose: To invoke blessings, attract positive energy, and bring harmony.

Clarity and Focus Incense: Ingredients: Peppermint leaves, lemon verbena leaves, and white sage leaves. Purpose: To enhance mental clarity, improve focus, and aid in decision-making.

Cleansing and Purification Incense: Ingredients: White sage leaves, cedarwood chips, and frankincense resin. Purpose: To purify energy, cleanse space, and remove negative influences.

Court Case Incense: Ingredients: Calendula petals, basil leaves, and frankincense resin. Purpose: To gain favor in legal matters, receive a fair judgment, and protect against injustice.

Divination Incense: Ingredients: Mugwort leaves, frankincense resin, and lavender buds. Purpose: To enhance psychic abilities, facilitate divination practices, and receive clear insights.

Energy Clearing Incense: Ingredients: Palo Santo wood chips, white sage leaves, and lavender buds. Purpose: To clear stagnant or negative energy from a space, purify the aura, and promote a sense of calm and clarity.

Healing Incense: Ingredients: Eucalyptus leaves, lavender buds, and chamomile flowers. Purpose: To promote physical and emotional healing, soothe ailments, and restore balance.

Inner Strength Incense: Ingredients: Dragon's Blood resin, rosemary leaves, and bay leaves. Purpose: To enhance personal power, build resilience, and boost confidence.

Love Attraction Incense: Ingredients: Rose petals, lavender buds, and damiana leaves. Purpose: To attract love, enhance romance, and promote passion.

Love Reconciliation Incense: Ingredients: Red rose petals, patchouli leaves, and catnip leaves. Purpose: To mend broken relationships, promote forgiveness, and restore love and harmony.

Money Drawing Incense: Ingredients: Cinnamon powder, patchouli leaves, and dried orange peel. Purpose: To attract wealth, abundance, and financial opportunities.

Prosperity Incense: Ingredients: Allspice berries, basil leaves, and cinnamon powder. Purpose: To attract abundance, wealth, and financial prosperity.

Protection Incense: Ingredients: Mugwort, rosemary, sage, frankincense resin. Instructions: Mix equal parts of the dried herbs and optionally add a few drops of essential oil. Burn this herbal blend on charcoal discs or use it as a smudge to cleanse and protect your space from negative energies.

Protection Incense: Ingredients: Frankincense resin, myrrh resin, and dried rosemary. Purpose: To ward off negative energies, protect the home, and create a protective barrier.

Protection from Evil Spirits Incense: Ingredients: Angelica root, black salt, and myrrh resin. Purpose: To ward off evil spirits, protect against negative influences, and create a safe and sacred space.

Psychic Power Incense: Ingredients: Mugwort leaves, rosemary leaves, and lavender buds. Purpose: To enhance psychic abilities, intuition, and spiritual insight.

Road Opener Incense: Ingredients: Lemongrass leaves, bay leaves, and cinnamon sticks. Purpose: To clear obstacles, open new opportunities, and invite positive changes.

Spiritual Protection Incense: Ingredients: Angelica root, frankincense resin, and juniper berries. Purpose: To create a protective shield against spiritual attacks, negative entities, and psychic harm.

Success and Achievement Incense: Ingredients: Bay leaves, cinnamon sticks, and dried orange slices. Purpose: To attract success, achieve goals, and enhance confidence.

Uncrossing Incense: Ingredients: Hyssop leaves, lemon balm leaves, and black salt. Purpose: To remove crossed conditions, break hexes, and eliminate negative influences.

Remember to use these incense blends with caution, following proper safety measures, and always respect the traditions and practices associated with Hoodoo.

How to Use Hoodoo Incense

Intention: Set your intention for using the herbal incense. Determine the purpose or goal you wish to achieve, such as cleansing, protection, love, or prosperity. Focus your thoughts and visualize the desired outcome as you prepare to use the incense.

Selection and Preparation: Choose the appropriate herbal incense blend that aligns with your intention. You can either purchase handmade herbal incense from trusted sources or make your own by blending the desired herbs and resins together. Ensure that the herbs are properly dried and prepared for burning.

Incense Holder: Place the handmade herbal incense on a heat-resistant incense holder or a non-flammable surface. You can use a traditional incense holder, a metal dish filled with sand, or any other suitable container that can safely hold and burn the incense.

Ignition: Light the tip of the herbal incense with a match or lighter until it catches fire. Allow the flame to burn for a few seconds, then gently blow it out, leaving the incense smoldering and releasing fragrant smoke.

Smoke Purification: Pass the incense over yourself, your tools, or the area you wish to cleanse or purify. Move the incense in a circular motion or wave it around to ensure the smoke reaches all areas. Visualize the smoke purifying and cleansing the energy.

Affirmations and Prayers: While using the herbal incense, recite affirmations or prayers that align with your intention. Speak your desires out loud, expressing gratitude for the blessings and protection you are inviting into your life. This helps to amplify the energy and intention behind the incense.

Ritual or Metaphysical work: If you are performing a specific ritual or working, incorporate the use of the herbal incense as instructed in your practice. You can use the smoke to consecrate objects, draw symbols or sigils in the air, or simply allow the smoke to fill the space and create a sacred atmosphere.

Disposal: Once you have finished using the herbal incense, let the remaining embers burn out naturally or gently extinguish them in a fire-safe container. Dispose of the ashes in a respectful manner, such as burying them in the earth or scattering them in a natural setting.

Hoodoo Candles

In Hoodoo practices candles are used as a focal point for intention-setting, manifestation, and connecting with spiritual energies. Candles are seen as a symbol of light, transformation, and spiritual illumination. They can be used to represent individuals or entities, serving as a medium for communication with spirits or divine forces. Candles are also believed to carry the energy of the practitioner's intention and act as a channel to manifest desires or bring about change.

Why would you need a recipe for a candle? Candle recipes involve anointing or dressing candles with oils, herbs, or other substances to enhance their energy and align them with specific intentions. Recipes can vary based on the desired outcome, such as love, protection, prosperity, or spiritual growth. The choice of oils, herbs, and colors is crucial, as each ingredient carries its own symbolic or energetic properties.

Candle workings refer to specific rituals or works performed using candles to manifest intentions or work towards a desired outcome. This can involve lighting a prepared candle, focusing on the intention, and allowing the candle to burn completely or for a specific duration.

Various techniques can be incorporated, such as visualization, recitation of prayers, Psalms, or affirmations, or the use of additional tools like crystals or sigils. The process may also include monitoring the behavior of the candle flame, such as the way it flickers, sputters, or burns, as it is believed to convey messages or signs from the spiritual realm.

Candle workings in Hoodoo are versatile and can be personalized to suit individual needs and intentions. They are considered a potent tool for spiritual transformation, manifestation, and connection with higher energies or spirits.

Hoodoo Candle Recipe

Breakthrough and New Beginnings Candle: Ingredients: Purple or white candle, geranium essential oil, and dried lavender buds. Purpose: To break through barriers, invite new opportunities, and embrace fresh starts.

Blessing Candle: Ingredients: White candle, myrrh essential oil, and dried rose petals. Purpose: To invoke blessings, attract positive energy, and bring harmony.

Blessing of the Home Candle: Ingredients: White candle, cedarwood essential oil, and dried lavender buds. Purpose: To bless and purify the home, invite positive energy, and create a sacred space.

Communication and Clarity Candle: Ingredients: Light blue or white candle, eucalyptus essential oil, and dried chamomile flowers. Purpose: To enhance communication skills, promote clear and effective expression, and improve understanding.

Court Case Candle: Ingredients: Purple or white candle, hyssop essential oil, and calendula petals. Purpose: To gain favor in legal matters, receive a fair judgment, and protect against injustice.

Energy Clearing Candle: Ingredients: White candle, palo santo essential oil, and white sage leaves. Purpose: To clear stagnant or negative energy from a space, purify the aura, and promote a sense of calm and clarity.

Fertility and Pregnancy Candle: Ingredients: Green or white candle, jasmine essential oil, and dried lavender buds. Purpose: To promote fertility, support healthy pregnancy, and invite the blessings of motherhood.

Healing Candle: Ingredients: Blue or white candle, lavender essential oil, and dried chamomile flowers. Purpose: To promote physical and emotional healing, soothe ailments, and restore balance.

Love Attraction Candle: Ingredients: Pink or red candle, rose essential oil, and rose petals. Purpose: To attract love, enhance romance, and promote passion.

Money Drawing Candle: Ingredients: Green candle, cinnamon essential oil, and dried bay leaves. Purpose: To attract wealth, abundance, and financial opportunities.

Protection Candle: Ingredients: Black candle, frankincense essential oil, and black salt. Purpose: To ward off negative energies, protect against harm, and create a protective barrier.

Protection from Psychic Attacks Candle: Ingredients: Black candle, myrrh essential oil, and black salt. Purpose: To shield against psychic attacks, negative energies, and spiritual harm.

Psychic Power Candle: Ingredients: Indigo or purple candle, frankincense essential oil, and mugwort leaves. Purpose: To enhance psychic abilities, intuition, and spiritual insight.

Reconciliation Candle: Ingredients: Pink or white candle, patchouli essential oil, and dried rose petals. Purpose: To heal and mend relationships, promote forgiveness, and restore harmony.

Road Opener Candle: Ingredients: Yellow or orange candle, lemongrass essential oil, and dried rosemary. Purpose: To clear obstacles, open new opportunities, and invite positive changes.

Road Safety Candle: Ingredients: Orange or yellow candle, bergamot essential oil, and dried marigold petals. Purpose: To protect against accidents, ensure safe travels, and ward off road-related dangers.

Spiritual Protection Candle: Ingredients: Black candle, angelica essential oil, and juniper berries. Purpose: Create a shield of spiritual protection around an individual, space, or object. Wards of negative energy.

Success and Achievement Candle: Ingredients: Orange or gold candle, bergamot essential oil, and dried bay leaves. Purpose: To attract success, achieve goals, and enhance confidence.

Uncrossing Candle: Ingredients: Black and white or reversible candle, lemon essential oil, and black salt. Purpose: To remove crossed conditions, break hexes, and eliminate negative influences.

Wisdom and Guidance Candle: Ingredients: Indigo or purple candle, sandalwood essential oil, and dried sage leaves. Purpose: To seek wisdom, receive guidance from higher powers, and enhance spiritual awareness.

Remember to set your intentions clearly and focus your energy as you work with these candles. Practice candle safety and respect the traditions associated with Hoodoo.

Prosperity's Candle

In a dimly lit room, the rootworker's hands dance with the flame,
As the candle's flickering dance takes on a life of its own,
She whispers ancient secrets, coaxing luck and wealth to play the game,
The fire's gentle whispers seem to echo her intent, sown.

The wax melts and reforms, a symbol of transformation and rebirth,
As she imbues it with her will, coaxing fortune's hand to turn,
The shadows flicker and twist, a dance of hope upon the earth,
As she tends to the candle, her energy begins to burn.

With each passing moment, the candle's light grows stronger,
A beacon of prosperity, a signal to the universe's throng,
She watches with knowing eyes, as the ritual lingers longer,
For in this quiet ritual, she knows she can't go wrong.

The room is filled with the scent of herbs and ancient lore,
As the rootworker weaves her magick, calling on forces unseen,
She knows that in this moment, she's opening a brand new door,
To a future filled with abundance, where prosperity will convene.

The candle's steady flame reflects the passion in her eyes,
As she channels her intentions, weaving spells with skillful hands,
She feels the energy shift, as the universe complies,
To her earnest plea for riches, as the candlelight expands.

With a knowing smile, she releases the energy into the night,
Trusting in the universe to heed her heartfelt plea,
For she knows that in due time, her world will be alight,
With the wealth and prosperity she's summoned with her decree.

-Rootwoker Kye

How to Use Hoodoo Candle Recipes

Select the Candle: Choose a candle that corresponds with your intention or goal. Distinct colors have different meanings in Hoodoo. For example, a green candle can be used for money and abundance, a red candle for love and passion, and a white candle for purification and spiritual work.

Cleanse and Prepare the Candle: Before using the candle, cleanse it by passing it through the smoke of sacred herbs like sage or palo santo. This helps to remove any negative or unwanted energies. You can also wash the candle with a mild soap and water or spiritual waters to cleanse it physically.

Gather the Ingredients: Prepare the ingredients specified in the Hoodoo candle recipe. This may include specific oils, herbs, powders, or other items. Ensure that your ingredients are of high quality and properly prepared.

Dressing the Candle: Begin by anointing the candle with a suitable oil. Use a few drops and rub it onto the candle in a specific direction, such as from the bottom to the top for drawing energy or from the top to the bottom for banishing energy. Visualize your intention as you do this. Next, roll or sprinkle the herbs, powders, or other ingredients onto the oiled candle, focusing on your desired outcome.

Set the Intention: Hold the dressed candle in your hands and take a moment to set your intention. Visualize your goal, affirm your desires, and infuse the candle with your energy and intention. Speak your intention out loud or silently in your mind.

Lighting the Candle: Place the dressed and prepared candle in a safe and fireproof holder. Light the candle while focusing on your intention and desired outcome. You may choose to recite a prayer, affirmation, or specific Hoodoo chant as you light the candle.

Candle Vigil: Allow the candle to burn completely in one sitting if possible. During this time, maintain a focused and positive mindset, keeping your intention in mind. Avoid blowing out the candle; instead, snuff it out gently if necessary and relight it later.

Disposal: Once the candle has burned down completely, collect the remnants, including any leftover wax, herbs, or other materials. You can bury them in your yard, dispose of them in running water, or keep them for further workings, depending on your specific tradition and beliefs in Hoodoo. Some practitioners choose to bury the remnants near their front doorstep for protection, while others may dispose of them at a crossroads to symbolize the completion of the working.

Follow-Up Action: After the candle has burned down, it's important to take action in alignment with your intention. This may involve performing additional rituals or metaphysical work, taking practical steps towards your goal, or simply remaining open and receptive to opportunities and manifestations related to your intention.

Repeating the Process: If your intention or goal requires ongoing work, you can repeat the process with a new candle and follow the same steps as outlined above. Some practitioners prefer to work with the same candle for multiple sessions, gradually dressing it more with each repetition.

Remember, Hoodoo candle recipes are just one tool within the practice of Hoodoo. It's essential to approach your work with respect, intention, and a deep understanding of your desired outcome. Adapt the recipes to suit your personal beliefs, intuition, and the specific circumstances of your situation.

CHAPTER 9

Journey to Two-Headed Doctor

I woke up that morning feeling a knot of unease in my stomach. It was as if the weight of the world had settled on my shoulders overnight. Little did I know this day would mark the beginning of a transformative journey that would lead me to become a Two-Headed Doctor in Hoodoo. It all started when an ex-friend stole my business idea to start my own metaphysical business. Detaching myself from her became an essential step in reclaiming my power and protecting myself. It was a painful realization that someone I had trusted had not only betrayed me but also attempted to steal my business idea.

I vividly remember the moment I discovered her deceit. After she had asked me to train her in the art of Hoodoo and I had shared my plans to create a Hoodoo business offering handmade products and services, I could never have anticipated her audacious move. Two days later, as I innocently scrolled through my Facebook feed, my heart sank. There it was, an advertisement from her, claiming that she would be pursuing the opening of her own metaphysical business. The timing was too uncanny to be a mere coincidence.

She, who had never practiced a day in her life, had swiftly purchased a few books and materials, and just two days later, had the audacity to announce her official intention for her venture. The anger and disappointment I felt were overwhelming, but I knew that I had to detach myself from her, both personally and professionally leaving me feeling betrayed and hurt. I had put my heart and soul into those ideas, and to see them snatched away by someone I once considered a friend was a hard blow.

A few weeks passed, and it was during this time that I noticed a strange occurrence. I wore a beautiful crystal necklace, a symbol of positivity and protection. But one day, without any warning, it fell from my neck and my shattered into pieces, as if a force beyond my understanding had deliberately broken its energy. I checked the clasp, but it was not broken, there was no reason for it to fall from my neck. It was a clear sign that something was amiss.

That very night, I had a vivid and unsettling dream. In the dream, I found myself at an award ceremony, where I was meant to receive recognition for my accomplishments. But she, the one who had stolen my business ideas, appeared and deliberately made me late for the event. As a result, I missed my chance to receive the award, my moment of triumph stolen away by her actions. The months that followed were a series of unfortunate events. I experienced a string of bad luck that seemed unwavering. My car, my only means of transportation, was stolen, leaving me stranded and vulnerable. And then, the worst blow of all,

I received an eviction notice. My life was in shambles, and I felt as if I was being swallowed by a dark cloud of misfortune. To make matters worse, flies began to invade my apartment in alarming numbers. They quite literally covered my windows scaring my children and myself. No matter how diligently I tried to rid myself of them, they persisted, their constant presence serving as a constant reminder of the chaos that had befallen me.

It was in this moment of despair and desperation that I realized I had been cursed. The day that necklace fell off my neck and I had that dream months prior was my warning. I knew immediately I had to find a way to protect myself and send the work back from where it came. Already a practitioner of Hoodoo, though initially focused only on lighter work, I realized that I needed to delve deeper into the practice to defend myself against her. Determined to protect myself and restore balance to my life, I embarked on a journey to become a Two-Headed Doctor - a practitioner who works with both the light and dark aspects of Hoodoo, maintaining a balance between the two. I sought out mentors who could teach me the deeper and more powerful rituals of Hoodoo, and I researched my ass off.

I was guided through the intricacies of working with darker energies, cautioning me to always maintain a sense of responsibility and respect for the forces I was harnessing. With their guidance, I learned to channel my intentions with precision and purpose. Armed with newfound knowledge and a deeper connection to the spiritual realm, I began to counteract the negative energy that had plagued me. I crafted powerful protection, uncrossing, and "return to sender" workings, calling upon the strength of ancestors and the spirits that dwelled within the roots and herbs of Hoodoo.

Slowly but surely, the tides began to turn in my favor. The misfortunes that had befallen me started to recede, and a sense of empowerment and balance was restored to my life. I felt a renewed sense of purpose and clarity, no longer bound by the negativity that had once consumed me.

With this renewed determination, I focused all my energy on building my own shop, pouring my heart and soul into every aspect of it. I refused to let her actions define me or derail my dreams. I worked tirelessly, creating unique and handmade products, infusing them with the power of my Hoodoo practice. As word spread about my genuine and authentic offerings, customers began flocking to my shop. They could sense the difference, the sincerity in my work that set it apart from the mass-produced or unauthentic offerings of others.

My dedication and passion were rewarded as my business flourished, attracting a loyal clientele who recognized the authenticity and integrity behind what I provided. In time, I realized that her attempt to steal my business idea had unintentionally pushed me to reach new heights. It lit a fire within me, driving me to excel and prove that success could be attained through hard work, dedication, and a genuine connection to the spiritual practices I held dear.

Looking back, I am grateful for the painful lesson she taught me. It taught me the importance of discernment, trust, and self-reliance. It reminded me that not everyone who seeks guidance or knowledge has pure intentions. But most importantly, it reinforced my commitment to remaining true to myself and my craft. Detaching from her allowed me to fully embrace my journey as a Two-Headed Doctor. I channeled my energy into honing my skills.

As I continued to grow as a Two-Headed Doctor, I found solace in the equilibrium between light and dark, understanding the importance of maintaining balance in my practice. I vowed to use my newfound abilities to not only protect myself but also to help others who may find themselves in similar situations.

It was through the hardships and challenges I faced that I discovered my true strength and purpose. And while the scars of betrayal still lingered, they served as a constant reminder of my resilience and the power I held within me. Now, armed with the knowledge of both light and dark, I stand as a beacon of balance, ready to face any challenge that comes my way. My journey as a Two-Headed Doctor has just begun, and I am determined to use my abilities to bring positivity, protection, and healing to those who seek it.

What is a Two-Headed Doctor?

In Hoodoo, a Two-Headed Doctor refers to a practitioner who is skilled in both light and dark work, possessing knowledge and proficiency in a broad range of spiritual practices. The term "Two-Headed" is symbolic and represents the ability to work with both positive and negative energies, maintaining a balance between them.

A Two-Headed Doctor is someone who has honed their skills and understanding of various aspects of Hoodoo, including both light work and dark work. They have extensive knowledge of herbs, roots, candles, oils, and other tools used in Hoodoo practices. They are adept at performing rituals, metaphysical workings, medicinal and physical workings, and spiritual cleansings, and are well-versed in the use of charms, amulets, and talismans.

Two-Headed Doctors possess the ability to address a wide range of needs and situations. They can offer healing, protection, and blessings through their light work, while also having the knowledge and expertise to confront and address negative energies, hexes, or harmful situations through their "dark" work. They understand the importance of balance and discernment, knowing when each type of work is appropriate and how to navigate the complexities of different situations.

In essence, a Two-Headed Doctor is a versatile and experienced practitioner who can draw upon a broad range of spiritual practices to help themselves and others. They are skilled in both light and dark work, utilizing their knowledge and abilities to create effective and holistic solutions tailored to the specific needs of their clients or their own personal spiritual journey.

Lightwork Vs Dark work

Balancing light work and dark work in Hoodoo is important for several reasons. Firstly, Hoodoo is a complex and multifaceted practice that encompasses a range of spiritual traditions, beliefs, and practices. It acknowledges the existence of both light and dark energies and recognizes the need for balance between them.

Light work in Hoodoo involves working with positive, healing, and uplifting energies. It focuses on bringing blessings, protection, and prosperity into one's life and the lives of others. This can include practices such as candle blessings, spiritual cleansing, and prayer. Light work aims to promote harmony, positivity, and spiritual growth.

On the other hand, dark work in Hoodoo involves working with shadow energies, which may include aspects such as protection from harm, justice, and the removal of obstacles. Dark work acknowledges that there are times when one may need to confront and address negativity or harmful situations. This can involve practices such as hexing, uncrossing, or banishing. The balance between light and dark work in Hoodoo is crucial because life itself is a mixture of positive and negative experiences. Just as light cannot exist without darkness, the concept of balance recognizes that both aspects have their place and purpose.

Hoodoo practitioners understand that there are times when it is necessary to confront and address challenging situations, and at other times, to focus on healing, growth, and positivity. By maintaining this balance, Hoodoo practitioners can navigate the complexities of life, addressing challenges and obstacles while also fostering personal growth and spiritual well-being. It is important to note that the intention behind the work is crucial. Practitioners should approach both light and dark work with respect, ethical considerations, and a deep understanding of the potential consequences of their actions.

Ultimately, the balance between light and dark work in Hoodoo allows practitioners to harness the full spectrum of energies available to them, enabling them to create holistic and effective spiritual practices that align with their intentions and needs.

Karma In Hoodoo

I debated whether or not to share this story, fearing the judgment and skepticism that might come my way. But I made a promise to myself that I would share my experiences to help others who might find themselves in similar situations. So, here it goes...

It all started when my daughter began facing relentless bullying at school. It was heartbreaking to see her come home each day, her spirit crushed by the hurtful words and actions of her peers. But things took a sinister turn when rumors began circulating, claiming that both my daughter and I were promiscuous women, engaging in immoral behavior. These fabrications couldn't have been further from the truth. Our lives revolved around our home, work, and running errands. Any time I left the house, it was for legitimate reasons – whether it was for work or to take care of necessary tasks.

If I attended any social events, it was strictly for business purposes and networking. But the rumors grew worse with each passing day, spreading like wildfire throughout the community. It felt as if there was no escape from the malicious gossip. I couldn't bear to see my daughter suffer any longer, so I knew I had to take action. Turning to my knowledge of Hoodoo, I decided to perform an uncrossing working with a return to sender twist. I crafted a special charm, infusing it with my intentions to protect my daughter and myself from the harm caused by these false rumors. I whispered my Psalms of protection, calling upon my ancestors for their guidance and assistance.

The very next day, a tragic accident occurred at the school. My next-door neighbor, an elderly woman who was a frequent substitute teacher at the school, was involved in a freak accident and tragically passed away three days later. It was a shocking turn of events, and I couldn't help but feel a mix of emotions, she was always so nice to me. She spoke to me every day when I would go for my morning walks.

A couple of weeks later, I stumbled upon undeniable evidence that my late neighbor had indeed been the one behind the vicious rumors about my children and me. She had been spreading malicious and completely fabricated rumors about my household. Telling anyone who would listen that I had men running in and out of my house, and I was allowing my oldest daughter who was only sixteen at the time to sleep with adult men. No man who wasn't a family member had ever stepped foot inside my home. I barely even dated at that time. Looking back at the incident, if I could go back in time, I am not sure if I would have performed the return to sender or not. That is the truth.

This is a cautionary tale reminding you of the power and consequences of our actions. This experience taught me a profound lesson about the importance of being mindful of the energy we put into the world. It's a reminder that every word we speak, every action we take, has the potential to create ripples that can impact not only ourselves but also those around us.

While I sought protection for my daughter and myself, I hadn't anticipated the severity of the consequences that would befall the person responsible for spreading those hurtful rumors. It made me reflect on the responsibility that comes with practicing Hoodoo or any form of spiritual work.

Now, I share this cautionary tale not to encourage revenge or harmful intentions but to remind others of the power of their actions and the importance of using our ancestral power responsibly. It is crucial to approach metaphysics with respect, understanding, and consideration for the potential consequences.

My purpose in sharing this story is to shed light on the complexities of Hoodoo and its potential effects. It is a reminder to harness the power of spirituality, not for personal gain or vengeance, but to promote healing, protection, and positive change in our lives and the lives of those around us. With that being said, always protect yourself, your family, and those that you love.

To be completely honest in the aftermath of these events, I found myself contemplating the idea of karma and the repercussions of my actions. It was important for me to understand that seeking protection for myself and my daughter was not an act of vengeance or revenge, but rather an act of self-defense and preservation.

Karma, often misunderstood, is not simply about punishment or payback for our actions. It is a complex concept that encompasses the consequences of our intentions and actions, both positive and negative. While it is true that every action, we take has an effect, it is crucial to remember that the intention behind our actions plays a significant role in determining the karmic outcome.

When I performed the uncrossing working with a return to sender twist, my heart was focused on protection – not on seeking harm or revenge. I didn't even know where the rumors were coming from at that time. I just wanted to shield my daughter and myself from the destructive impact of the rumors, to restore our sense of safety and well-being. It was an act of self-defense, not an act of ill-will.

In the realm of spirituality and metaphysics, protection work is a means of establishing boundaries, defending oneself against harm, and promoting a sense of security. It is not about causing harm to others, but about safeguarding our own energy and preserving our well-being. The heart-centered intention to protect oneself and loved ones from harm is fundamentally different from seeking vengeance or inflicting harm upon others.

In working with Hoodoo and other spiritual practices, it is essential to approach workings with a clear understanding of our intentions and the potential consequences. When our intentions are rooted in love, protection, and the desire for positive change, we can engage in spiritual practices without creating negative karma. It is also important to note that karma is not an instantaneous or linear system of cause and effect. It is a complex interplay of energies that may unfold over time and in ways that are sometimes beyond our comprehension.

Therefore, it is best to approach our actions with mindfulness and respect for the interconnectedness of all things. So, as I reflect on my experience, I am confident that seeking protection through the uncrossing work was not an act that created bad karma. It was an act of self-preservation, guided by a heart-focused on protecting my daughter and myself from the harm caused by the rumors. It serves as a reminder that, in our spiritual practices, our intentions must always be rooted in love, compassion, and the greater good.

In sharing my story, I hope to dispel any misconceptions about protection (justice) work and highlight the importance of understanding the true nature of karma. It is important to recognize that protection is not synonymous with revenge or vengeance. When we work with the heart focused on protection, we are aligning ourselves with the universal principle of self-preservation and the preservation of others. In this interconnected web of existence, we are all entitled to live free from harm and fear.

Protection work is an acknowledgement of this inherent right and a proactive step towards safeguarding ourselves and those we care about. It is an act of empowerment, asserting our boundaries and asserting our worth. When our intention is to shield ourselves from harm, we are not seeking to harm others. Our actions are driven by love, compassion, and the desire to create a safe and nurturing environment.

By working from a place of protection, we are not perpetuating a cycle of negativity or adding to the karmic debts in the universe. It is also important to understand that karma is not a system of punishment, but rather a mechanism for growth and learning. The consequences of our actions are not meant to be seen as retribution but as opportunities for personal development and evolution.

When we approach protection work with a genuine heart and a clear intention, we are aligning ourselves with the positive forces of the universe and promoting harmony. Ultimately, it is the intent behind our actions that shapes the karmic outcome. The energy we put into protecting ourselves and others can have a ripple effect, inspiring others to do the same and creating a more compassionate and empathetic world. By focusing on protection with a heart rooted in love and understanding, we can transcend the notion of revenge and contribute to the collective well-being. I know I keep repeating myself in different ways, but I just want to give a clear understanding.

In conclusion, protection work is not an act that generates bad karma when approached with genuine intentions. It is not about seeking revenge or inflicting harm upon others, but rather about creating a safe and nurturing space for ourselves and those we care about. By understanding the true nature of karma and working with a heart focused on protection, we can navigate the complexities of life with compassion and integrity.

Consent, Harm Reduction & Accountability

Consent, harm reduction, and accountability are important principles in any spiritual or metaphysical practice, including Hoodoo. They provide a framework for ethical conduct, respect, and responsible use of one's spiritual powers.

Here's why these principles are significant in Hoodoo practice:

Consent: Consent is crucial in any form of spiritual work, as it respects the autonomy and boundaries of individuals. In Hoodoo, practitioners should always seek the consent of the person they are working on behalf of or with. This includes obtaining permission before performing any workings, rituals, or evocation on someone else's behalf. Consent ensures that individuals have agency over their own spiritual practices and are actively participating in the work being done.

Harm Reduction: Hoodoo practitioners are mindful of the potential consequences and impacts of their actions. Harm reduction involves taking measures to minimize harm or negative repercussions. This can include ethical considerations, such as refraining from performing rituals or workings that could cause undue harm or suffering to others. It also involves using discernment and wisdom to ensure that one's actions align with the principles of justice, fairness, and compassion.

Accountability: Accountability is essential in Hoodoo practice to ensure that practitioners take responsibility for their actions and the effects they may have. It involves being aware of the potential consequences of one's work and being prepared to address any unintended harm or negative outcomes. Practitioners should be willing to reflect on their practices, learn from their mistakes, and make amends if necessary. Accountability fosters integrity, growth, and ethical conduct within the Hoodoo community.

By embracing these principles, Hoodoo practitioners create a safe and respectful environment for themselves and others. They promote ethical and responsible use of their spiritual powers, ensuring that their work is aligned with the well-being and autonomy of all involved. Consent, harm reduction, and accountability help practitioners cultivate a deep sense of integrity, compassion, and respect in their Hoodoo practice.

Take Care of Yourself

Once I embarked on, the journey to help others by utilizing protection work, justice work, and removal of negative energies those services began to take off in my business. My work spoke for itself and was always effective. The more work I did for my clients, the more people sought me out.

Little did I know, this path was not without its challenges. Without hesitation, I dived into spiritual work, eager to make a difference in people's lives. However, as the months went by, I soon discovered the toll it could take on my own well-being. I began to focus on my client's physical and spiritual health more than my own. I started to neglect my meditations, cleansings, and personal workings. I started to put all my time and effort into my clients. However, the universe has a way of slowing you down when you will not do it on your own.

One week I found myself cleansing two individuals who had negative energies attached to themselves. One in the form of a generational curse, and the other client had a negative entity that was sent to her by an ex who practices. I made the foolish decision to perform works on both clients in the same week, back-to-back. One on Wednesday and one on Thursday. I did these rituals not realizing that I had neglected to protect and cleanse myself.

The consequences were severe. The weight of the energies I had absorbed overwhelmed me, and my body began to show signs of strain. It was as if I had been dealt a blow that mirrored the effects of a stroke, and it landed me in the hospital. This experience served as a valuable lesson, reminding me of the paramount importance of self-care and caution in the realm of spiritual work. I learned that while we may have the power to heal and cleanse, we must always prioritize our own protection and well-being.

So, my dear readers, future Hoodoos, and spiritualist if you ever find yourself on a similar path, remember to take care of yourself. Stay vigilant, cleanse, and protect yourself. Don't let the burden of negativity weigh you down. Embrace the power of Hoodoo with caution, knowing that your own well-being is of utmost importance. Stay safe on your journeys, and may your experiences be filled with light and positivity.

Rootworker Kye's After Work Cleanse

Gather your supplies:

1. You'll need a white candle.
2. cleansing herbs (such as sage, rosemary, or lavender)
3. a small bowl of salt or black salt, and a small bowl of water

Set the intention:

1. Light the white candle and take a moment to focus your energy.
2. State your intention clearly, emphasizing the need to cleanse and protect yourself after assisting others.

Cleanse with smoke:

1. Take the cleansing herbs and light them, allowing the smoke to fill the space around you.
2. Move the smoke over your body, starting from your head and working your way down to your feet.
3. Visualize the smoke removing any residual energies or negativity.

Salt cleanse:

1. Dip your fingers into the bowl of salt or black salt and gently touch your forehead, each shoulder, and the soles of your feet.
2. As you do this, imagine the salt forming a protective barrier around you, sealing in positive energies and repelling any negative influences.

Water cleanse:

1. With clean hands, dip your fingertips into the bowl of water.
2. Touch your forehead, each shoulder, and the soles of your feet once again.
3. Envision the water washing away any lingering energetic residue, leaving you cleansed and refreshed.
4. Express gratitude: Thank the universe or any spiritual beings you work with for their guidance and assistance throughout this cleansing process.
5. Acknowledge the cleansing and protective energies that surround you.

Close the ritual:

1. Extinguish the white candle, expressing your gratitude once again.
2. Allow any remaining smoke from the herbs to disperse naturally.

Remember, this ritual is just a guideline, and you can modify it to fit your personal beliefs and practices. Hoodoo is a spiritual practice not a religion! Trust your intuition and do what feels right for you. Take care of yourself.

Father Simms the Two-Headed Doctor

Despite the title Father Simms, he was a Protestant preacher, he had gained quite a reputation as a Rootworker and Two-Headed Doctor in the vibrant city of New Orleans. Many called him the "Frizzly Rooster" due to his uncanny ability to break any curse, regardless of who had placed it or who it was aimed at.

Contrary to his religious role, Father Simms, whose real name was Joe Watson, had a deep understanding of the mystical arts and metaphysics. Known for his exceptional intuition, it was said that he could read anyone at any given moment, peering into their souls as if he held the key to their deepest secrets. One of his most astounding feats was predicting his own death, precisely down to the hour and minute, a staggering nineteen years before it would occur. Though he had been a robust and healthy man throughout his life, Father Simms claimed that God had personally revealed to him the precise moment he would depart from this earthly realm. He often shared this story with those who sought his guidance, emphasizing the importance of living each day to its fullest.

Aside from his spiritual insights, Father Simms also offered unique services to those seeking his aid. One of his most popular offerings was his "Sweet and Sour Jars." In his humble kitchen, he kept a jar filled with honey and sugar, representing all the sweet works and petitions made by his clients after payment. This jar symbolized the positive aspects of life and served as a vessel for their hopes and dreams.

However, Father Simms also had another jar, known as the "Break Up Jar." This jar contained a concoction of vinegar and unsweetened coffee, representing the bitterness and negative energy associated with discord and separation. Clients who sought his assistance with more challenging situations would provide him with their petitions for negative work, which he carefully placed inside the Breakup Jar.

Father Simms stated that these jars held a unique power, amplifying the intentions placed within them. By focusing on the positive aspects of life, he aimed to bring sweetness, harmony, and success to those who sought his help. Conversely, the Breakup Jar served as a tool to address situations where negativity and discord needed to be dissolved. While his methods may have seemed unconventional to some, Father Simms never wavered in his belief that he was providing a valuable service to those in need. He saw himself as a bridge between the spiritual and physical realms, utilizing his knowledge and connection with the divine to bring about positive change in the lives of others.

His reputation as the "Frizzly Rooster" grew, and people from far and wide sought his jars, spiritual guidance, and blessings. Over time, Father Simms became known not only for his abilities but also for his kind and compassionate nature. He had a deep understanding of the human condition and a genuine desire to help those in need, regardless of their background or beliefs. People flocked to him, not just for his mystical services, but also for his comforting presence and wise counsel.

Father Simms's impact extended far beyond the realm of New Orleans. His name became synonymous with hope and resilience, and stories of his miraculous interventions spread throughout the country. People shared tales of how their lives had been transformed after seeking his assistance, and his jars became cherished relics, passed down through generations. Even after his passing, the legend of Father Simms endured. Visitors to New Orleans would seek out his grave, leaving offerings and prayers, hoping to channel his extraordinary power. His name became a symbol of faith, strength, and the ability to overcome any obstacle, just as he had promised with his legendary "Road Opener" keys. That had the ability to open any door that stood in the way of his clients.

To this day, Father Simms's story continues to inspire those who believe in the power of the spiritual realm and the potential for positive change. His legacy serves as a reminder that even the most unconventional paths can lead to profound impact and that true power lies in the ability to offer compassion, guidance, and a helping hand to those in need.

And so, the tale of Father Sims, the Protestant preacher who defied expectations, the Rootworker and Two-Headed Doctor, lives on as a testament to the extraordinary and mysterious nature of the human spirit. His jars, his predictions, and his unwavering faith in the divine continue to captivate the hearts and minds of all who hear his story.

CHAPTER 10

Workings of a Two-Headed Doctor

In this chapter, we delve into the workings of the Two-Headed Doctor, embracing the essence of Hoodoo while offering a flexible and adaptable approach to suit practitioners of various beliefs and practices. Each work presented here has been intentionally crafted to be basic, providing a solid foundation for customization and personalization according to your individual style.

As a Two-Headed Doctor, you are a practitioner who embodies the duality of two spiritual forces, often symbolized by the two-headed snake or two-headed animal imagery. This duality represents the balance and harmony needed to navigate the complexities of life and metaphysics. The workings shared in this chapter are designed to be versatile, allowing you to add or subtract elements based on your personal beliefs, ancestral connections, and spiritual guidance.

As a practitioner, you have the freedom to adapt and modify these rituals to align with your unique understanding and relationship with Hoodoo. While these workings may be basic, they provide a solid framework for you to build upon. Feel free to incorporate additional herbs, roots, candles, prayers, or other tools that resonate with you and your intentions.

Remember, the true power of Hoodoo lies in the authenticity and intention behind your actions. Before engaging in any work, it is essential to cleanse your body, mind, and soul. Take the time to purify yourself through ritual baths, smudging, or personal prayer. This process helps to remove any negative energies or spiritual impurities that may hinder the effectiveness of your metaphysical workings. As you embark on this journey, remember to approach each work with respect, humility, and a deep connection to your spiritual roots. Seek guidance from your ancestors, spirits, or deities that resonate with you, inviting their presence and assistance in your spiritual endeavors.

Throughout this chapter, you will find a collection of foundational workings, each exploring a different aspect of two-headed work. Embrace these teachings as a starting point, a springboard for your own personal exploration and growth within the Hoodoo tradition. May these workings serve as a catalyst for your own unique practice, allowing you to tap into the vast reservoir of ancestral wisdom, personal intuition, and the power of the unseen forces that surround us.

Remember, you are the conduit, the channel through which the energy flows. Embrace your role as the Two-Headed Doctor and let the magick unfold. So let us begin this journey together, exploring the workings of the Two-Headed Doctor within the realm of Hoodoo, with an open heart, a curious mind, and the willingness to adapt and grow. May your path be illuminated, and your endeavors blessed with the transformative power of the Hoodoo practice.

Covering Your Head in White

In Hoodoo, covering the head in white during ceremonies, rituals, and workings is often done for spiritual and symbolic reasons.

Sign of purity and spiritual protection: Wearing white is often associated with purity, cleanliness, and spiritual protection. By covering the head in white, practitioners aim to create a sacred space and protect themselves from negative energies or influences during their rituals or workings.

Connection to ancestral traditions: Wearing white during ceremonies and rituals is a practice that can be traced back to various African diasporic traditions. In some of these traditions, white clothing is worn as a symbol of spiritual purity and reverence for ancestors. By wearing white, Hoodoo practitioners may be honoring their ancestral heritage and connecting with the spiritual practices of their lineage.

Symbol of spiritual elevation and authority: Wearing white can also be seen as a symbol of spiritual elevation and authority. It is believed that white garments enhance one's spiritual connection and signal a readiness to engage in sacred work. By covering the head in white, practitioners may be acknowledging their role as spiritual intermediaries and demonstrating their commitment to their practice. Regarding the practice of covering the head and wearing white before giving divinations or performing rituals, it is seen as a way to create a focused and spiritually aligned atmosphere.

It can help to establish a sense of reverence and ritual purity, allowing the practitioner to connect more deeply with the spiritual forces they are working with and to access the wisdom and guidance they seek to provide. It is also a way to visually signify their role as a spiritual authority and to create a clear boundary between the mundane and the sacred.

It is important to note that practices and traditions within Hoodoo can vary among individual practitioners and communities, so interpretations and practices may differ.

Rootworker Kye's 7-day Cleanse

In Hoodoo, the practice of cleansing the body, mind, and soul before performing workings is considered important for several reasons:

Clearing Negative Energies: Cleansing rituals help to remove negative energies or spiritual impurities that may be present within oneself. These energies can hinder the effectiveness of magical workings and block the flow of positive energy. By purifying oneself, it creates a clean and receptive state, allowing for a stronger connection to the spiritual realm.

Enhancing Focus and Intention: Cleansing rituals help to clear the mind and focus one's intention on the desired outcome of the magical workings. When the mind is cluttered, it can be challenging to concentrate and direct energy effectively. By purifying the mind, it becomes easier to align one's thoughts and intentions with the desired goal, increasing the potency of the Hoodoo work.

Creating Sacred Space: Cleansing rituals help to create a sacred and consecrated space for workings. By purifying the body, mind, and soul, one establishes a connection to the spiritual realm and opens oneself up to receiving guidance and assistance from spiritual forces. This sacred space allows for a deeper connection to one's ancestors, spirits, or deities that are often invoked in Hoodoo practices.

Releasing Emotional Baggage: Cleansing rituals can also help in releasing emotional baggage or negative emotions that may hinder the effectiveness of workings. Emotional disturbances can create blocks in the energy flow, affecting the outcome of the work. By purifying the soul and letting go of negative emotions, one can approach their work with a clearer and more balanced state of being.

Cleansing the body, mind, and soul in Hoodoo is seen as a way to prepare oneself for spiritual work, ensuring that one is in a receptive, focused, and purified state. It allows for a stronger connection to the spiritual realm and enhances the effectiveness of spiritual work.

Rid the body of negative energy and physical impurities

With this cleanse each day you will be able to add something new to the diet! For example, on the first day you can eat fruit and vegetables. The second day you can eat fruits, vegetables, and whole gains...and you keep on with that pattern every day adding something new!

Preparing for the Diet: - Take some time to set your intentions for the diet. Reflect on why you want to cleanse your body of negative energy and physical impurities. - Make a grocery list of the foods and ingredients you will need for the week. - Clear out your pantry and refrigerator of any processed or unhealthy foods that may tempt you during the diet.

Day-by-Day Approach: - Each day, focus on the specific food group or theme mentioned in the diet plan. - Plan your meals and snacks, accordingly, ensuring they align with the designated food group for the day. - Prioritize fresh, whole foods and try to incorporate a variety of colors, flavors, and textures into your meals. - Listen to your body's hunger and fullness cues, and eat mindfully, savoring each bite. - Stay hydrated throughout the day by drinking water, herbal teas, and detox drinks.

Mindful Practices: - Alongside the diet, incorporate mindful practices such as meditation, deep breathing exercises, or gentle yoga. - Take time each day to reflect on your intentions and connect with the purpose of the cleanse. - Consider journaling your experiences, emotions, and any insights that arise during the process. - Engage in activities that bring you joy, relaxation, and a sense of connection with yourself and the world around you.

Self-Care and Rest: - Prioritize self-care during the cleanse. Get enough restful sleep each night to support your body's healing and detoxification processes. - Practice self-care activities such as taking spiritual baths, engaging in gentle exercise, or spending time in nature. - Be gentle with yourself and practice self-compassion throughout the process.

If you have any setbacks or slip-ups, simply acknowledge them and continue with the diet. Remember, this diet plan is designed to support your body's natural cleansing processes and promote overall well-being. Listen to your body, make adjustments as needed, and consult with a healthcare professional if you have any concerns or specific health conditions. Enjoy the journey of cleansing and nourishing your body, mind, and spirit!

Day 1: Fruits and Vegetables

Focus on consuming a variety of fresh fruits and vegetables throughout the day. These are rich in vitamins, minerals, and antioxidants that help detoxify the body and promote overall well-being. Drink plenty of water and herbal teas to stay hydrated.

Day 2: Whole Grains

Opt for whole grains such as brown rice, quinoa, oats, and whole wheat bread. These provide fiber, essential nutrients, and sustained energy. Avoid processed grains and refined carbohydrates.

Day 3: Plant-Based Proteins

Choose plant-based protein sources like legumes (lentils, chickpeas, black beans), tofu, tempeh, and nuts. These protein-rich foods support muscle repair and provide essential amino acids without the added burden of digesting animal products.

Day 4: Herbal Teas and Detox Drinks

Spend a day focusing on hydrating and detoxifying beverages. Drink herbal teas like dandelion, nettle, ginger, or green tea throughout the day. You can also prepare detox drinks with ingredients like lemon, cucumber, mint, and ginger to support cleansing and elimination.

Day 5: Raw Foods

Consume a variety of raw foods such as salads, sprouts, raw vegetables, and fruits. Raw foods are rich in enzymes and nutrients that support digestion, detoxification, and overall vitality. Be mindful to properly wash and prepare these foods to ensure safety.

Day 6: Healthy Fats

Incorporate healthy fats into your diet, such as avocados, nuts, seeds, and cold-pressed oils like olive oil or coconut oil. These fats provide essential fatty acids and promote satiety while supporting brain function and overall health.

Day 7: Cleansing Soups and Herbal Broths

Prepare homemade cleansing soups and herbal broths using fresh vegetables, herbs, and spices. Opt for light, nourishing soups that are easy to digest and promote detoxification. Include ingredients like garlic, turmeric, cayenne pepper, and ginger for their cleansing properties.

Throughout the week:

1. Avoid processed foods, refined sugars, and artificial additives.
2. Minimize or eliminate caffeine, alcohol, and smoking.
3. Practice mindful eating, savoring each bite, and chewing food thoroughly.
4. Engage in daily meditation, deep breathing exercises, or yoga to promote mental and emotional detoxification.
5. Get adequate restful sleep each night to support the body's natural healing and detoxification processes.
6. Don't eat meat. (the flesh of an animal)

Remember, this seven-day spiritual and holistic diet is intended to cleanse the body of negative energy and physical impurities. It is important to listen to your body and make adjustments as needed. If you have any underlying health conditions or dietary restrictions, consult with a healthcare professional before starting any new diet plan.

Additionally, along with the diet, consider incorporating spiritual practices such as journaling, gratitude exercises, energy healing, or connecting with nature to enhance the cleansing process on a deeper level. This holistic approach will support not only the physical body but also the mind, emotions, and spirit.

Cleanse Your Space

Before diving into any Hoodoo workings, it is vital to cleanse and purify your space and home. This process helps to remove any lingering negative energies, create a sacred environment, and establish a harmonious atmosphere for your spiritual endeavors.

Set your intention: Before you begin, take a moment to set your intention for the cleansing. Focus on your desired outcome, whether it's to clear negative energies, create a sacred space, or invite positive vibes into your home.

Declutter and clean: Start by decluttering your space and tidying up. Remove any unnecessary items, clear out physical clutter, and ensure that your space is clean and organized. This step helps to create a clear and open energy flow.

Open windows and doors: Open all windows and doors to allow fresh air and natural light to enter your space. This helps to disperse stagnant energies and invite in positive energy.

Smudging: Light a bundle of sage, palo santo, or any other cleansing herb that resonates with you. Begin at the entrance of your home and walk clockwise, moving through each room while gently wafting the smoke into the air. As you do so, visualize the smoke purifying and cleansing the space. Pay extra attention to corners, doorways, and windows. You can also recite a prayer, psalm, scripture, or affirmation that aligns with your intention.

Sound cleansing: Use sound vibrations to further cleanse your space. You can ring a bell, play a singing bowl, or use a drum or rattles to create sound waves that break up stagnant energy. Again, move through each room while focusing on clearing the space and harmonizing the energy.

Salt or herbal cleansing: Sprinkle salt or a mixture of cleansing herbs, such as rosemary or lavender, around the perimeter of each room or on windowsills and doorways. As you do so, visualize the salt or herbs creating a protective barrier and absorbing any negative energies. Leave it for a short period before sweeping or vacuuming it away.

Blessing and protection: Once you have completed the cleansing process, it is essential to seal the space with positive energy and protection. You can do this by reciting a blessing or prayer that resonates with you, asking for divine guidance and protection in your metaphysical workings. You may also place protective talismans or objects, such as crystals or amulets, in strategic locations throughout your home, or even create a protective and blessing floor wash to cleanse your home.

Remember, cleansing is an ongoing process, and it's essential to regularly maintain the positive energy in your space.

Additional Cleansing Tips

Regularly smudge or cleanse your space. You can do this weekly, monthly, or whenever you feel the energy needs a refresh. Trust your intuition to guide you.

Keep your space clean and organized. Clutter can create stagnant energy, so make an effort to keep things tidy and organized. Regularly dust, vacuum, and declutter your space to maintain a clear and open energy flow.

Use essential oils or cleansing sprays. You can create your own cleansing spray by diluting essential oils like lavender, sage, or frankincense with water. Spray this mixture around your space to refresh and cleanse the energy.

Practice regular energy clearing techniques. Meditation, visualization, and energy healing practices can help you maintain a positive and balanced energy in your space. Incorporate these practices into your routine to keep the energy flowing harmoniously.

Invite positive energy. Set the intention to invite positive energy into your space. You can do this through affirmations, prayers, or by placing symbols of positivity and abundance, such as fresh flowers, crystals, or meaningful artwork.

By regularly cleansing and maintaining your space, you create an environment that supports and enhances your Hoodoo workings. Remember to trust your instincts and adapt these instructions to suit your personal beliefs and preferences.

Return To Sender

In the context of Hoodoo and other spiritual practices, "return to sender" refers to a working or ritual that is intended to send negative energy or intentions back to the person who originally sent them. It is a form of spiritual protection and a way to defend oneself against harmful actions or intentions. The purpose of a "return to sender" work is to reverse any negative energy, curses, hexes, or harm that has been directed towards you.

The work is performed with the intention of reflecting the negative energy back to its source, effectively turning it back on the person who sent it. The specific methods and ingredients used in a "return to sender" work can vary depending on individual practices and traditions. However, it commonly involves the use of a candle, such as a black candle to absorb and dispel negative energy, along with herbs, oils, or other materials associated with protection and reversal.

During the working, the practitioner focuses their intention on sending the negative energy back to its source, visualizing it returning and causing no harm to themselves. They may recite specific prayers, psalms, or affirmations to reinforce the intention and strengthen the working's effectiveness.

It is important to note that performing a "return to sender" work should be done with caution and ethical consideration. While it can be a form of self-defense and protection, it is generally advised to use such works responsibly and with the understanding that harm may be caused to the original sender.

Rootworker Kye's Seven-day Return to Sender Ritual

Materials needed:
1. A black seven-day glass-encased candle
2. A white seven-day glass-encased candle
3. A protective oil (such as Uncrossing Oil or Fiery Wall of Protection (Flying Devil) Oil)
4. A cleansing herb (such as white sage or rosemary)
5. A small piece of paper and a pen
6. A fireproof container or bowl
7. Matches or a lighter.

Day 1:

1. Begin the ritual on a Saturday, which is associated with removing negativity and protection.
2. Set up your sacred space, ensuring you have a calm and quiet environment.
3. Cleanse yourself and the area using the cleansing herb, such as white sage.
4. Visualize any negative energy being removed from your space.
5. Take the black seven-day candle and anoint it with the protective oil. As you do so, state your intention aloud, such as "I cleanse and remove any hex or curse that has been placed upon me."
6. Light the black candle and focus on the flame, visualizing it consuming and neutralizing any negative energy or hex that has affected you.
7. Write down your intention on the piece of paper, stating that the hex or curse is being removed and returning to its source. Fold the paper and place it under the candle.
8. Allow the candle to burn for at least one hour, focusing on your intention and visualizing the hex or curse being removed and returned to its origin.
9. Safely extinguish the candle, either by snuffing it out or letting it burn down completely.

Days 2-6:

1. Repeat steps 2-8 of Day 1, using the black candle and reaffirming your intention to remove the hex or curse each day.
2. Each day, spend a few moments reflecting on the progress and visualizing the hex or curse being completely removed and returning to its source.

Day 7:

1. On the final day, replace the black candle with a white seven-day candle, representing purity and protection.
2. Anoint the white candle with the protective oil, stating your intention aloud, such as "I am now protected from any returning hex or curse."
3. Light the white candle and visualize a bright, protective light surrounding you, shielding you from any negative energy that may attempt to return.
4. Safely extinguish the candle, either by snuffing it out or letting it burn down completely.

Additional Steps: (To Return to Sender)

On the last day, after extinguishing the white candle, take the folded piece of paper that was placed under the black candle.

1. Hold the paper in your hands and visualize all the negative energy and hex or curse returning to its original source.
2. Speak aloud your intention, stating something like, "By the power of this ritual, I return this hex or curse to its source. May it be neutralized and rendered harmless."
3. Safely burn the paper in a fireproof container or bowl, visualizing the hex or curse being consumed by the flames and transformed into neutral energy.
4. Once the paper has completely burned, dispose of the ashes in a natural body of water or bury them in the earth, symbolizing the permanent removal and dissolution of the hex or curse.

Remember, during the seven-day ritual, maintain a positive mindset, trust in the power of your intentions, and stay focused on the desired outcome of removing and returning the hex or curse to its source. It is important to perform this ritual with respect and belief in its efficacy.

Candle Working with Hot Foot Powder:

Ingredients:

1. Black candle (represents banishing and protection)
2. Hot Foot Powder (used to drive away unwanted energies or individuals)
3. Herbs such as black pepper, cayenne pepper, and red pepper flakes (optional for added potency)

Instructions:

1. Carve the name or description of the person or energy you wish to send back on the black candle.
2. Dress the candle with Hot Foot Powder by sprinkling it on the candle or rolling the candle in the powder.
3. Light the candle and visualize the negative energy or person being driven away.
4. As the candle burns, repeat an incantation or prayer that emphasizes returning the unwanted energy or person to its source.
5. Allow the candle to burn completely and dispose of the remains far away from your home or sacred space.

Herb Sachet with Mirror:

Ingredients:

1. Black fabric or cloth pouch
2. Herbs such as agrimony, rue, and angelica (known for their protective and banishing properties)
3. Small mirror (represents reflection and reversal of negative energy)
4. Thread or string to seal the pouch.

Instructions:

1. Combine the herbs in the black fabric or cloth pouch, focusing on your intention to return the negative energy.
2. Place the small mirror in the pouch, facing inward to reflect the negative energy back to its source.
3. Seal the pouch with thread or string, visualizing the energy being trapped and sent back.
4. Keep the sachet in a safe place, such as under your pillow or near your front door.
5. You can also bury it on the property of the unwanted energy or person, symbolically returning it to them.

Evocation Ritual with Banishing Herbs:

Ingredients:

1. White candle (symbolizes purity and protection)
2. Banishing herbs such as sage, hyssop, and rosemary
3. Charcoal disc for burning herbs.
4. A small cauldron or fireproof dish
5. Pen and paper

Instructions:

1. Begin by writing a clear and concise statement of your intention to return the negative energy or person to its source.
2. Set up your ritual space, lighting the white candle and preparing the charcoal disc in the cauldron.
3. Burn the banishing herbs on the charcoal disc, allowing the smoke to fill the space.

4. Close your eyes, visualize the energy or person leaving your life, and recite your written.
5. Visualize the negative energies or influences being surrounded by a swirling vortex of banishing energy, getting pushed away and dissipated.
6. Place the pouch in the cauldron or fireproof dish, and carefully light the banishing herbs on fire using the flame of the incense.
7. As the herbs burn, visualize the banishing energy intensifying and purifying the space.
8. Repeat a banishing incantation or prayer while the herbs burn, affirming your intention for the negative energies to be banished.
9. Allow the ashes to cool, and then bury them in the earth or scatter them in a body of running water, symbolically releasing and removing the banished energies.

Remember to always practice rituals and workings with respect, intention, and caution. Adapt and modify the steps as needed to align with your personal beliefs and preferences.

Protection

Protection work in Hoodoo refers to the practice of employing various spiritual techniques and rituals to safeguard oneself, loved ones, or spaces from negative energies, influences, and harm. It is an essential aspect of Hoodoo, as it aims to create a shield of spiritual protection and maintain personal safety. Here are some common forms of protection work in Hoodoo:

Spiritual Cleansing: This involves using herbs, washes, or baths to cleanse oneself or a space from negative energies to remove any harmful influences and create a clean and protected environment.

Mojo Bags: Mojo bags are small fabric pouches filled with specific herbs, roots, and other items that possess protective properties. These bags are carried or worn on the body to provide ongoing protection.

Amulets and Talismans: Various objects, such as crystals, charms, or religious symbols, can be used as amulets or talismans for protection. These are often worn or carried to ward off negative energies and provide a sense of security.

Candle Workings: Burning protective candles, such as black or white candles, can be used to create a shield of spiritual protection. Specific oils, herbs, or powders may be used to enhance the candle's protective properties.

Prayer and Affirmations: Reciting prayers or affirmations that invoke spiritual protection is a common form of protection work in Hoodoo. This practice establishes a connection with higher powers or spiritual entities, seeking their assistance in shielding from harm.

Crossroads Work: Working at crossroads (the place where two roads meet), a significant symbol in Hoodoo, offers protection. This can involve burying protective items or performing rituals at crossroads to ward off negative energies and deflect harm.

Protection Candle Working with Bay Leaves:

Ingredients:

1. White candle (symbolizes purity and protection)
2. Bay leaves (known for their protective properties)
3. Protection oil (such as a blend of olive oil and essential oils like frankincense or rosemary)

Instructions:

1. Anoint the white candle with the protection oil, starting from the middle and moving towards the ends, focusing on your intention for protection.
2. Write your name or the name of the person you wish to protect on a bay leaf.
3. Light the candle and hold the bay leaf in your hand, visualizing a shield of protective energy surrounding you or the person.
4. Place the bay leaf in the flame of the candle, allowing it to burn and release its protective energy.
5. Repeat a protection psalm or prayer while the candle burns, envisioning the desired outcome.
6. Allow the candle to burn out completely in a safe space.

Herb Bath for Protection:

Ingredients:

1. Protective herbs such as basil, rosemary, and bay leaves
2. Epsom salt or sea salt
3. A large pot of water

Instructions:

1. Boil a large pot of water and add the protective herbs.
2. Allow the herbs to steep in the water for a few minutes, releasing their protective energies. Add a handful of Epsom salt or sea salt to the pot, stirring it clockwise to incorporate the protective properties.
3. Let the mixture cool down to a comfortable temperature.
4. Take a bath or shower as you normally would, and then pour the herb-infused water over your body, from head to toe.
5. As you pour the water, visualize a shield of protection forming around you, repelling any negative energies or influences.
6. Afterward, air dry or lightly towel dry to allow the protective energy to remain on your body.

Evocation Ritual with Protective Talisman:

Ingredients:

1. A small protective talisman, such as a piece of black tourmaline, Ankh, Cross, or a Hamsa
2. A white cloth or pouch
3. Protection incense (such as a blend of frankincense, myrrh, and sandalwood)
4. A small cauldron or fireproof dish
5. Pen and paper

Instructions:

1. Begin by writing a clear and concise statement of your intention for protection on paper.
2. Set up your ritual space, lighting the protection incense and preparing the cauldron.
3. Place the small protective talisman in the white cloth or pouch, symbolizing its containment and activation.
4. Hold the pouch in your hands, close your eyes, and recite your written intention for protection.
5. Visualize a sphere of protective energy surrounding you or the person you wish to protect, growing stronger and impenetrable.
6. Place the pouch in the cauldron or fireproof dish, and carefully light it on fire using the flame of the incense.
7. As the pouch burns, visualize the protective energy being released and activated.

7. Repeat a protection psalm or prayer while the pouch burns, affirming your intention for protection.
8. Allow the ashes to cool, and then bury them in the earth or scatter them in a body of running water, symbolically grounding and spreading the protective energy.

Energy Shielding & Cleansing

In Hoodoo, energy shielding refers to the practice of creating a protective barrier or shield of energy around oneself, a space, or an object. It is used to repel and block negative or harmful energies, influences, and entities. Energy shielding in Hoodoo is often done to maintain spiritual protection and prevent the intrusion of negative forces.

It can be used in various situations, such as when entering unfamiliar or potentially hostile environments, when dealing with negative people or situations, or when engaging in spiritual work that may attract unwanted energies. Here are some common techniques used for energy shielding in Hoodoo:

Visualization: One common method is to visualize a shield of white or golden light surrounding you or the space you want to protect. Visualize this shield as impenetrable and reflective, bouncing off any negative energy or intentions sent towards you.

Prayer and Affirmations: Recite prayers or affirmations that invoke the protection of a higher power or spiritual entities. This can strengthen your intention and establish a spiritual connection for added protection.

Protective Amulets and Talismans: Carry or wear protective amulets or talismans, such as mojo bags, black tourmaline, or other crystals that have protective properties. These items can absorb or repel negative energies and provide ongoing protection.

Herbal Baths and Washes: Use herbs with protective properties, such as rosemary, bay leaves, or hyssop, to create cleansing baths or washes. These can be used to physically cleanse yourself or your space and create a protective barrier.

Anointing with Oils: Use protective oils, such as frankincense, myrrh, or basil oil, to anoint your body, objects, or entrances to your space. This creates a protective barrier and wards off negative influences.

Remember, energy shielding in Hoodoo is a personal practice, and the specific techniques and rituals used may vary. It is important to trust your intuition and adapt these practices to suit your beliefs and individual needs. Hoodoo is a spiritual practice not a religion.

Ritual of Cleansing and Protection:

Ingredients:

1. White sage bundle or palo santo stick
2. Small bowl or dish filled with sea salt or Epsom salt.
3. A white candle
4. Pen and paper

Instructions:

1. Begin by lighting the white candle, symbolizing purity and light.
2. Sit in a quiet and comfortable space, taking a few deep breaths to center yourself.
3. Write down any negative energies or influences that you wish to combat on paper.
4. Hold the white sage bundle or palo santo stick in one hand and the paper in the other.
5. Pass the paper through the smoke of the sage bundle or palo santo, visualizing the smoke cleansing and purifying the negative energy.
6. Place the paper in the bowl or dish filled with salt, imagining the salt absorbing and neutralizing the negative energy.
7. Lightly wave the sage bundle or palo santo stick around your body, starting from the top of your head and moving down to your feet, while visualizing any negative energy being banished.
8. Place the paper in the flame of the white candle and let it burn, releasing the negative energy.
9. Close the ritual by expressing gratitude for the cleansing and protection.

Ritual of Energy Shielding:

Ingredients:

1. Clear quartz crystal or black tourmaline
2. A small dish of saltwater or a bowl of earth
3. A white or black candle
4. Pen and paper

Instructions:

1. Light the white or black candle, symbolizing purification or grounding, depending on your preference.
2. Sit in a peaceful space and take a few moments to ground yourself.
3. Write down your intention to create a strong energy shield that repels negative energy on the paper.
4. Hold the clear quartz crystal or black tourmaline in your hand, focusing on its protective energy.
5. Visualize a radiant shield of light or a dense shield of protective energy surrounding you.
6. Place the crystal in the dish of saltwater or bowl of earth, allowing it to absorb the cleansing and grounding properties.
7. Take the crystal and, starting from the top of your head, slowly move it down your body, imagining it creating an impenetrable shield that repels negative energy.
8. Repeat your intention out loud or silently, reinforcing your shield of protection.
9. Place the crystal back in the dish of saltwater or bowl of earth to cleanse and recharge it.
10. Close the ritual by expressing gratitude for the shielding and protection.

Psalm 91 Shielding

Ingredients:

1. A Bible
2. A white candle
3. A small dish of saltwater or a bowl of earth Pen and paper

Instructions:

1. Begin by lighting the white candle, symbolizing purity and divine light.
2. Open the Bible to Psalm 91, which is often associated with protection, and read it aloud or silently.
3. Take a moment to reflect on the words and allow their meaning to resonate within you.
4. Write down specific verses or phrases from the Psalm that resonate with you and evoke a sense of protection and security.
5. Hold the paper with the selected verses in your hands, visualizing a radiant shield of divine light forming around you.
6. Place the paper in the dish of saltwater or bowl of earth, symbolizing the grounding and purifying properties of these elements.
7. Close your eyes and recite the selected verses from Psalm 91, either out loud or in your mind, with conviction and faith.

8. Visualize the shield of divine light growing stronger and more impenetrable with each recitation.
9. Take a moment to express your gratitude for the protective shield that has been created.
10. Close the ritual by extinguishing the candle, knowing that the shield of protection remains in place.

Remember to always trust your intuition and adapt these rituals to suit your personal beliefs and preferences. Regularly practicing these rituals can help you maintain a positive and protected energy field. It's important to approach these rituals with focus, intention, and respect.

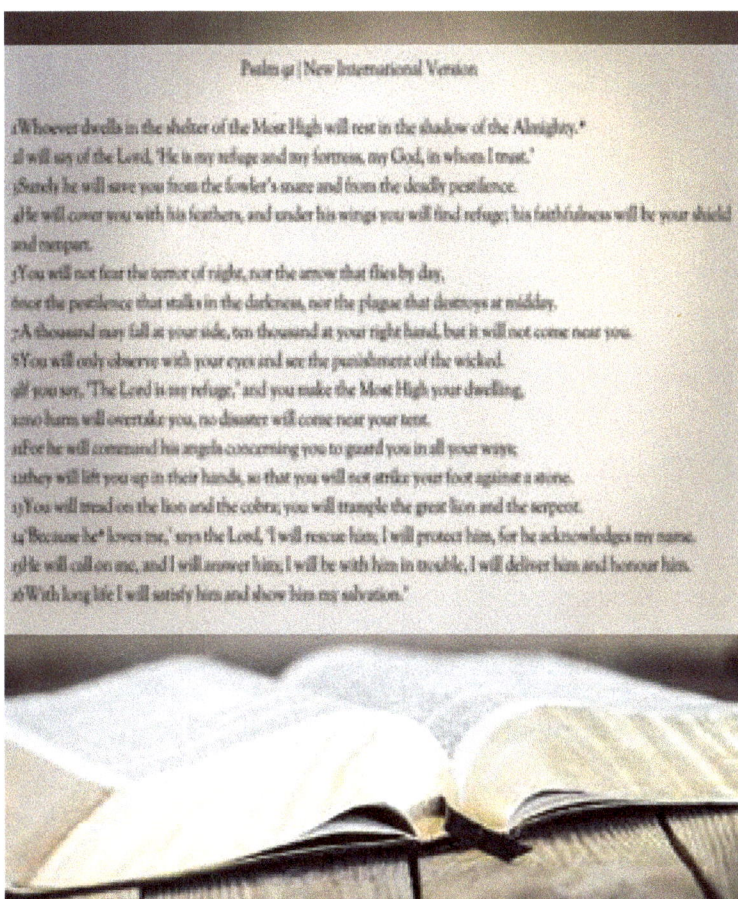

CHAPTER 11
Living in my Power

It was a time in my life when I found myself entangled in a toxic relationship. My boyfriend, if you could even call him that, was far from being a good person. He had a knack for deceit, a reputation as a serial cheater, and an addiction to manipulating people's emotions. Looking back, I still wonder why I ever allowed myself to be with him in the first place.

One day, amidst the chaos of our dysfunctional relationship, he confessed something that sent shivers down my spine. He revealed to me his involvement in Satanism and shared that he had once made a blood pact with his previous girlfriend. Odd occurrences had been happening around his house, and he attributed them to a curse she had supposedly placed upon him. Though I had never witnessed any of these strange events myself, I couldn't shake off the eerie feeling that lingered whenever I was at his place.

On one fateful evening, I stood in his kitchen, preparing dinner for him. The lights in the room began flickering, but it wasn't the typical flicker that occurs due to electrical issues. It was something else entirely, something that sent chills down my spine. As the unnatural phenomenon continued, I looked over at him, sitting at the kitchen table, his eyes wide with a mix of fear and confusion. An overwhelming sense of certainty washed over me – a knowing that I couldn't explain.

Without thinking, I walked out of the kitchen and positioned myself in the center of the room. I took a deep breath, feeling an inner strength begin to rise within me. With a surge of confidence, I clapped my hands together, creating a sharp and resounding sound that cut through the air. I clapped again, even louder, commanding the spirit to leave the house immediately. To my astonishment, the flickering lights ceased instantaneously, as if responding to my command. The room fell into a hushed silence, and I turned to face my boyfriend, who stared at me with a mixture of disbelief and awe. In that profound moment, I discovered something within myself – a power I had never recognized before. It was a revelation that transcended the boundaries of logic and reason. I knew deep within my being that there was something extraordinary residing within me, something that allowed me to tap into unseen forces and command them to my will. It was a power that stemmed from a place of intuition, of raw instinct, and of belief in the extraordinary.

That experience marked another turning point in my life. It was the moment I truly recognized my own power and the immense potential that lay dormant within me. The realization that I could influence the energy around me in such a profound way filled me with a newfound sense of purpose and determination.

I discovered that I possessed an uncanny intuition, a heightened sense of empathy, and a natural ability to rid any space or person of negative energy. With this newfound understanding of my capabilities, I began to take control of my own destiny.

I let go of toxic relationships (including that one) and negative influences, realizing that I deserved so much more than what I had settled for. I embraced my inner power and used it to create a life filled with love, joy, and abundance. As I continued to explore my spirituality, I discovered the importance of self-care and self-love. I learned to set boundaries and prioritize my own well-being.

Through meditation, I found a sense of peace and clarity that allowed me to tap into my intuition even more profoundly. Over time, I began to share my experiences and insights with others who were also seeking their own paths of empowerment. I became a guide, a mentor, and a source of inspiration for those who were searching for their own inner strength. It is a humbling and fulfilling role that I embrace with open arms... most of the time.

Through my journey, I realized that we all possess an innate power within us. We have the ability to shape our lives, to manifest our desires, and to create positive change in the world. It is a power that transcends the physical realm and taps into the depths of our souls. It is a power that can be harnessed through belief, intention, and unwavering faith in ourselves.

As I reflect on that particular experience in my life, I am filled with gratitude. It was a moment of darkness that led me to uncover my own light. It was a moment of fear that propelled me to embrace my own strength. And it was a moment of realization that opened the door to a life of purpose, authenticity, and limitless possibilities.

So, I invite you to embrace your own inner power. Trust in yourself and the incredible abilities that reside within you. Know that you have the capacity to overcome any challenge, to manifest your dreams, and to create a life that is truly extraordinary. The journey may not always be easy, but with belief, determination, and a deep connection to your own power, you can accomplish anything you set your mind to.

Enhancing Your Power

In Hoodoo, enhancing spiritual power is important because it strengthens your connection to the spiritual realm, heightens your intuition, and allows you to manifest your desires more effectively. By incorporating practices such as chakra balancing, tools, meditation, and shadow work, you can deepen your spiritual practice and align your energy for greater success in Hoodoo.

Chakra balancing: Chakras are energy centers within the body that correspond to various aspects of our being. Balancing and aligning the chakras helps to ensure a free flow of energy, promoting overall well-being and enhancing spiritual power. By working with chakra balancing techniques, you can clear any blockages, increase your energy flow, and strengthen your connection to higher realms.

Tools: Tools such as candles, herbs, crystals, and oils are commonly used in Hoodoo to focus intention and amplify energy. They can serve as powerful aids in workings and rituals, enhancing your spiritual power by harnessing the energy of these tools in alignment with your intentions. Selecting and using the appropriate tools can help you to channel and direct energy more effectively.

Meditation: Meditation is a practice that cultivates mindfulness, relaxation, and spiritual awareness. By incorporating meditation into your Hoodoo practice, you can quiet the mind, attune to your inner wisdom, and develop a deeper connection to your spiritual guides and ancestors. Regular meditation helps to strengthen your spiritual power and intuition, allowing you to work with greater clarity and intention.

Shadow work: Shadow work involves exploring and integrating the aspects of yourself that are often hidden or repressed. By addressing and healing your shadow aspects, you can release blockages, fears, and limiting beliefs that may be hindering your spiritual growth and personal power. Shadow work allows you to embrace your whole self and tap into your authentic power, which can greatly enhance your effectiveness in Hoodoo practices.

By incorporating these practices into your Hoodoo practice, you can deepen your spiritual connection, align your energy, and amplify your power for more potent workings and manifestation. Remember, it's important to adapt these practices to your own beliefs and preferences, finding what resonates with you and supports your spiritual growth.

Meditation in Hoodoo

Meditation can be a valuable tool to enhance one's Hoodoo practice in several ways:

Focusing the Mind: Meditation helps quiet the mind and cultivate focus and concentration. In Hoodoo, having a clear and focused mind is essential for effective workings, divination, and connecting with spiritual energies.

Heightening Intuition: Regular meditation practice can help strengthen your intuitive abilities. Intuition plays a significant role in Hoodoo as practitioners rely on their inner knowing and guidance to make decisions, choose the right herbs and ingredients, and interpret signs and symbols.

Connecting with Ancestors and Spirits: Hoodoo often involves working with ancestors, spirits, and deities. Through meditation, you can develop a deeper connection with these entities, allowing for clearer communication, guidance, and support in your Hoodoo practice.

Raising Vibrational Energy: Meditation helps raise your personal vibrational energy, allowing you to align yourself with higher frequencies, which can enhance the effectiveness of your workings, rituals, and manifestations in Hoodoo.

Cultivating Inner Power: Hoodoo practitioners believe in harnessing personal power to influence their reality. Regular meditation practice can help you tap into your inner power, build self-confidence, and develop a stronger sense of personal agency in your Hoodoo work.

Managing Emotions and Energy: Hoodoo often involves working with emotions and energy. Through meditation, you can cultivate emotional balance, release negative energies, and develop a greater awareness of the energetic dynamics at play in your Hoodoo practice.

Enhancing Visualization: Visualization is a crucial aspect of Hoodoo work. By incorporating meditation techniques that focus on visualization, you can strengthen your ability to vividly imagine and manifest your desired outcomes in Hoodoo.

Cultivating Mindfulness: Mindfulness, a key component of meditation, involves being fully present in the moment and aware of your thoughts, feelings, and surroundings. Practicing mindfulness can help you become more attuned to the subtle energies, signs, and synchronicities that are integral to Hoodoo.

It's important to note that meditation is a personal practice, and different techniques may resonate with different individuals. Experiment with different meditation styles, such as breath awareness, guided visualization, or mantra repetition, to find what works best for you and supports your Hoodoo practice.

Rootworker Kye's Meditation Technique

1. Find a quiet and comfortable space where you won't be disturbed. You may want to dim the lights or light a candle to create a calming atmosphere. (Optional: play music that puts you in a heightened emotional state.)
2. Sit in a comfortable position, either on a chair or on the floor with a cushion. Keep your spine straight, but not rigid, and relax your body.
3. Close your eyes and take a few deep breaths, inhaling slowly through your nose and exhaling through your mouth. Allow your body to relax with each breath.
4. Begin to focus on your breath. Notice the sensation of the air entering and leaving your body. As thoughts or distractions arise, gently acknowledge them and let them go, bringing your attention back to your breath.
5. As you continue to breathe, imagine each breath carrying relaxation and peace into your body. Visualize the tension and stress leaving your body with each exhale.
6. Now, imagine yourself in a serene and natural setting, such as a peaceful forest, a beach, or a mountain. Engage your senses and imagine the sounds, scents, and textures of this environment.
7. Continue to deepen your relaxation and focus by repeating a calming phrase or affirmation silently or out loud. For example, you can say, "I am calm and centered" or "I am open to receiving guidance and insight."
8. As you remain in this relaxed state, allow your mind to wander and explore. You may start to receive images, symbols, or messages. Pay attention to any insights or intuitive thoughts that arise.
9. Stay in this meditative state for as long as you feel comfortable, allowing yourself to fully embrace the experience. When you are ready to end the meditation, slowly bring your awareness back to your physical surroundings.
10. Take a moment to express gratitude for the experience and any insights you gained during the meditation. Slowly open your eyes and return to your day feeling refreshed and centered.

Remember, meditation is a personal practice, and it may take time to find what works best for you. Explore different techniques, adjust the ritual to your preferences, and be patient with yourself as you develop your meditation practice.

Chakra Work in Hoodoo

In Hoodoo, the practice of balancing chakras may not be as commonly emphasized as it is in other spiritual traditions that specifically focus on the chakra system. However, some practitioners may choose to incorporate chakra balancing techniques into their Hoodoo practice for various reasons. The significance of balancing chakras in Hoodoo can vary depending on the individual practitioner's beliefs and intentions.

Energetic Alignment: Balancing the chakras is believed to align and harmonize the body's energy centers, promoting holistic well-being. By incorporating chakra balancing into their Hoodoo practice, individuals may seek to enhance their overall energetic alignment and promote a sense of balance and harmony in their lives.

Spiritual Connection: Hoodoo practitioners may use chakra balancing as a means to deepen their spiritual connection. Balancing the chakras can help clear energetic blockages and enhance the flow of vital life force energy throughout the body, potentially facilitating a deeper spiritual connection and opening pathways for spiritual growth and intuition.

Healing and Manifestation: Balancing the chakras is often associated with promoting physical, emotional, and spiritual healing. By working with crystals and focusing on each chakra's corresponding qualities, Hoodoo practitioners may seek to address specific areas of imbalance or blockages in their lives and invite healing and positive transformation.

Enhancing Workings: Some individuals may incorporate chakra balancing techniques into their Hoodoo workings as a way to enhance the effectiveness of their rituals. When the chakras are balanced and aligned, it is believed that energy can flow more freely, potentially amplifying the intentions and outcomes of their work.

Chakras are energy centers within our bodies that are believed to be aligned along the spine, from the base to the crown of the head. These energy centers are associated with different aspects of our physical, emotional, and spiritual well-being. There are seven main chakras, each connected to specific organs, emotions, and characteristics.

Root Chakra (Muladhara): Located at the base of the spine, the root chakra represents our foundation, stability, and sense of security. It is associated with the color red and governs our basic survival instincts, grounding us to the physical world.

Sacral Chakra (Svadhisthana): Positioned just below the navel, the sacral chakra is linked to our creativity, sexuality, and emotions. It is associated with the color orange and is responsible for our ability to experience pleasure, passion, and intimacy.

Solar Plexus Chakra (Manipura): Situated in the upper abdomen, the solar plexus chakra governs our personal power, confidence, and sense of self-worth. It is associated with the color yellow and influences our ability to take action and make decisions.

Heart Chakra (Anahata): Located in the center of the chest, the heart chakra is the bridge between the lower and higher chakras. It represents love, compassion, and emotional balance. It is associated with the color green and influences our ability to give and receive love.

Throat Chakra (Vishuddha): Positioned at the throat, the throat chakra is associated with our communication, self-expression, and ability to speak our truth. It is associated with the color blue and governs our ability to express ourselves authentically and communicate effectively.

Third Eye Chakra (Ajna): Located between the eyebrows, the third eye chakra is associated with our intuition, inner wisdom, and spiritual insight. It is associated with the color indigo and governs our ability to perceive and understand deeper truths beyond the physical realm.

Crown Chakra (Sahasrara): Situated at the crown of the head, the crown chakra is the highest energy center. It represents our connection to higher consciousness, spirituality, and universal wisdom. It is associated with the color violet or white and symbolizes our transcendence and spiritual enlightenment.

These chakras, when balanced and in harmony, contribute to our overall well-being and vitality. However, imbalances or blockages in these chakras can lead to physical, emotional, or spiritual issues. Practices such as meditation, yoga, energy healing, or chakra balancing techniques can help restore the balance and flow of energy within these energy centers. Balancing your chakras before engaging in Hoodoo work can help ensure that your energy centers are aligned and functioning optimally.

It's important to note that Hoodoo is a versatile and eclectic practice, and not all practitioners may incorporate chakra balancing into their work. The significance and approach to balancing chakras in Hoodoo can vary among individuals, so it's essential to follow your own intuition and adapt the practices to align with your personal beliefs and goals. Hoodoo is a spiritual practice not a religion.

How do I Know if My Chakra is Unbalanced?

Physical symptoms: Chronic pain or discomfort in specific areas of the body, frequent illnesses or weakened immune system, digestive issues, or unexplained fatigue.

Emotional imbalances: Frequent mood swings, feeling emotionally overwhelmed, difficulty expressing emotions, or feeling disconnected from your emotions.

Mental imbalances: Difficulty concentrating, feeling scattered or restless, excessive worrying, or lack of mental clarity.

Relationship challenges: Struggles with establishing healthy boundaries, difficulty connecting with others on an emotional level, or feeling a lack of trust or love in relationships.

Creativity and expression issues: Feeling creatively blocked, difficulty expressing yourself authentically, or a lack of inspiration and passion in your life.

Spiritual disconnection: Feeling disconnected from your higher self or spiritual guidance, experiencing a lack of purpose or meaning in life, or feeling a sense of disconnection from the world around you.

Lack of balance and harmony: Feeling ungrounded, unstable, or experiencing a lack of balance in various aspects of your life.

If you notice any of these signs, it may indicate that your chakras are unbalanced. Balancing your chakras can help restore harmony and flow of energy within your system, promoting overall well-being and alignment.

Simple Chakra Balancing Ritual

Create a calm and sacred space: Find a quiet space where you won't be disturbed. Light candles, burn incense, put on peaceful music, or use any other tools that help create a peaceful atmosphere.

Ground and center yourself: Take a few moments to ground and center yourself. You can do this by taking deep breaths, visualizing roots growing from the base of your spine into the earth, or by connecting with your body and the present moment.

Start with the Root Chakra: Begin at the base of your spine, focusing on your Root Chakra, which is associated with stability, grounding, and survival. Visualize a bright red light at the base of your spine, spinning and radiating energy. Take a few moments to breathe into this area and imagine any blockages or imbalances being released and replaced with vibrant, balanced energy.

Move up to the Sacral Chakra: Shift your attention to the area just below your navel, which is associated with creativity, passion, and pleasure. Visualize a warm, orange light in this area, spinning and expanding. Breathe into this chakra.

Move up to the Sacral Chakra: Shift your attention to the area just below your navel, which is associated with creativity, passion, and pleasure. Visualize a warm, orange light in this area, spinning and expanding. Breathe into this chakra, allowing any tension or blockages to dissolve and be replaced with a balanced and harmonious energy.

Proceed to the Solar Plexus Chakra: Focus on the area above your navel, where the Solar Plexus Chakra is located. This chakra is associated with personal power, confidence, and willpower. Visualize a bright yellow light in this area, spinning and glowing with vitality. Breathe into this chakra, releasing any doubts or fears and inviting in a sense of empowerment and balance.

Move to the Heart Chakra: Shift your attention to the center of your chest, where the Heart Chakra is located. This chakra is associated with love, compassion, and emotional well-being. Visualize a beautiful green or pink light in this area, radiating love and healing energy. Breathe deeply into your heart, allowing any emotional blockages or pain to dissolve and be replaced with a balanced and open heart.

Proceed to the Throat Chakra: Focus on the throat area, where the Throat Chakra is located. This chakra is associated with communication, self-expression, and authenticity. Visualize a bright blue light in this area, expanding and spinning freely. Breathe into this chakra, releasing any inhibitions or fears around speaking your truth and inviting clear and authentic communication.

Move up to the Third Eye Chakra: Shift your attention to the space between your eyebrows, where the Third Eye Chakra is located. This chakra is associated with intuition, insight, and spiritual awareness. Visualize a deep indigo light in this area, shining brightly. Breathe into this chakra, letting go of any mental clutter or confusion and inviting clarity and heightened intuition.

Finally, focus on the Crown Chakra: Direct your attention to the top of your head, where the Crown Chakra is located. This chakra is associated with spiritual connection, divine guidance, and higher consciousness. Visualize a pure white or violet light in this area, expanding and connecting you to the divine. Breathe into this chakra, releasing any attachments or limitations and inviting in a sense of spiritual alignment and connection.

After balancing each chakra, take a few moments to sit with the energy and allow it to integrate into your being. You can conclude the ritual with a prayer, affirmation, or any other closing that feels meaningful to you.

Using Crystals & Stones in Hoodoo

Crystals are used in Hoodoo for their energetic properties and symbolism. They hold specific vibrations that can be harnessed to support various intentions and goals. They can amplify intentions, enhance energy, and provide specific energetic properties that align with your desired outcomes.

Amplifying Energy: Crystals are known to amplify energy and intentions. In Hoodoo, practitioners use crystals to enhance the energy they are working with. Crystals can intensify the power of workings, rituals, or intentions by magnifying their energy. By holding or placing a crystal on your altar during your Hoodoo rituals, workings, or meditations, you can infuse it with your intention and use it as a focal point to magnify your desired outcome.

Protection and Cleansing: Crystals are often used for protection and cleansing purposes in Hoodoo. Certain crystals, such as Black Tourmaline or Obsidian, are believed to absorb and transmute negative energies, ward off malevolent spirits, and create a protective shield around the practitioner or space. Amethyst is also a commonly used crystal in Hoodoo as it is known for its protective properties. Hoodoo practitioners who are empathic or intuitive use it to guard against psychic attacks.

Spiritual Connection: Crystals are used to enhance spiritual connection and intuition in Hoodoo. Some crystals, like Amethyst or Labradorite, are believed to open the third eye chakra, stimulate psychic abilities, and deepen spiritual insight. They can assist in divination, meditation, and connecting with higher realms.

Healing and Well-being: Many crystals have healing properties and are used in Hoodoo for physical, emotional, and spiritual healing. Crystals, such as Rose Quartz or Green Aventurine, are associated with love, healing emotional wounds, and promoting overall well-being.

Attracting Specific Energies: Different crystals attract specific energies or qualities. Hoodoo practitioners may choose crystals based on their metaphysical properties to support their intentions. For example, Citrine is often used to attract abundance and prosperity, while Carnelian is used to enhance motivation and creativity.

Energy Cleansing: Crystals, like clear quartz or selenite, have purifying properties. They can be used to cleanse and purify your energy, ritual tools, or sacred space in Hoodoo, ensuring that you are working with a clean and clear energetic slate.

Chakra Alignment: Crystals are associated with different chakras or energy centers in the body. By using crystals that correspond to specific chakras in your Hoodoo practice, you can balance and align your energy system, promoting overall well-being and enhancing the effectiveness of your work.

Manifestation and Abundance: Crystals such as citrine, pyrite, or green aventurine are known for their properties of abundance and manifestation. Utilizing these crystals in your Hoodoo practice can help attract prosperity, wealth, and opportunities for success.

Love and Relationships: Crystals like rose quartz or rhodochrosite are often associated with love, romance, and relationships. Incorporating these crystals into your Hoodoo rituals or love workings can help attract love, enhance existing relationships, or promote self-love and compassion.

Divination and Intuition: Crystals such as amethyst, labradorite, or lapis lazuli are believed to enhance psychic abilities and intuition. Using these crystals in your Hoodoo divination practices, such as scrying or tarot readings, can help deepen your connection to the spiritual realm and enhance your intuitive insights.

Grounding and Centering: Some crystals, like hematite or smoky quartz, have grounding properties. They can be used in Hoodoo to help anchor and stabilize your energy, promoting a sense of calm, focus, and stability during your practice.

When working with crystals in your Hoodoo practice, it's important to cleanse and charge them regularly. This can be done by placing them under running water, burying them in the earth, or using smoke from incense or sage to cleanse their energy. You can also charge them by placing them in sunlight or moonlight for a few hours.

Once your crystals are cleansed and charged, you can incorporate them into your Hoodoo rituals, workings, or altar setups. There are many ways to incorporate crystals into your workings.

Altar: Place relevant crystals on your Hoodoo altar to represent specific intentions or energies. For example, if you're working on a money working, you may place citrine or green aventurine on your altar to attract abundance.

Mojo Bags: Add a crystal or two to your mojo bags or gris-gris bags to enhance their energy and intention. Choose crystals that align with the purpose of the bag, such as love stones for a love mojo bag or protection stones for a protection mojo bag.

Candle Work: Place crystals around your candles during Hoodoo candle rituals. You can choose crystals that correspond to the intention of your working or use clear quartz to amplify the energy of the candle flame.

Energy Charging: Use crystals to charge or infuse items with specific energies. For example, you can place a crystal on top of a jar of herbs or oils to infuse them with the crystal's properties.

Meditation and Visualization: Hold a crystal in your hand during meditation or visualization exercises to enhance your focus, intention, and spiritual connection. You can also place crystals on your third eye or heart chakra to deepen these practices.

Remember, crystals are tools that can support and enhance your Hoodoo practice, but they are not the sole source of power. Your intention, energy, and the work you put into your rituals are what truly manifest your desired outcomes. Use crystals in a way that feels authentic and aligned with your own spiritual practice, and always trust your intuition when selecting crystals for your Hoodoo work.

Crystals & Stones in Hoodoo

AGATE
Promotes stability, balance, and grounding. Enhances strength and courage.

BLACK TOURMALINE
Offers protection against negative energies, psychic attacks, and electromagnetic smog. Grounds and purifies energy.

CARNELIAN
Boosts creativity, motivation, and confidence. Enhances passion and vitality.

CITRINE
Attracts wealth, success, and positive energy. Promotes abundance and manifestation.

GARNET
Boosts energy, passion, and motivation. Enhances love, sexuality, and protection.

AMETHYST
Enhances intuition, spiritual growth, and protection against negative energies. Soothes and calms the mind.

BLOODSTONE
Enhances strength, courage, and vitality. Protects against negative energies and promotes healing.

CLEAR QUARTZ
Amplifies energy, enhances spiritual clarity, and promotes healing and protection. Cleanses and purifies energy.

FLUORITE
Enhances mental clarity, focus, and decision-making. Balances and harmonizes energy.

HEMATITE
Provides grounding, protection, and strength. Enhances focus and concentration.

HOWLITE
Promotes calmness, patience, and stress relief. Aids in communication and emotional healing.

JASPER
Grounds and stabilizes energy. Enhances courage, strength, and protection.

LAPIS LAZULI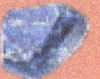
Enhances wisdom, intuition, and spiritual growth. Boosts communication and self-expression.

MOONSTONE
Enhances intuition, psychic abilities, and feminine energy. Promotes emotional healing and harmony.

ONYX
Enhances strength, protection, and self-control. Promotes grounding and stability.

PYRITE
Attracts abundance, success, and prosperity. Enhances confidence and manifestation.

RHODONITE
Enhances love, compassion, and emotional healing. Promotes forgiveness and harmony.

RUBY
Enhances passion, vitality, and courage. Promotes abundance and protection.

SMOKY QUARTZ
Provides grounding, protection, and stress relief. Enhances clarity and removes negativity.

JADE
Enhances abundance, luck, and harmony. Promotes emotional balance and peace.

LABRADORITE
Enhances intuition, psychic abilities, and spiritual connection. Protects and balances energy.

MALACHITE
Promotes transformation, protection, and abundance. Enhances emotional healing and balance.

OBSIDIAN
Provides protection against negative energies, psychic attacks, and emotional blockages. Grounds and cleanses energy.

OPAL
Enhances intuition, creativity, and emotional healing. Promotes inspiration and transformation.

RED JASPER
Provides grounding, protection, and stability.

ROSE QUARTZ
Attracts love, promotes self-love and compassion. Enhances peace and harmony in relationships.

SELENITE
Cleanses and purifies energy. Enhances spiritual connection and psychic abilities.

SODALITE
Enhances intuition, mental clarity, and communication. Promotes harmony and self-expression.

TIGER'S EYE
Enhances courage, strength, and motivation. Promotes abundance and protection.

TOURMALINATED QUARTZ
Combines the properties of Clear Quartz and Black Tourmaline. Enhances spiritual clarity, protection, and grounding.

UNAKITE
Promotes emotional healing, balance, and harmony. It is often used for fertility, grounding, and manifesting abundance.

WHITE AGATE
Brings peace, tranquility, and harmony. It is used for grounding, protection, and promoting clarity of thought.

XANTHITE
A type of pyrite, it is known for its protective properties and ability to shield against negative energies. It promotes confidence, abundance, and manifestation.

YELLOW JASPER
Enhances self-confidence, courage, and personal power. It is used for protection, grounding, and bringing joy and positivity.

ZEBRA JASPER
Encourages balance, grounding, and connection with the Earth. It promotes harmony, relaxation, and protection against negativity.

VESUVIANITE
Also known as Idocrase, it enhances spiritual growth, manifestation, and creativity. It is used for protection, abundance, and attracting positive energy.

Crystal Workings

Love Drawing Ritual:
1. Select a Rose Quartz crystal, known for its associations with love and relationships.
2. Hold the crystal in your hands, close your eyes, and visualize the love and relationship you desire.
3. Speak your intentions, focusing on attracting love into your life.
4. Place the Rose Quartz crystal on your altar or carry it with you to amplify your intentions and attract love energy.

Protection Ritual:
1. Choose a Black Tourmaline crystal, known for its protective properties.
2. Cleanse the crystal by placing it under running water or smudging it with sage.
3. Hold the crystal in your hands, envisioning a protective shield forming around you.
4. Recite a protection affirmation, psalm or prayer, infusing your intentions into the crystal.
5. Place the Black Tourmaline crystal near your front door or carry it with you to ward off negative energy and protect yourself and your space.

Abundance Ritual:
1. Select a Citrine crystal, associated with abundance and prosperity.
2. Cleanse the crystal by smudging it with sage or placing it in sunlight.
3. Hold the crystal in your hands and visualize your financial goals and desires.
4. Speak affirmations, scripture, or prayers related to abundance and prosperity.
5. Place the Citrine crystal in your wallet, purse, or on your altar to attract wealth and prosperity energy.

These rituals are just examples, and you can adapt them to your own personal beliefs and practices. Remember this is a spiritual practice not a religion.

Rootworker Kye's Chakra Balancing Ritual

Preparation:

1. Gather the crystals associated with each chakra: Clear Quartz (Crown), Amethyst (Third Eye,) Blue Lace Agate (Throat), Rose Quartz (Heart), Citrine (Solar Plexus), Carnelian (Sacral), and Red Jasper (Root).
2. Cleanse the crystals using your preferred method, such as smudging with sage or placing them in sunlight.
3. Find a quiet and comfortable space where you can sit or lie down.

Grounding and Centering:

1. Begin by grounding yourself. Take a few deep breaths, feeling your connection with the earth beneath you. Visualize roots growing from the soles of your feet, reaching deep into the earth, grounding and stabilizing you.
2. Crown Chakra (Clear Quartz): - Place the Clear Quartz crystal on the top of your head or hold it in your hands. - Visualize a bright white light entering through the crown of your head, filling your entire body with pure, divine energy. - Repeat affirmations related to spiritual connection and higher consciousness.
3. Third Eye Chakra (Amethyst): - Place the Amethyst crystal on your forehead, between your eyebrows (the location of the third eye). - Close your eyes and focus on your third eye area. - Visualize a deep indigo light spinning and balancing the energy of your third eye. - Repeat affirmations related to intuition, insight, and clarity.
4. Throat Chakra (Blue Lace Agate): - Place the Blue Lace Agate crystal on your throat or hold it in your hand. - Take a few deep breaths and focus on your throat area. - Visualize a vibrant blue light spinning and clearing any blockages in your throat chakra. - Repeat affirmations related to clear communication and self-expression.
5. Heart Chakra (Rose Quartz): - Place the Rose Quartz crystal on your heart center, in the center of your chest. - Take deep breaths and direct your attention to your heart area. - Visualize a soft green light expanding from your heart, radiating love, compassion, and healing. - Repeat affirmations related to love, forgiveness, and emotional healing.
6. Solar Plexus Chakra (Citrine): - Place the Citrine crystal on your solar plexus, just above your navel. - Take a few deep breaths and focus on your solar plexus area. - Visualize a bright yellow light spinning and balancing the energy of your solar plexus. - Repeat affirmations related to personal power, confidence, and abundance.
7. Sacral Chakra (Carnelian): - Place the Carnelian crystal on your lower abdomen, below your navel. - Take deep breaths and direct your attention to your sacral area. - Visualize a vibrant orange light spinning and clearing any blockages in your sacral chakra. - Repeat affirmations related to creativity, passion, and emotional balance.
8. Root Chakra (Red Jasper): - Place the Red Jasper crystal at the base of your spine. - Take deep breaths and focus on your root area. - Visualize a deep red light spinning and grounding your energy into the earth. - Repeat affirmations related to stability, security, and grounding.

Closing:

1. Take a few moments to sit or lie quietly, feeling the balanced energy in your chakras. Express gratitude for the healing and balancing experience.
2. Gently remove the crystals from each chakra, thanking them for their assistance.
3. Ground yourself once again, feeling your connection to the earth.

Suggested Chakra Affirmations

1. Root Chakra (Muladhara): "I am grounded, safe, and secure in my body and in the world."
2. Sacral Chakra (Svadhisthana): "I embrace my creativity and sensuality, allowing my emotions to flow freely."
3. Solar Plexus Chakra (Manipura): "I am confident, empowered, and worthy of all the success and abundance that comes my way."
4. Heart Chakra (Anahata): "I give and receive love unconditionally, opening my heart to compassion and forgiveness."
5. Throat Chakra (Vishuddha): "I express my truth with clarity and confidence, speaking my authentic voice."
6. Third Eye Chakra (Ajna): "I trust my intuition and inner wisdom, allowing it to guide me on my path."
7. Crown Chakra (Sahasrara): "I am connected to the divine, and I am open to receiving divine guidance and spiritual enlightenment."

Remember, these affirmations can be personalized and tailored to resonate with you and your unique journey.

Empowered Enchantment

In the realm of spirit, she delves deep,
A woman of wisdom, her journey takes a leap.
With crystals in hand, she seeks their embrace,
Enhancing her power, with each step she takes.

Dream work and shadow work, she diligently explores,
Unveiling the secrets that lie within her core.
Meditation, her sanctuary of peace,
Connecting with the divine, her soul finds release.

Through the pages of books, she seeks knowledge's light.
Studying diligently, day and night.
Her dedication unwavering, her passion aflame,
She's determined to master her Hoodoo's flames.

With every ritual, every work she tasks,
She's weaving her magick, her power amassed.
A practitioner on a quest to grow,
To become the best version of herself, she knows.

Her hard work and studying, a testament true,
To the depth of her spirit and all that she'll do.
A beacon of light, a healer so bright,
She's transforming her practice, with all her might.

So let her inspire, let her story be told,
Of a woman on a journey, so brave and bold.
With crystals, dream work, and spiritual healing,
She's embracing her power, the spirit is revealing.

-Rootwoker Kye

Shadow Work in Hoodoo

Shadow work is a process of exploring and integrating the unconscious aspects of ourselves, including our fears, repressed emotions, and limiting beliefs. It involves shining a light on the parts of ourselves that we often keep hidden or deny and working through them to achieve healing and personal growth.

Journaling: Start by setting aside dedicated time for journaling. Begin by reflecting on any patterns, emotions, or behaviors that you feel may be rooted in your shadow aspects. Write freely and honestly about your experiences, fears, and any memories that come to mind. Allow yourself to express your thoughts and emotions without judgment or censorship.

Inner Child Work: Our inner child represents our early experiences and emotions that may have influenced our beliefs and behaviors. By connecting with your inner child, you can uncover and heal unresolved wounds. Visualize yourself as a child and have a conversation with this inner aspect, asking about their needs, fears, and desires. Offer love, compassion, and reassurance to your inner child, and commit to meeting their needs and healing any past hurts.

Meditation and Visualization: Set aside time for meditation and visualization specifically focused on shadow work. Find a quiet and comfortable space, close your eyes, and take deep breaths to relax. Visualize yourself descending into a dark and safe space, representing your subconscious mind. As you explore this space, allow any emotions, memories, or images to arise. Sit with these experiences, observe them without judgment, and offer yourself compassion and understanding.

Dialogue with Your Shadow: Engage in a dialogue with your shadow aspects. You can do this through visualization or writing exercises. Create a separate space or invite your shadow aspects to speak through automatic writing. Ask questions like, "What do you need me to know?", "What fears or beliefs are holding me back?", and "How can I integrate and heal you?" Allow the answers to come naturally, without trying to control or judge them.

Seek Support: Shadow work can be challenging, so seeking support from a therapist, counselor, or spiritual guide can be beneficial. They can provide guidance, offer a safe space for exploration, and help you navigate any difficult emotions or memories that arise during the process.

Shadow Integration Ritual: Create a ritual to symbolize the integration of your shadow aspects. This can be done in a way that is meaningful to you, such as lighting a candle, gathering symbolic objects, or creating artwork. Set an intention to honor and accept all parts of yourself, including the shadow aspects. Visualize yourself merging with your shadow, embracing its gifts and acknowledging its presence as an integral part of your being.

Dream Analysis: Pay attention to your dreams as they often contain symbolic messages from the unconscious. Keep a dream journal and write down any dreams you remember upon waking. Reflect on the symbols, emotions, and themes present in your dreams. Explore how they may relate to your shadow aspects and what insights they may offer. Consider working with a dream therapist or participating in dream analysis workshops to deepen your understanding.

Shadow Dance or Movement: Engage in a physical practice, such as dance or movement, to explore and express your shadow aspects. Put on some music that resonates with your emotions and allow your body to move freely. Imagine yourself embodying different aspects of your shadow, expressing their energy and releasing any repressed emotions. This can be a powerful way to release and integrate your shadow aspects.

Shadow Work with Art: Engage in artistic practices that allow you to explore and express your shadow aspects. This can include painting, drawing, sculpting, or collaging. Allow your intuition to guide you as you create art that represents your shadow. Notice any emotions, symbols, or themes that arise during the process. Reflect on the artwork and journal about what it reveals about your shadow aspects.

Remember, shadow work is a lifelong process, and it is normal to encounter resistance or discomfort along the way. Be patient and compassionate with yourself as you navigate this journey of self-discovery and healing. Celebrate your courage to explore the depths of your being and embrace the transformative power of shadow work.

Shadow work is a deeply personal and individual journey. It's important to approach it with self-compassion, patience, and a willingness to confront and heal your shadow aspects. Be gentle with yourself and take breaks if needed. As you integrate and heal your shadow, you may experience a greater sense of wholeness, self-acceptance, and inner peace.

Rootworker Kye's Shadow Work Ritual

Set up a sacred space: Find a quiet and comfortable space where you won't be disturbed. Set up an altar or a designated area with items that hold personal significance to you, such as crystals, symbols, or objects that represent your intentions for shadow work.

Prepare the candles: Place two candles on your altar or in a safe space. Choose one candle to represent your conscious self, and the other to represent your shadow aspects. You can use different colored candles or add personal touches like carving symbols or affirmations onto them.

Begin with meditation: Sit comfortably, close your eyes, and take a few deep breaths to center yourself. Set the intention to explore and integrate your shadow aspects. Visualize a warm, golden light enveloping you, providing a safe and loving space for your shadow work.

Journaling: Take out your journal and pen, and begin writing freely about any patterns, fears, or limiting beliefs that you suspect may be rooted in your shadow. Explore any emotions or memories that come up without judgment. Write as honestly and openly as you can, allowing your thoughts and feelings to flow onto the pages.

Dialogue with your shadow: After journaling, imagine yourself in a dialogue with your shadow. Ask questions like, "What do you need me to know?", "How have you influenced my life?", and "How can we work together for our mutual growth and healing?" Write down any insights or responses that come to you during this process.

Lighting the candles: Light the candle representing your conscious self and say a few words, or a prayer acknowledging your commitment to explore and integrate your shadow aspects. Then, light the candle representing your shadow and express your willingness to embrace and learn from these aspects of yourself.

Meditation with the candles: Sit in front of the lit candles, gazing at the flames. Allow yourself to feel the presence of your conscious self and your shadow self. Notice any emotions or sensations that arise. As you focus on the flames, visualize the light from both candles merging and intertwining, symbolizing the integration of your shadow aspects with your conscious self.

Closing the ritual: Take a few deep breaths, expressing gratitude for the insights and experiences gained during the ritual. Blow out the candles, symbolizing the release of any resistance or fear around embracing your shadow aspects. Reflect on your journaling and consider any action steps or self-care practices that will support your ongoing shadow work.

Integration: In the following days and weeks, continue to explore your shadow through journaling, meditation, and other practices. Be gentle with yourself as you integrate these aspects into your daily life. Seek support from a therapist, counselor, or trusted friend if needed.

Remember, this ritual is meant to be adapted and personalized to your own needs and beliefs. Feel free to modify any steps or add elements that resonate with you. Trust your intuition and allow the process to unfold naturally.

The Purple Place

As a child, I had recurring dreams of a place I can only describe as "The Purple Place." These dreams began when I was around six or seven years old (I really can't remember the age they began), transporting me to a world filled with various shades of purple and lavender. In this ethereal realm, there stood a house inhabited by three mysterious figures, whom I can only refer to as witches or spiritual beings. They spoke to me, imparting knowledge about the universe and the world that still lingers within me today.

In these dreams, the three beings allowed me to freely explore this magical land. I roamed wherever my heart desired, relishing the vibrant hues that painted the surroundings. However, there was one place they adamantly forbade me from entering—an ominous portal that emanated a deep, dark purple, almost black, aura. Curiosity gnawed at me as I grew older, and during my teenage years, I finally mustered the courage to venture into the forbidden realm.

As I stepped through the portal, I found myself in a vast field adorned with breathtaking purple flowers. But to my surprise, a new color had emerged—a vibrant shade of green. It blended harmoniously with the purples, creating a mesmerizing sight. Yet, beyond the field, darkness loomed, swallowing all light. Something inexplicably drew me towards this void, and I found myself inching closer, compelled by an unseen force. Just as I reached the edge of the darkness, a piercing scream shattered the silence.

Startled, I turned around to find a man standing before me. His voice trembled with urgency as he demanded to know what in the world, I thought I was doing. Confusion etched across my face, I tried to explain my inexplicable compulsion, but before I could utter a word, I abruptly woke up, the dream fading away like a wisp of smoke.

Years later, fate intervened in a peculiar way. I stumbled upon the man from my dream on Facebook. Intrigued, I reached out to him, sharing the details of my dream and the encounter we had within it. To my astonishment, he revealed that he was the very man I had encountered as a teenager. He explained that he was a Dreamwalker—a person who traverses the realms of dreams and the Astro-world.

Through this revelation, I finally understood the significance of my dreams and the encounters within them. The purple place, the witches, and the man were not merely figments of my imagination.

They were gateways to a realm beyond our waking world, a realm where dreams hold truths and connections can transcend the boundaries of consciousness. The man, whom I now knew as a Dreamwalker, shared his own experiences and insights with me. He explained that Dreamwalkers possess the ability to navigate the vast expanse of dreams and other dimensions, and unraveling the mysteries that lie within. As I delved deeper into conversations with the Dreamwalker, memories flooded back to me, memories of those childhood dreams that seemed so surreal at the time. I recalled the wisdom imparted by the three spirit beings, the profound understanding of the universe they had shared.

It became apparent that my dreams had served as a conduit for knowledge, a means of connecting with a realm beyond our waking lives. I found out that the three beings that I encountered often change their appearance depending on who they are sharing knowledge with. At that time, I was obsessed with the movie "Hocus Pocus." So, when I entered that world, they appeared to me as three witches. With newfound clarity, I embarked on a journey of self-discovery, exploring the depths of my own dreams and unlocking the hidden truths they held. The Dreamwalker became my guide in this quest, offering guidance and support as I navigated the intricate landscapes of my subconscious mind. Through this exploration, I began to understand the significance of the purple place and its connection to my waking life.

The hues of purple and lavender represented intuition, spirituality, and inner wisdom. It was a realm where the boundaries of reality blurred, where I could access profound insights and discover hidden facets of myself. As I embraced my role as a dream explorer, I started to tap into the power of my dreams. They became a wellspring of inspiration, a source of guidance during times of uncertainty.

The Dreamwalker taught me to interpret the symbols and messages within my dreams, unlocking their hidden meanings and applying them to my waking life. Today, I continue to embrace the world of dreams and the knowledge it bestows upon me. The purple place remains a symbol of the profound connection between the conscious and subconscious realms, a reminder that there is more to our existence than meets the eye.

...And the Dreamwalker, though I lost contact with him and haven't heard from him in over a decade, he remains a constant presence, guiding me through the ever-shifting landscapes of my dreams, reminding me of the limitless potential that lies within the realm of dreams. In sharing my story, I hope to inspire others to embrace the power of their own dreams. For within the realm of dreams, we may find the answers we seek, the guidance we crave, and the connection to a higher truth that can shape our lives in ways we never thought possible.

Kyesha The Dreamwalker

Contrary to popular belief, this path was far from easy or idyllic. It was filled with darkness, pain, and unimaginable struggles. I battled physical and emotional abuse, endured the trauma of sexual abuse, and faced the harsh reality of homelessness. There were moments when the weight of my experiences pushed me to the brink of despair, making me question the purpose of my existence. Thoughts of ending it all seemed like a tempting escape from the relentless hardships I faced.

During those tumultuous times, my dreams became my refuge. Whenever I closed my eyes, I would enter the dreams of others or find myself navigating through the intricate tapestry of humanity's past and future. Occasionally, I would even glimpse fragments of my own past lives, connecting with soulmates in this ethereal realm. Yet, even with this extraordinary gift, happiness eluded me. I couldn't find solace or contentment in these experiences.

However, amidst the chaos, I discovered something profound. I found my purpose. Emerging from the fog of despair, I shed the identity of Kyesha, the lost Dreamwalker who was forever lost in the clouds. Instead, I embraced the strength and empowerment of Rootworker Kye. This transformation marked a turning point in my life.

I understand that some of the stories I share in this book may sound unbelievable, even crazy, to some readers. I recognize that others may doubt the authenticity of my experiences. But this is my truth, my story. It is my hope that by sharing it, it can offer some solace, inspiration, or guidance to those who may be walking their own challenging paths. So, I invite you to join me on this journey, as I navigate through the depths of this world in search of enlightenment. Together, let us explore the intricate tapestry of dreams, past lives, and the resilience of the human spirit. May my story serve as a beacon of hope and understanding, reminding us all that even in our darkest moments, there is a glimmer of light waiting to guide us home.

Dream Warnings: The Struggle of Being Heard

I have always had vivid dreams, and sometimes they take me on unexpected journeys. But there's a particular aspect of my dreams that has made it difficult for me to share them with my friends and family. It's as if they become skeptical or dismissive when I mention dreaming about them. Perhaps they think I'm crazy, or maybe they simply don't understand the significance dreams hold for me. You see, in my dreams, I often find myself in the body of someone else. It's like I enter their dreams, experiencing their lives firsthand.

Once I realized I am not dreaming of myself, I always look for a mirror in the dream and look at myself, this became a way for me to decipher who I'm dreaming about and potentially offer them guidance or a warning. One incident stands out vividly in my memory. I dreamt that I was my ex-boyfriend, surrounded by his friends, having a good time. But suddenly, the dream took an unexpected turn. The police barged in and arrested all of us; we had been caught smoking weed. The intensity of the dream left me unsettled, and I knew I had to share it with my "then" boyfriend. The following morning, I mustered the courage to tell him about the dream and expressed my concerns about him spending time with his friends that day.

However, he misconstrued my intentions. He believed that I was merely making excuses to keep him from leaving, as we had been grappling with issues of quality time in our relationship. That day and the next passed by without any communication from him. I started to worry, hoping that my dream was nothing but a figment of my imagination. However, my phone eventually rang, and it was my boyfriend on the line.

He told me something that sent chills down my spine - he had indeed been arrested, just as I had foreseen. Experiences like these have taught me that not everyone will readily listen to warnings stemming from dreams. It takes discernment to decide whether to share these visions or keep them to oneself. It can be disheartening when people label you as crazy or brush off your concerns. But I've learned to remain steadfast, holding onto the belief that dreams hold meaning and the potential to offer guidance.

I remind myself that I possess a unique gift, even if it's not always understood or accepted by those around me. Dreams have shown me a unique perspective, allowing me to tap into a realm beyond the waking world. So, if you find yourself in a similar predicament, don't lose hope. Embrace your ability and trust your intuition. Understand that not everyone will be receptive to the messages you receive through dreams. It's a personal journey, and you alone have the power to decide how to navigate it.

Over time, I have come to realize that it's not about convincing others or seeking their validation. It's about honoring the wisdom and insight that dreams offer me. Dreams have become a source of guidance and understanding in my life, and I have learned to trust in their messages. While it can be disheartening when others dismiss or label me as crazy, I have come to accept that not everyone is open to the idea of dreams having significance beyond the realm of sleep. Some may view it as mere coincidence or attribute it to an overactive imagination. But for me, it goes deeper than that.

Dreams have offered glimpses into the hidden corners of our lives, revealing truths and possibilities that may have otherwise remained concealed. They have the power to tap into our subconscious, bringing to light our deepest fears, desires, and unresolved issues. I have also learned the importance of discernment when it comes to sharing these dream warnings, because not everyone is ready or willing to receive such information.

It is a delicate balance between caring for others and respecting their choices. There are times when I choose to keep the dreams to myself, letting life unfold as it may.

Other times, when the sense of urgency or potential danger is strong, I feel compelled to speak up, even if there's a risk of being dismissed. Ultimately, it is essential to remain true to myself and my experiences. Dreams are a part of who I am, and they provide me with insights that can impact the lives of others. While it may be challenging at times, I have learned to embrace my unique perspective and not let the opinions of others discourage me.

So, if you find yourself in a comparable situation, where you have dreamt of someone you care about and feel the need to share your experience, trust your instincts. Approach the conversation with compassion and understanding, knowing that not everyone will grasp the significance of your dreams.

But remember, it is not your responsibility to convince or persuade them. Your role is simply to offer your perspective and insights, leaving the choice of whether to heed your warning in their hands.

Dreams are a mysterious and fascinating part of our human experience. They hold the potential to guide us, reveal hidden truths, and provide a deeper understanding of ourselves and the world around us. So, don't be discouraged if others call you crazy or dismiss your dreams. Embrace your gift, trust your intuition, and let your dreams be a source of guidance and inspiration in your own life.

Dream Interpretation

In Hoodoo, interpreting dreams involves seeking to understand the symbolic messages, guidance, and insights that dreams may hold. Dream interpretation is seen as a way to connect with the spiritual realm, receive guidance from ancestors or spirits, and gain a deeper understanding of oneself and one's life circumstances.

Dreams are believed to be a form of communication from the spirit world, and interpreting their symbolism can provide guidance, warnings, or insights into various aspects of life, such as relationships, health, work, and spiritual growth. The interpretation process involves analyzing the symbols, themes, emotions, and events within the dream to uncover their hidden meanings and messages.

Dreams are seen as a reflection of the subconscious mind, and Hoodoo practitioners believe that by paying attention to dreams and interpreting their symbolism, one can gain valuable insights into their current life situations, challenges, and opportunities. Dream interpretation in Hoodoo often involves using traditional symbolism and cultural associations to understand the meaning of specific symbols. However, it is also important to consider subjective experiences, emotions, and intuition when interpreting dreams, as they may hold unique meanings for each individual.

Overall, dream interpretation in Hoodoo is a practice that aims to tap into the spiritual realm, gain guidance from ancestors and spirits, and unlock the hidden wisdom and messages contained within dreams. It is a way to deepen one's understanding of oneself, navigate life's challenges, and seek guidance for spiritual growth and personal development.

Dream Journaling: Keep a dream journal by your bedside to record your dreams as soon as you wake up. Write down as many details as you can remember, including people, objects, colors, emotions, and any noteworthy events or symbols.

Symbolism: Pay attention to symbols and recurring themes in your dreams. In Hoodoo, symbols often hold specific meanings. For example, seeing a snake may represent transformation or deceit, while a white dove can symbolize peace and harmony. Researching the traditional symbolism of certain animals, objects, or events can provide insights into your dream's messages.

Intuition and Emotion: Connect with your intuition and the emotions you experienced during the dream. In Hoodoo, emotions carry significance and can help guide the interpretation. Consider how you felt during the dream and if any emotions stood out to you, as they may be key in understanding the dream's meaning.

Ancestor Communication: In Hoodoo, dreams are seen as a channel for communication with ancestors. If you dream of deceased loved ones or ancestors, it may be a sign that they are trying to convey a message or offer guidance. Pay attention to their presence, what they say or do in the dream, and any emotions you feel when interacting with them.

Divination Tools: Hoodoo practitioners often use divination tools, such as playing cards, tarot cards, or pendulums, to assist in dream interpretation. These tools can help provide additional insights and clarification regarding the symbols and messages within your dreams.

Seek Guidance: If you're struggling to interpret a dream or are unsure about its meaning, consider seeking guidance from an experienced Hoodoo practitioner or spiritual advisor. They can offer their expertise and provide insights and guidance based on their knowledge of Hoodoo practices and symbolism.

Rituals and Offerings: In Hoodoo, rituals and offerings can be performed to honor and seek clarity from the spirits or deities associated with dream interpretation. This can involve lighting candles, offering specific herbs or foods, or creating an altar dedicated to dream work. These practices can help create a sacred space for connecting with the spiritual realm and seeking guidance.

Meditation and Visualization: Before going to sleep, engage in meditation or visualization practices to focus your intention on receiving meaningful dreams. Clear your mind, set your intention to receive guidance or insight through your dreams, and visualize yourself receiving and understanding the messages. This can help enhance your dream experiences and make them more vivid and memorable.

Remember, dream interpretation in Hoodoo is a deeply personal practice. While there are cultural and traditional associations with symbols, it is also important to trust your own intuition and individual experiences when interpreting your dreams. The symbolism and messages within your dreams may hold unique meanings for you, so approach dream interpretation with an open mind and a willingness to explore the depths of your subconscious.

Dream Symbolism: Common Symbols in Dreams

Water: Emotions, unconscious mind, purification, cleansing.

Flying: Freedom, liberation, transcendence, empowerment.

Falling: Insecurity, loss of control, fear, instability.

Teeth: Communication, self-expression, confidence, vulnerability.

Snakes: Transformation, healing, sexuality, hidden fears, an enemy.

Death: Change, transformation, endings, new beginnings.

Ocean: Deep emotions, vastness, the subconscious.

Thunderstorms: Turbulence, emotional intensity, release.

Ghosts: Unresolved issues, past traumas, unfinished business.

Desert: Isolation, loneliness, personal introspection.

Bubbles: Playfulness, childlike joy, temporary nature of things.

Rainbows: Hope, positivity, harmony, divine connection.

Animals: Instincts, primal desires, aspects of the self.

Fire: Passion, creativity, destruction, renewal.

Money: Abundance, self-worth, power, material concerns.

Trees: Growth, stability, rootedness, connection to nature.

Houses: Self-identity, personal space, security, family.

Bridges: Transition, connection, crossing obstacles.

Keys: Access, opportunities, unlocking potential.

Masks: Hiding true self, deception, personas.

Clocks: Time, deadlines, awareness of mortality.

Mirrors: Self-reflection, self-perception, self-image.

Roads: Life journey, direction, choices, challenges.

Doors: Opportunities, new beginnings, opportunities.

Babies: New beginnings, innocence, vulnerability.

Mountains: Obstacles, challenges, personal growth.

Rainbows: Hope, positivity, harmony, divine connection.

Stars: Guidance, inspiration, dreams, aspirations.

Clouds: Uncertainty, confusion, lack of clarity.

Light: Awareness, enlightenment, guidance, truth.

Shadows: Hidden aspects, fears, unacknowledged emotions.

Books: Knowledge, wisdom, learning, exploration.

Beach: Relaxation, leisure, emotional boundaries, transitions.

Mirror: Self-reflection, self-perception, self-image.

Spider: Creativity, weaving dreams, intricate connections.

Car: Personal drive, ambition, progress, control.

Clocks: Awareness of time passing, deadlines, urgency.

Forest: Exploration, mystery, the unknown, primal instincts.

Ghosts: Unresolved issues, past traumas, unfinished business.

Wedding: Union, commitment, partnership, harmony.

Balloons: Joy, lightness, celebration, letting go.

Tornado: Chaos, upheaval, uncontrollable emotions.

Labyrinth: Confusion, feeling lost, seeking direction.

Keys: Unlocking potential, access to new opportunities.

Bridges: Transition, connection, crossing obstacles.

Masks: Deception, hidden intentions, social masks.

Flowers: Beauty, growth, blossoming, new beginnings.

Thunderstorms: Turbulence, emotional intensity, release.
Bridges: Transition, connection, crossing obstacles.

Ocean: Deep emotions, vastness, the subconscious.

Thunder: Power, transformation, divine intervention.
School/Classroom: Learning, personal growth, self-development.

Rain: Cleansing, emotional release, renewal, fertility.

Fireworks: Celebration, excitement, joy, unexpected surprises.

Moon: Intuition, emotions, feminine energy, cycles.
Sun: Vitality, energy, life force, consciousness.

Stars: Hope, inspiration, guidance, aspirations.

Caves: Hidden emotions, inner exploration, self-discovery.

Birds: Freedom, spirituality, transcendence, communication.

Mountains: Challenges, obstacles, personal growth, strength.

Remember, dream symbolism can be subjective, and it's important to consider your own personal associations and emotions connected to these symbols when interpreting your dreams.

Common Colors in Dreams

Red: Passion, energy, anger, intensity, power.

Yellow: Happiness, positivity, optimism, clarity.

Orange: Creativity, enthusiasm, vitality, motivation.

Brown: Grounding, stability, practicality, earthiness.

Blue: Tranquility, calmness, peace, emotional healing.

Green: Growth, renewal, harmony, balance.

Black: Mystery, the unknown, hidden aspects, transformation.

Pink: Love, affection, compassion, nurturing.

Silver: Intuition, reflection, feminine energy, emotional balance.

Magenta: Passion, creativity, self-confidence, boldness.

Lavender: Healing, relaxation, spiritual growth, tranquility.

Maroon: Intensity, passion, endurance, strength

Coral: Emotional warmth, nurturing, connection.

Olive: Peace, wisdom, growth, fertility.

Burgundy: Sophistication, elegance, luxury, refinement.

Rose: Love, romance, tenderness, beauty.

Slate: Stability, grounding, practicality, reliability.

Mauve: Creativity, imagination, inspiration, artistic expression.

Mustard: Energy, vitality, confidence, assertiveness.

Purple: Spirituality, intuition, mystery, higher consciousness.

White: Purity, innocence, new beginnings, spiritual awakening.

Gray: Indecision, neutrality, ambiguity, uncertainty.

Gold: Success, wealth, abundance, divine guidance.

Turquoise: Communication, emotional healing, self-expression.

Indigo: Intuition, deep inner wisdom, spirituality.

Beige: Neutrality, blending in, conformity.

Navy: Authority, power, discipline, control.

Teal: Emotional balance, healing, self-expression.

Peach: Gentleness, innocence, vulnerability, sensitivity.

Chartreuse: Creativity, uniqueness, originality, innovation.

Enhance Your Dreams with Herbs

Mugwort:

Mugwort is known for its ability to enhance dreams and promote vivid and prophetic experiences. It is often used to enhance dream recall, increase intuition, and deepen spiritual connections.

Uses:
1. To use mugwort for dream interpretation, you can create a dream pillow by stuffing dried mugwort leaves into a small fabric pouch and placing it under your pillow.
2. This can help promote vivid and meaningful dreams.

Mugwort Tea Recipe:

Ingredients:
1. 1 teaspoon dried mugwort leaves
2. 1 cup of boiling water

Instructions:
1. Place the dried mugwort leaves in a tea infuser or a small teapot.
2. Pour the boiling water over the mugwort leaves.
3. Let the tea steep for about 5-10 minutes.
4. Strain the tea into a cup.
5. You can sweeten the tea with honey or add a squeeze of lemon if desired.
6. Drink the mugwort tea before bed to enhance dream experiences and promote dream recall.

Mugwort Incense Blend Recipe:

Ingredients:
1. 1-part dried mugwort leaves
2. 1-part dried lavender flowers
3. 1-part dried rosemary leaves
4. 1-part dried sage leaves

Instructions:
Mix equal parts of dried mugwort leaves, lavender flowers, rosemary leaves, and sage leaves in a bowl.

1. Gently crush the herbs together using your hands or a mortar and pestle to release their aromatic properties.
2. Once the herbs are well combined, you can use this blend as a smudging or incense material.
3. Light a charcoal disk or use an incense burner.
4. Sprinkle a small amount of the mugwort smoke blend onto the charcoal or place it in an incense burner.
5. Allow the herbs to smolder and release their fragrant smoke.
6. Use the smoke to cleanse your space before dream work or to prepare yourself for a dream-enhancing environment.
7. Remember to exercise caution when burning herbs and ensure proper ventilation in the room.
8. Always follow safety guidelines when working with fire or smoke.

Lavender:

Lavender is often used for its calming and relaxing properties, making it beneficial for promoting restful sleep and encouraging dream recall. It is believed to help purify and protect the mind, allowing for clearer and more insightful dreams.

Uses:

To incorporate lavender into your dream practices, you can create a lavender-infused oil or sachet to place near your bedside. This can help create a soothing and conducive environment for dream work.

Hops:

Hops are commonly associated with promoting peaceful sleep and relieving anxiety. They are believed to help facilitate deep and restorative dreams, making them ideal for dream interpretation.

Uses:

To utilize hops for dream work, you can create a dream tea by steeping dried hops flowers in hot water. Drinking this tea before bed can help promote peaceful sleep and enhance dream experiences.

Rosemary:

Rosemary is often used for its cleansing and protective properties. It is believed to help ward off negative energies and promote clarity and insight in dreams.

Uses:

1. To incorporate rosemary into dream interpretation, you can create a rosemary-infused water spray.
2. Spray this mixture around your bedroom or onto your pillow before sleep to create a protective and spiritually conducive atmosphere for dream work.

Jasmine:

Jasmine is associated with love, spirituality, and psychic abilities. It is believed to enhance dream recall, promote prophetic dreams, and deepen spiritual connections during dream experiences.

Uses:

1. You can incorporate jasmine into your dream interpretation practices by creating a jasmine-infused oil.
2. Apply a small amount to your temples or pulse points before sleep to enhance dream experiences.

Cinnamon:

Cinnamon is known for its stimulating and energizing properties. It is believed to increase psychic awareness and stimulate vivid dreams.

Uses:

1. To incorporate cinnamon into dream interpretation, you can create a dream sachet by combining dried cinnamon bark with other dream-enhancing herbs like mugwort and lavender.
2. Place this sachet under your pillow to enhance dream recall and promote meaningful dreams.

Remember, these are just a few examples of herbs commonly used in Hoodoo for dream interpretation. Feel free to explore and experiment with different herbs and combinations to find what works best for you. It is important to research and ensure that you are using herbs safely and responsibly. Additionally, always trust your intuition and firsthand experiences when working with dream interpretation in Hoodoo.

CHAPTER 12
Christianity in Hoodoo

Christianity played a significant role in the development of Hoodoo, as it became intertwined with African spiritual beliefs and practices in a unique and syncretic manner. The origins of Hoodoo can be traced back to the forced migration of African slaves to the Americas during the era of the transatlantic slave trade. As slaves were brought to the New World, they were forcibly introduced to Christianity by their captors. However, the enslaved Africans managed to preserve their traditional spiritual beliefs and practices by incorporating elements of Christianity into their own traditions. This blending of African spirituality and Christian symbolism laid the foundation for the development of Hoodoo

.

In the context of Hoodoo, Christianity serves as a framework or container for African spiritual beliefs. African slaves, who were often denied the freedom to practice their ancestral religions openly, found ways to adapt their traditions within the scope of Christianity. They incorporated Christian prayers, biblical verses, and the symbolism of saints into their rituals and workings. Christianity provided a familiar language and imagery that allowed African Americans to express their spiritual beliefs and engage in their true spiritual practices while appearing to conform to the dominant Christian culture.

This syncretism allowed them to maintain their spiritual connections with their African ancestors and spirits while outwardly conforming to the expectations of their oppressors. Within Hoodoo, Christian elements are often used for protection, healing, and empowerment. The Bible is considered a sacred text and is frequently consulted for divination purposes. Psalms, in particular, are utilized for their spiritual power and are recited as prayers or incorporated into metaphysical workings.

Saints also play a significant role in Hoodoo practices. African ancestors and spirits are often associated with specific Christian saints, allowing practitioners to establish a connection between the two belief systems. For example, the Yoruba Orisha Oshun is often associated with the Catholic saint Our Lady of Charity, while Ogun is linked to Saint Peter. It is important to note that while Christianity has influenced Hoodoo, it is not the sole religious or spiritual foundation of the practice. Hoodoo also draws from various African spiritual traditions, Native American practices, and a few European spiritual practices. The combination of these diverse influences has resulted in a rich and complex system of Hoodoo that continues to be practiced by many African Americans today.

The Power of the Psalms

Hoodoo practitioners often incorporate Psalms from the Bible into their practice for assorted reasons. The use of Psalms in Hoodoo can be attributed to several factors, including historical, cultural, and spiritual significance.

The Book of Psalms is a significant part of the Bible, which holds religious and spiritual authority for many people. Hoodoo practitioners often incorporate biblical elements into their practice, and the Book of Psalms provides a rich source of prayers, hymns, and spiritual guidance. It is believed to possess powerful metaphysical properties., and each psalm is considered to have its own unique energy and purpose. Hoodoo practitioners use specific psalms for various intentions, such as protection, healing, love, prosperity, and spiritual guidance.

The Book of Psalms contains a wide range of themes and emotions, making it versatile for different spiritual purposes. Whether one seeks comfort, strength, or divine intervention, there is likely a psalm that resonates with their specific needs. Hoodoo practitioners often emphasize their connection to God and the spiritual realm. The Book of Psalms provides a means to communicate with the divine and seek assistance in various aspects of life. By reciting or meditating on specific psalms, practitioners can establish a deeper connection to their spirituality.

Furthermore, the use of the Book of Psalms in Hoodoo has a long-standing historical tradition. African slaves brought their spiritual practices, including Hoodoo, to the Americas, and they incorporated elements of Christianity into their rituals. The Book of Psalms became a central text for Hoodoo practitioners, blending African spirituality with Christian beliefs. The poetic and symbolic language used in the Book of Psalms resonates with many Hoodoo practitioners. The metaphors, imagery, and prayers found in the psalms evoke deep emotions and spiritual connections. This symbolic language allows practitioners to express their desires, hopes, and fears in a profound and meaningful way.

The use of the Book of Psalms in Hoodoo is not only a personal practice but also a communal one. It is a shared cultural and spiritual tradition that connects practitioners to their ancestors and the larger Hoodoo community. By using the same psalms, practitioners establish a sense of unity and continuity with those who came before them.

The reasons for using the Book of Psalms in Hoodoo may vary among practitioners. Some may emphasize the religious and spiritual aspects, while others may focus more on the metaphysical properties. Ultimately, Psalms in Hoodoo is not limited to strict adherence to religious dogma. Instead, practitioners often interpret and adapt the verses to align with their specific intentions and cultural context. The Psalms serve as a spiritual tool, offering guidance, solace, and empowerment to those who incorporate them into their Hoodoo practice.

The Use of Psalms

Protection: Psalms are often used for protection against negative energies, evil spirits, or harmful intentions. Certain psalms, such as Psalm 91, are believed to have strong protective qualities and are recited or written down as a form of spiritual defense.

Healing and Health: Psalms are utilized for healing purposes, both physical and emotional. Specific psalms, such as Psalm 103, are believed to have the power to restore health, alleviate pain, and bring comfort to those who are suffering.

Love and Relationships: Hoodoo practitioners turn to the Book of Psalms for matters of love, romance, and relationships. They may recite or meditate on psalms like Psalm 45 or Psalm 139 to attract love, strengthen existing relationships, or resolve conflicts.

Prosperity and Abundance: Psalms associated with abundance and prosperity, such as Psalm 23 or Psalm 112, are used to attract financial success, wealth, and material blessings. Hoodoo practitioners may recite these psalms or incorporate them into money-drawing rituals.

Divination and Guidance: The Book of Psalms is also consulted for divination and seeking guidance. Practitioners may open the book randomly or use specific psalms, such as Psalm 119, as a form of bibliomancy to receive insights, answers, or spiritual direction.

Cleansing and Purification: Psalms are used for spiritual cleansing and purification purposes. Certain psalms, like Psalm 51, are recited or incorporated into rituals to remove negative energies, purify the spirit, and seek forgiveness.

Manifestation and Intention Setting: Hoodoo practitioners use the power of psalms to manifest their desires and set intentions. By reciting or meditating on specific psalms that align with their goals, they believe they can attract positive outcomes and bring their desires into reality.

Once again it is important to remind you that the use of psalms in Hoodoo is not limited to these specific purposes. Hoodoo is a diverse and individualized practice, and practitioners may adapt and incorporate psalms into their rituals and work based on their personal beliefs and needs.

Psalms Commonly used in Hoodoo

Psalm 3:
For protection against enemies and to overcome fear.

Psalm 7:
For protection against slander, false accusations, and enemies.

Psalm 10:
For protection against evil and to overcome feelings of despair.

Psalm 18:
for protection against enemies and overcoming obstacles. It is believed to provide strength, courage, and victory in challenging situations.

Psalm 35:
for protection against enemies and to overcome unjust situations. It is believed to invoke divine assistance in times of conflict and to bring about justice.

Psalm 51:
To seek forgiveness, cleansing, and to overcome guilt.

Psalm 5:
To seek divine guidance and justice in legal matters.

Psalm 9:
To seek justice and victory over enemies.

Psalm 13:
To seek comfort and relief from distress or sorrow.

Psalm 23:
for guidance and protection. It is believed to provide comfort and assurance, allowing the two-headed doctors to feel supported and guided in their work.

Psalm 37:
for justice and protection against enemies or adversaries. It is believed to bring about a sense of justice and fairness, while also providing spiritual defense against those who may seek to harm or interfere with the two-headed doctors' work.

Psalm 56:
for protection against adversaries and to overcome fear. It is believed to grant courage, resilience, and the ability to face and conquer challenges.

Psalm 57:
for divine favor and grace. It is believed to bring about blessings, mercy, and positive outcomes in various aspects of life.

Psalm 71:
To seek protection, healing, and support in times of trouble.

Psalm 103:
To express gratitude, seek blessings, and attract divine favor.

Psalm 118:
For victory, success, and to overcome obstacles or enemies.

Psalm 121:
for travel and journeying. It is believed to provide protection and guidance during travel, whether physical or spiritual.

Psalm 125:
for stability and security. It is believed to provide a strong foundation and protection against instability or threats.

Psalm 70:
for quick help and urgent situations. It is believed to invoke swift divine intervention and assistance in times of immediate need.

Psalm 91:
is known as the "Psalm of Protection" and is commonly used to invoke divine protection and safety. It is believed to create a shield of spiritual defense, guarding against negative energies and harm.

Psalm 109:
for justice and to overcome slander or false accusations. It is believed to bring about truth and vindication, while also protecting against harmful intentions.

Psalm 120:
For protection against enemies and to overcome gossip or slander.

Psalm 122:
for peace and harmony. It is believed to promote unity, reconciliation, and a sense of tranquility in relationships and situations.

Psalm 139:
for its emphasis on divine knowledge and omnipresence. It is often used to seek guidance and wisdom from the divine, allowing the two-headed doctors to connect with higher powers and receive insights for their work.

Psalm 144:
for victory and success. It is believed to bring about triumph over obstacles, enemies, and challenges, granting strength and favor.

These Psalms can be incorporated into various Hoodoo workings, such as candle work, prayer rituals, or even written petitions. Remember to approach them with reverence and an open heart, understanding their spiritual significance and seeking their divine assistance in your specific needs.

Bible Verses Relevant in Hoodoo

Genesis 1:1-2:
For spiritual cleansing and opening the way for new beginnings.

Exodus 20:12:
To honor and seek blessings from parents and elders.

Numbers 6:24-26:
To invoke blessings and divine favor.

Joshua 1:9:
To overcome fear and gain courage in challenging situations.

1 Samuel 17:45-47:
For victory over enemies and protection in battles.

1 Kings 3:5:
For wisdom, discernment, and guidance in decision-making.

Job 5:12:
To seek divine wisdom and understanding.

Proverbs 10:22:
For attracting blessings, abundance, and prosperity.

Ecclesiastes 3:1-8:
For understanding and acceptance of life's seasons and cycles.

Isaiah 41:10:
For protection, comfort, and overcoming fear.

Exodus 14:14:
For protection against enemies and to overcome obstacles.

Exodus 23:20:
For divine guidance and protection on a journey.

Deuteronomy 28:1-14:
For attracting abundance, prosperity, and blessings.

Judges 16:28:
To invoke strength and power in times of weakness.

2 Samuel 22:33:
To seek divine strength and refuge in times of trouble.

2 Kings 20:5:
For healing and restoration of health.

Proverbs 3:5-6:
For guidance, trust, and surrender to divine will.

Proverbs 16:3:
To seek divine guidance and success in endeavors.

Isaiah 40:31:
To invoke strength, endurance, and renewal of energy.

Jeremiah 29:11:
For hope, guidance, and assurance of a positive future.

Ezekiel 37:1-14:
For spiritual renewal, revival, and transformation.

Hosea 6:6:
For seeking mercy, compassion, and forgiveness.

Micah 6:8:
For guidance in walking humbly, seeking justice, and showing mercy.

Mark 11:24:
For faith, belief, and manifestation of miracles.

John 14:27:
For peace, tranquility, and release from anxiety or stress.

Romans 8:31:
For protection against enemies and to invoke divine support.

Romans 12:21:
For overcoming evil with good and attracting positive energy.

1 Corinthians 13:4-7:
For attracting and cultivating love, harmony, and healthy relationships.

Galatians 5:22-23:
For attracting the fruits of the spirit, such as love, joy, and peace.

Philippians 4:13:
For invoking strength and confidence in achieving goals and overcoming obstacles.

Daniel 3:17-18:
To invoke divine protection and courage in the face of adversity.

Joel 2:25:
To invoke restoration and reclaim lost blessings.

Matthew 7:7-8:
For manifestation of desires and seeking divine guidance.

Luke 10:19:
For protection against evil and to overcome spiritual attacks

Romans 8:28:
For seeking divine purpose and understanding in difficult circumstances.

Romans 12:2:
To seek transformation, renewal of mind, and divine guidance in decision-making.

1 Corinthians 10:13:
For strength and endurance in times of temptation or challenges.

2 Corinthians 12:9:
For seeking divine strength and power in times of weakness.

Ephesians 6:10-11:
For protection against spiritual warfare and negative energies.

Thessalonians 5:17:
For cultivating a consistent and powerful prayer practice.

Hebrews 11:1:
For strengthening faith and belief in the manifestation of desires.

James 1:5:
For seeking divine wisdom and guidance in decision-making.

1 Peter 5:7:
For casting worries and anxieties upon the divine and seeking comfort.

1 John 4:18:
For releasing fear and attracting divine love and peace.

Colossians 3:23-24:
For attracting success, abundance, and divine favor in work or endeavors.

2 Timothy 1:7:
For invoking courage and overcoming fear or anxiety.

Hebrews 11:6:
For seeking divine reward and favor through faithfulness and trust.

James 4:7:
For protection against negative influences and spiritual attacks.

1 John 1:9:
For seeking forgiveness, cleansing, and restoration of spiritual purity.

Revelation 3:20:
For inviting divine presence and guidance into one's life.

As stated earlier in this book, the use of scriptures in Hoodoo is not limited to strict adherence to religious dogma. Instead, practitioners often interpret and adapt the verses to align with their specific intentions and cultural context. They serve as a spiritual tool, offering guidance, solace, and empowerment to those who incorporate them into their Hoodoo practice.

Saints in Hoodoo

Saint Anthony: Patron saint of lost items and finding love, often invoked for guidance in matters of the heart and to locate lost or stolen objects.

Saint Expedite: Patron saint of urgent causes and fast solutions, known for his ability to bring quick results and speed up the resolution of problems.

Saint Jude: Patron saint of desperate or impossible cases, often called upon when facing seemingly insurmountable challenges or when in need of divine intervention.

Saint Michael: Archangel associated with protection, justice, and spiritual warfare. Often called upon for defense against negative energies, spiritual attacks, or for general protection.

Saint Martha: Known for her strength, assistance with domestic matters, and mastery over difficult situations. She is often invoked for assistance in matters of work, home, and relationships.

Saint Peter: Considered the gatekeeper of heaven, associated with opening doors and opportunities, protection, and assistance with legal matters.

Saint Rita: Patron saint of impossible causes abused women, and difficult marriages. She is often called upon for healing, restoration, and resolving relationship issues.

Saint Joseph: Patron saint of the home and family, often invoked for assistance with selling or buying property, finding employment, and maintaining a harmonious household.

Saint Cyprian: Associated with magic, occultism, and divination. Often called upon for help with metaphysical workings, spiritual insight, and protection from negative forces.

Saint Dymphna: Patron saint of mental and emotional health, invoked for assistance with anxiety, depression, and other psychological challenges.

Saint Anne: Mother of the Virgin Mary, often invoked for fertility, motherhood, and protection during pregnancy and childbirth.

Saint Jude Thaddeus: Patron saint of lost causes, desperate situations, and hope. Often called upon for assistance in seemingly impossible or hopeless circumstances.

Saint Christopher: Patron saint of travelers and those seeking protection during journeys. Often invoked for safe travel, protection from accidents, and guidance on long journeys.

Saint Lucy: Patron saint of vision, clarity, and protection of the eyes. Often called upon for assistance with eye-related ailments, clarity of vision, and protection against evil eyes or negative influences.

Saint Francis of Assisi: Known for his connection to nature and animals, often called upon for assistance with animal-related matters, ecology, and connection to the natural world.

Saint Agatha: Patron saint of breast cancer, invoked for healing and protection against diseases and ailments related to the breasts.

Saint Rita of Cascia: Patron saint of abused women, difficult marriages, and impossible causes. Often called upon for assistance in resolving marital or relationship issues and finding peace.

Saint Martin de Porres: Known for his compassion and healing abilities, often invoked for matters of health, physical healing, and racial harmony.

Saint Barbara: Patron saint of protection against lightning, storms, and sudden death. Often called upon for protection from natural disasters, accidents, and sudden dangers.

Saint Helen: Known for her discovery of the True Cross, often invoked for assistance with finding lost or hidden objects, uncovering secrets, and seeking truth.

Remember, these are just a few examples, and there are many more saints that can be incorporated into Hoodoo practices based on individual needs and cultural influences.

Gospel Music in Hoodoo

Practitioners of Hoodoo often incorporate gospel songs into their work for several reasons, including the power of music, the emotional resonance of gospel, and the spiritual connection it fosters.

Emotional Resonance: Gospel music is known for its powerful and emotive qualities. The lyrics and melodies evoke strong emotions and create a deep connection to the spiritual realm. Hoodoo practitioners recognize the potency of these emotional states and use gospel songs to amplify their intentions and connect with the divine.

Spiritual Connection: Gospel music is deeply rooted in African American spiritual traditions and has its origins in African musical and spiritual practices. The songs often express themes of faith, hope, and perseverance, resonating with the experiences and struggles of African American communities. By incorporating gospel songs, practitioners tap into this spiritual heritage and foster a connection with their ancestors and the divine.

Vibrational Energy: Like other forms of music, gospel songs carry vibrational energy that can impact the energetic and emotional states of individuals. The uplifting and soul-stirring nature of gospel music can raise vibrations, shift energy, and create a conducive environment for spiritual work and manifestation.

Affirmations and Declarations: Gospel songs often contain affirmations, declarations of faith, and expressions of trust in a higher power. These affirmations can be used as spiritual tools in Hoodoo practice, reinforcing intentions, and calling upon divine assistance. By singing or reciting these affirmations, practitioners align themselves with the positive messages and vibrations of the gospel songs.

Cultural Significance: Gospel music is deeply intertwined with African American culture and history. Its use in Hoodoo practice honors and acknowledges the cultural and spiritual contributions of African American communities. By incorporating gospel songs, practitioners tap into the strength, resilience, and wisdom of their ancestors.

Community and Collective Consciousness: Gospel music often brings people together in worship and celebration. In Hoodoo, the use of gospel songs can create a sense of community and shared spiritual experience. The collective energy and intention generated through group singing can enhance the power of rituals and workings.

Gospel songs in Hoodoo are not limited to adherence to any particular religious doctrine. Instead, practitioners embrace the spiritual and cultural significance of gospel music and allow its power to support and enhance their intention and connection to the divine. Gospel songs serve as a vehicle for spiritual expression, healing, empowerment, and connection with the ancestral and divine realms, making them a powerful tool in the practice of Hoodoo.

Commonly used Gospel songs

"Down By the Riverside" - This traditional gospel song is often used for cleansing and purifying purposes. It can be used to wash away negativity, clear obstacles, and bring about a fresh start.

"Wade in the Water" - Also a traditional gospel song, it is often used for spiritual cleansing and protection. The lyrics reference the biblical story of the Israelites crossing the Red Sea. It can be used to cleanse and purify oneself or a space from negative energy and provide spiritual protection.

"Oh, Happy Day" - This song, popularized by the Edwin Hawkins Singers, is a joyful and uplifting gospel anthem. It is often used to invoke positive energy, bring happiness, and celebrate divine blessings.

"Amazing Grace" - A well-known traditional hymn, "Amazing Grace" is often used for spiritual healing, forgiveness, and redemption. It can be used to seek divine intervention, find solace, and release burdens.

"Take My Hand, Precious Lord" - Made famous by Mahalia Jackson, this song is often used for guidance, comfort, and strength. It can be used to seek divine guidance in difficult situations and find solace in times of trouble.

"I Shall Not Be Moved" - This traditional gospel song carries a powerful message of resilience and unwavering faith. It is often used to invoke determination, steadfastness, and protection against obstacles or negative influences.

"This Little Light of Mine" - A joyful and empowering gospel song, it is often used to affirm one's spiritual light and purpose. It can be used to amplify personal power, dispel darkness, and radiate positive energy.

"Go Down Moses" - This traditional spiritual is often used for liberation, freedom, and overcoming oppression. It can be used to invoke divine intervention, break free from bondage, and bring about justice.

"Swing Low, Sweet Chariot" - A popular spiritual, this song is often used for spiritual guidance, protection, and transition. It can be used to seek divine assistance, protection during journeys, and guidance during challenging times.

"His Eye Is on the Sparrow" - A beautiful hymn popularized by Mahalia Jackson, it is often used for trust, faith, and surrender to divine providence. It can be used to find comfort in knowing that the divine is watching over and caring.

Biblical Figures Used in Hoodoo

These figures are often seen as spiritual allies or intercessors who can help practitioners achieve their desired outcomes.

Moses: Moses is revered for his leadership, wisdom, and ability to perform miracles. He is often called upon for assistance with matters of justice, guidance, and protection. For example, a Hoodoo practitioner may invoke Moses when seeking legal help or guidance in a difficult situation.

King Solomon: King Solomon is known for his wisdom and wealth. He is often invoked for matters related to prosperity, success, and finding solutions to complex problems. A Hoodoo ritual involving King Solomon may include the use of Solomon's Seal, a symbol associated with his wisdom and power.

Archangel Michael: Though not a biblical figure in the traditional sense, Archangel Michael is often invoked in Hoodoo for protection against spiritual and physical harm. He is seen as a powerful defender and can be called upon to banish negative energies, provide strength, and offer guidance in times of trouble.

Mary Magdalene: Known as a devoted follower of Jesus and a symbol of divine femininity, Mary Magdalene is honored in Hoodoo for matters related to love, relationships, and spiritual transformation. Her figure can be used in rituals or prayers for healing emotional wounds, attracting love, or seeking forgiveness.

Samson: Known for his immense physical strength, Samson is invoked in Hoodoo for matters related to strength, protection, and overcoming adversaries. His figure can be used in rituals or charms to enhance personal strength, defend against enemies, or break free from negative influences.

Elijah: Recognized as a powerful prophet in the Bible, Elijah is often invoked in Hoodoo for matters related to spiritual growth, enlightenment, and divine communication. His figure can be used in rituals or prayers to deepen spiritual connection, & receive guidance.

Saint Anne: Recognized as the mother of the Virgin Mary, Saint Anne is revered in Hoodoo for matters related to fertility, conception, and motherhood. Her figure can be used in rituals or petitions to seek blessings for conceiving a child, protection during pregnancy, or guidance in raising children.

David: Known for his bravery and defeating Goliath, David is invoked in Hoodoo for matters related to courage, strength, and victory over adversaries. His figure can be used in rituals or charms to enhance personal bravery, overcome challenges, or gain strength in difficult situations.

Ruth: Known for her loyalty and devotion, Ruth is invoked in Hoodoo for matters related to loyalty, love, and relationships. Her figure can be used in rituals or charms to attract loyal friends, strengthen existing relationships, or seek guidance in matters of the heart.

Biblical Figure Petition

In this ritual, an individual may write down their intention or desired outcome on a piece of paper, such as finding a job. They may then create an altar or sacred space with candles, herbs, and other items associated with their intention.

The practitioner may call upon a biblical figure like Moses or King Solomon, reciting prayers or psalms that align with their goal. They may ask for guidance, wisdom, or assistance in finding employment.

The written petition may be placed under a candle, which is then lit and allowed to burn down completely as a symbolic representation of the request being sent out into the universe.

It's important to note that the use of biblical figures in Hoodoo varies among practitioners, and rituals can be personalized based on one's specific spiritual beliefs and relationship with these figures.

Misconceptions: Christianity Vs. Hoodoo & ATRs

In embarking on my own personal journey with Hoodoo, I have encountered numerous misconceptions and misunderstandings surrounding this ancient practice. It is disheartening to witness the labeling of Hoodoo practitioners as demon worshipers, pagans, witches, or even as evil.

Disclaimer: there are some Hoodoo practitioners who identify as witches, or are also wiccans, or dive into witchcraft and there is nothing wrong with that. That is where their spiritual journey leads them, but they do not represent the majority.

The definition of a witch is a person thought to have magic powers, especially evil ones, popularly depicted as a woman wearing a black cloak and pointed hat and flying on a broomstick. That is not what a Hoodoo practitioner is. Witch is a term that was given to gifted women by their oppressors, and it is a term I do not resonate with.

These misrepresentations not only perpetuate fear and ignorance but also overshadow the true essence and purpose of Hoodoo. It is of utmost importance to debunk these misconceptions and shed light on the reality of Hoodoo. Hoodoo is not a form of worshiping demons or engaging in nefarious activities. It is a spiritual practice deeply rooted in African traditions.

Misconceptions about Hoodoo and other African diaspora traditions often stem from a lack of understanding and cultural biases. One common misconception is that these traditions are polytheistic or involve the worship of multiple gods. However, it is important to recognize that many African diaspora traditions, including Hoodoo, have a monotheistic belief system at their core.

While African diaspora traditions may incorporate the veneration of spirits, ancestors, and deities, they ultimately recognize a single supreme being or divine force. This supreme being is often referred to by different names, such as Olodumare in Yoruba traditions or Bondye in Haitian Vodou. These traditions acknowledge the existence of other spiritual entities but understand them as intermediaries or manifestations of the supreme being.

African diaspora traditions do not worship idols or objects as gods. Instead, they use symbolic representations, such as statues or sacred items, to connect with and honor the divine. These objects serve as focal points for devotion and are seen as conduits for spiritual communication, rather than being worshipped as gods themselves. African diaspora traditions have a rich and complex spiritual philosophy that encompasses deep wisdom and understanding of the human experience. These traditions often emphasize the interconnectedness of all beings and the importance of living in harmony with nature and the divine. They incorporate rituals, ceremonies, and practices that promote healing, empowerment, and spiritual growth.

African diaspora traditions have often been syncretized with Christianity due to historical circumstances, such as the forced conversion of enslaved Africans. This syncretism resulted in the blending of African spiritual practices with Christian beliefs and rituals. Many practitioners of African diaspora traditions see no contradiction between their ancestral traditions and their faith in a single supreme God. They view their practices as a way to connect with the divine within the context of their cultural heritage. While African diaspora traditions do incorporate metaphysical practices, they are not solely focused on metaphysics. These traditions encompass a holistic approach to spirituality, encompassing rituals, prayers, divination, healing, and community engagement. They emphasize personal growth, ethical conduct, and the pursuit of spiritual balance and harmony. It is important to approach African diaspora traditions with an open mind and a willingness to learn and understand their complexities. Recognizing the monotheistic nature of these traditions helps dispel misconceptions and fosters a deeper appreciation for their spiritual beliefs and practices.

It is also a huge misconception that Orishas and other African sprits are worshipped as gods in African diasporic practices. This belief couldn't be further from the truth. In Christianity, angels are believed to be celestial beings created by God to serve as messengers, protectors, and intermediaries between God and humans. They are often associated with specific tasks or responsibilities, such as guardian angels watching over individuals. In African diaspora traditions like Yoruba-based Orisha veneration and Haitian Vodou, Orishas and Lwa are considered divine entities or spirits. They are believed to be intermediaries between humans and the supreme being or divine forces. Each Orisha or Lwa has their own distinct personality, domain, and areas of influence. They are revered and called upon for guidance, protection, and assistance in various aspects of life.

Contrary to widespread belief, Hoodoo practitioners and followers of other African traditional and derived religions are not pagans. Paganism typically refers to belief systems that worship multiple gods without acknowledging a supreme being.

However, the presence of a supreme being in these African traditions aligns them more closely with monotheistic religions like Christianity, Islam, and Judaism. The misconception of paganism arises from a lack of understanding and cultural biases. Hoodoo, like other African traditional religions, places significant importance on spirituality, ancestral reverence, and the honoring of a supreme being. The practice is deeply rooted in African cultural heritage and has evolved over centuries, incorporating influences from various African tribes, as well as the experiences of enslaved Africans in the Americas.

It is crucial to recognize that the term "pagan" carries a Western-centric perspective and is often used to describe any belief system that deviates from the Abrahamic traditions. However, African traditional religions have their own distinct cosmologies, rituals, and beliefs that are far from the pagan label. In African traditional religions, spirituality is intertwined with everyday life, existing as an integral part of the community's customs and traditions.

It is not a separate entity, or a practice relegated to a specific day or time. The connection to the supreme being and the spiritual hierarchy is deeply ingrained in the fabric of their existence. By understanding and acknowledging the presence of a supreme being and the spiritual hierarchy within African traditional religions and African-American practices like Hoodoo, we can dispel the myth of paganism and appreciate the rich complexity of these belief systems. It is essential to approach the study of these religions and practices with cultural sensitivity and a willingness to challenge preconceived notions. It is vital to dispel the myth of paganism and to approach the study of African traditional religions with an open mind, cultural sensitivity, and a desire to learn. By doing so, we can gain a deeper understanding of these rich and diverse faiths.

Additional Information in Hoodoo

Hoodoo Sigils

Hoodoo does not have a standardized system of sigils like some other magical or occult traditions. However, there are symbols, seals, and metaphysical signs that are commonly used in Hoodoo practices. These symbols are often specific to the individual practitioner or passed down through family traditions.

Crossroads: The intersection of two roads is considered a symbol of power and a place where spirits and energies converge. It is often associated with opportunities, decisions, and the ability to connect with spiritual forces.

John the Conqueror Root: This root, often carried as a talisman or used in workings, is associated with personal power, confidence, and overcoming obstacles. Its image or representation can be used as a sigil for strength and success.

Black Cat Bone: The bone of a black cat is considered a potent item in Hoodoo. It is believed to bring luck, protection, and the ability to influence situations. The image of a cat or a cat bone can be used as a sigil for these purposes.

Veve Symbols: Veve symbols are intricate designs or patterns used in African diasporic religions and metaphysical practices, including Hoodoo. They represent specific spirits or deities and are often drawn or traced on the ground or other surfaces during rituals or works.

Ankh: An ancient Egyptian symbol representing eternal life and spiritual power. The ankh is sometimes used in Hoodoo to invoke protection, healing, and spiritual connection. It can be worn as a pendant, drawn on candles, or incorporated into ritual work.

Mojo Hand: Similar to a mojo bag, a mojo hand is a larger, often more complex, bundle of herbs, roots, and other items. It is typically created for a specific purpose, such as love, luck, or protection. Mojo hands are often carried or kept in a specific place, like an altar.

Candle: Candles play a significant role in Hoodoo rituals and workings. Different colored candles are used to represent various intentions and energies. For example, white candles symbolize purification and spiritual blessings, while red candles represent love and passion.

Cross: The cross is a Christian symbol that is sometimes incorporated into Hoodoo practices. It is used for spiritual protection, warding off evil, and invoking blessings. Crosses can be worn as jewelry, drawn on talismans, or placed on altars.

Lodestone: A naturally magnetic stone often used in Hoodoo for attracting love, money, or luck. Lodestones are believed to have a magnetic pull that draws in desired energies or circumstances. They are commonly used in attraction works or placed on altars.

Remember that symbols and sigils in Hoodoo can vary based on individual practices and regional traditions. It is always recommended to study and learn from experienced practitioners or reputable sources to gain a deeper understanding of the symbols and their meanings within Hoodoo.

Hoodoo Candle Color Meanings:

Red: Passion, love, courage, strength, vitality, and sexual energy.

Pink: Romance, friendship, emotional healing, self-love, and harmony.

White: Purity, spiritual cleansing, protection, healing, and divine guidance.

Black: Banishing negativity, protection against evil, breaking hexes, and absorbing negative energy.

Green: Prosperity, abundance, luck, money, fertility, and growth.

Yellow: Success, communication, creativity, clarity, and mental agility.

Orange: Attraction, stimulation, energy, confidence, and creativity.

Blue: Peace, tranquility, spiritual healing, intuition, and communication with spirits.

Purple: Spiritual power, psychic abilities, wisdom, spiritual protection, and spiritual growth.

Brown: Grounding, stability, home protection, and connecting with ancestral energies.

Gold: Wealth, success, achievement, abundance, and attracting positive energy.

Silver: Intuition, psychic abilities, lunar energy, feminine energy, and divination.

Gray: Neutralizing negative influences, compromise, and breaking through stagnation.

Lavender: Spiritual healing, purification, peace, and connecting with higher realms.

Turquoise: Emotional healing, balance, communication, and protection.

Indigo: Deep intuition, spiritual insight, divine guidance, and opening the third eye.

Maroon: Strength, courage, resilience, and protection against enemies.

Olive: Peace, harmony, fertility, and healing family or ancestral issues.

Burgundy: Personal power, assertiveness, leadership, and empowerment.
Teal: Emotional balance, clarity, healing, and renewal.

Rust: Grounding, stability, strength, and overcoming challenges.

Violet: Spiritual protection, enhancing psychic abilities, and connecting with higher realms.

Mauve: Spiritual intuition, divination, and psychic development.

Peach: Reconciliation, forgiveness, harmony, and healing of relationships.

Coral: Passion, energy, motivation, and attracting love and desire.

Aqua: Emotional healing, soothing, peaceful communication, and tranquility.

Magenta: Spiritual healing, manifestation, attracting desires, and personal power.

Salmon: Attracting love, emotional healing, and nurturing relationships.

Ivory: Healing, purification, and attracting positive energy.

Chartreuse: Attracting abundance, prosperity, and good luck.

It's important to note that while these color associations are commonly used in Hoodoo, individual practitioners may have their own personal interpretations or variations. Additionally, the specific intent and context of the working or ritual can also influence the choice of candle color. It is always recommended to trust your intuition and work with the colors that resonate with you and your intentions.

Types of Candles Used in Hoodoo

Seven-Day Candles: These are tall glass-encased candles that burn continuously for approximately seven days. They are often used for long-term works and rituals, as they provide a sustained energy throughout the duration. Different colors are used for different intentions, such as green for money, red for love, white for purification, and black for protection and banishing.

Figure Candles: These candles are shaped like human figures and are used in sympathetic metaphysics. They represent individuals or can be used as effigies to target a specific person in workings. They are often carved or dressed in oils, herbs, and personal items to enhance their effectiveness in the intended ritual.

Taper Candles: Taper candles are long, thin candles that are commonly used for focused workings, rituals, or candle workings. They can be easily inscribed with symbols or words, making them versatile for various intentions. Different colors are used to align with the specific purpose, such as yellow for communication, purple for spiritual power, or blue for healing.

Chime Candles: Chime candles are small, thin candles that burn for a relatively brief time, typically around 1-2 hours. They are often used for quick workings, rituals, or as an offering to deities or spirits. They come in assorted colors, each associated with specific intentions, such as gold for success, pink for love, or orange for creativity.

Vigil Candles: Vigil candles are similar to seven-day candles, but they have a shorter burn time, usually around 24-48 hours. They are often used for specific intentions that require focused energy for a shorter duration. They can be found in an assortment of colors based on the desired outcome of the ritual.

Reversal Candles: These candles are typically black on the outside and red on the inside. They are used for reversing or sending back negative energy, hexes, or curses that may have been directed towards you. The black outer layer absorbs and neutralizes the negativity, while the red inner layer represents the aggressive energy sent back to its source.

Remember, while these descriptions provide a general understanding of the various candles used in Hoodoo, it's important to research and study their symbolism and specific uses in more depth to align with your own practice and intentions.

Candle Interpretation

Flame Behavior:

Pay attention to the flame's size, movement, and behavior throughout the burning process. A strong, steady flame is generally considered positive, indicating that your intentions are being manifested. A flickering or dancing flame can suggest energy or resistance in the situation. A weak or struggling flame may indicate obstacles or challenges.

High, strong flame: A tall, powerful flame that burns steadily and produces a lot of light represents a favorable outcome. It suggests that your intentions are being received and that the work is manifesting successfully.

Low or weak flame: A flame that struggles to stay lit or appears weak and small can indicate obstacles or resistance. It may suggest that your desires are facing challenges, or that additional effort is required to overcome any opposition.

Flickering or dancing flame: If the flame flickers, dances, or moves erratically, it suggests energy or strong emotions in the situation. This could indicate that there are external influences or conflicting energies at play. It may be necessary to address these factors before your intentions can fully manifest.

Split flame: If the flame splits into two or more separate flames, it can symbolize division or conflicts. This could indicate that there are opposing forces or people involved in your desired outcome. Consider whether any mediation or resolution is needed to bring unity and harmony to your situation.

Sudden extinguishing: If the flame abruptly goes out before the candle has fully burned, it may indicate that your intentions are being blocked or rejected. This could suggest that the spell needs to be repeated, or that you may need to reconsider your approach and make adjustments before proceeding.

Smoke Behavior:

The presence and behavior of smoke can provide additional insights. Clear, clean smoke rising straight up is often considered a positive sign, indicating that the spell is progressing smoothly. Thick or heavy smoke may suggest that there are obstacles or negativity that need to be cleared. Pay attention to the direction the smoke moves and any shapes or patterns it may form, as these can hold symbolic meaning.

Clear and steady rising smoke: When the smoke from the burning candle rises straight up and is clear, it is generally seen as a positive sign. It suggests that your intentions are being received and that the spell is progressing smoothly.

Thick or heavy smoke: If the smoke is thick, heavy, or lingers around the candle, it may indicate the presence of obstacles, negativity, or resistance. This could suggest that there are external influences or energetic blockages that need to be addressed or cleared before your desires can manifest.

Smoke swirling or moving in a specific direction: Pay attention to the direction in which the smoke moves. If it moves towards you, it may indicate that the spell is drawing your desires closer to you. If it moves away or disperses quickly, it might suggest that there are external factors pushing your desires away or that more effort is needed to manifest your intentions.

Shapes or patterns in the smoke: Sometimes, the smoke may form shapes, symbols, or patterns as it rises. These can hold significant meaning and provide insights into your spell or ritual. For example, seeing a heart shape could indicate that love is on its way, while seeing a cross shape might represent spiritual protection or guidance.

Dispersing smoke: If the smoke disperses quickly or dissipates before reaching a significant height, it may suggest that your intentions need more time or effort to manifest fully. It could indicate that patience and persistence are required to achieve your desired outcome.

Candle Wax Behavior:

The way the wax melts and forms patterns can also provide valuable information. Look for any shapes, symbols, or figures that may appear in the melted wax. These can be interpreted as signs or messages related to your intentions. For example, seeing a heart shape may indicate love manifesting, while a cross shape could represent spiritual protection.

Clear and clean wax: When the wax burns cleanly and leaves no residue, it is generally seen as a positive sign. It suggests that your intentions are being received and that the spell is progressing smoothly.

Melting evenly and smoothly: If the wax melts evenly and smoothly without any irregularities or lumps, it indicates that your desires are flowing harmoniously and that your work is likely to bring about the desired outcome.

Wax residue forming shapes or symbols: Sometimes, as the wax melts, it may leave behind shapes, symbols, or patterns on the candle or in the container. These can hold significant meaning and provide insights into your working or ritual. For example, seeing a heart shape could indicate that love is on its way, while seeing a cross shape might represent spiritual protection or guidance.

Cracking or popping wax: If the wax cracks or pops loudly while burning, it may suggest that there are obstacles or challenges in manifesting your desires. It could indicate that there are external forces or energetic blockages that need to be addressed or cleared before your intentions can fully manifest.

Black, sooty, or smoky residue: If the wax leaves behind a lot of black, sooty, or smoky residue, it may indicate the presence of negativity or obstacles. This could suggest that there are external influences or energetic blockages that need to be addressed or cleared before your desires can manifest.

Residue Behavior:

After the candle has burned completely, examine any residue left behind. This can include herbs, remnants of personal items, or even soot on the glass or container. These remnants can offer further insights or messages related to your spell or ritual. Pay attention to any patterns or formations that may emerge.

Clear and clean residue: When the candle burns cleanly and leaves little to no residue, it is generally seen as a positive sign. It suggests that your intentions are being received and that the spell is progressing smoothly.

Black or sooty residue: If the candle leaves behind a significant amount of black or sooty residue, it may indicate the presence of negativity or obstacles. This could suggest that there are external influences or energetic blockages that need to be addressed or cleared before your desires can manifest fully.

Residue forming shapes or symbols: Sometimes, as the candle burns, residue may form shapes, symbols, or patterns. These can hold significant meaning and provide insights into your spell or ritual.

Residue dripping or running down the candle: If the wax drips or runs down the candle in a particular direction, it can indicate the flow or movement of energy. For example, if the wax drips down the front of the candle, it may suggest that your desires are being released and manifesting outwardly.

Residue pooling at the base of the candle: If the wax residue collects and pools at the base of the candle, it can suggest that there are unresolved issues or blockages that are preventing your desires from manifesting. This may indicate the need for additional work or spiritual intervention to overcome these obstacles.

Burn Time:

Take note of how long it takes for the candle to burn completely. If it burns quickly, it may indicate that your intentions are manifesting rapidly. A longer burn time might suggest that more time and patience are needed for your desires to come to fruition.

Quick burn: If a candle burns relatively quickly, it may indicate that your intentions are manifesting swiftly. This can be seen as a positive sign that your desires will be fulfilled soon.

Slow burn: If a candle takes longer than usual to burn, it might suggest that there are obstacles or delays in manifesting your desires. This could indicate the need for patience and perseverance in your workings.

Uneven burn: If a candle burns unevenly, with some parts melting faster than others, it may suggest that there are fluctuations or challenges in the energy surrounding your intention. This could indicate the need for additional focus or attention on certain aspects of your desires.

Long-lasting burn: If a candle burns for an exceptionally long time, it can indicate that your intention is deeply rooted and may require more time and effort to fully manifest. This could suggest the need for ongoing work or spiritual intervention to achieve your desired outcome.

Candle extinguishing prematurely: If a candle unexpectedly goes out before it has fully burned, it may indicate interference or resistance in your workings. This could suggest the need for protection or cleansing rituals to remove any negative energies or blockages.

Remember, interpreting candles is a highly intuitive process, and individual experiences and symbolism may vary. It is essential to develop your own understanding and relationship with the candles and their signs based on your own practice and experiences. Trust your instincts and the messages that resonate with you.

Divination Practices in Hoodoo

Tarot Cards: Hoodoo practitioners often use Tarot cards as a tool for divination. Tarot decks consist of 78 cards, each with its own symbolism and meaning. During the reading, the reader interprets the cards to gain insights into a person's past, present, or future. Tarot readings can provide guidance, clarity, and understanding of various aspects of life such as love, career, and spirituality.

Tea Leaf Reading: Also known as tasseography, this divination technique involves interpreting patterns and symbols formed by tea leaves in a cup. The reader examines the leaves' arrangement, shapes, and positions to provide insight into a person's life. The cup is usually divided into different sections representing different areas of life, and the symbols within each section are interpreted accordingly.

Pendulum Divination: A pendulum is a weighted object suspended on a string or chain. Hoodoo practitioners use pendulums to gain answers to yes or no questions or to seek guidance. The practitioner holds the pendulum over a question and observes its movement, which can be back and forth, side to side, or circular. The direction of the movement indicates the answer or response.

Numerology: Numerology is the study of numbers and their symbolic meanings. In Hoodoo, numbers can be used to gain insight into various aspects of life, such as personality traits, compatibility, and future events. Practitioners assign specific meanings to different numbers and use calculations based on birth dates, names, or other significant numbers to provide guidance and understanding.

Runes: Hoodoo practitioners may work with a set of runes, which are ancient symbols or letters carved onto stones or other objects. Each rune carries its own meaning and can be used for divination purposes. The practitioner may draw runes from a bag or scatter them and interpret their positions and meanings to gain insight into a person's situation or question.

Scrying: Scrying involves gazing into a reflective surface, such as a crystal ball, mirror, or water, to gain insights or visions. Hoodoo practitioners may use scrying as a method to connect with spirits, receive guidance, or gain clarity. The visions or symbols seen during scrying are interpreted by the practitioner to provide answers or understanding.

Playing Card Reading: Similar to Tarot reading, playing card reading utilizes a standard deck of playing cards for divination. Each playing card has its own symbolism and meaning. The reader interprets the cards drawn or laid out in a specific pattern to provide insights into a person's life, events, or potential outcomes.

Scrying with Flame: This divination technique involves focusing on the flame of a candle or fire to receive messages or visions. The practitioner gazes into the flame and observes the patterns, shapes, or movements. These can be interpreted to gain insights, receive guidance, or understand the energies surrounding a situation.

Bibliomancy: Bibliomancy is the practice of divination using a book, often a sacred text or a book of significant importance to the practitioner. The practitioner opens the book at a random page or selects a specific passage, and the words or phrases that catch their attention are interpreted to provide guidance or answers to questions.

Bone Reading: Bone reading involves working with a set of bones, shells, or other small objects with symbolic meaning. Each bone or object represents a certain aspect of life or carries its own significance. The practitioner casts or tosses the bones onto a surface and interprets their positions, orientations, and relationships to provide insights or guidance.

Coin Divination: Coin divination involves tossing or casting coins and interpreting the results to gain insight into a situation or question. Hoodoo practitioners may use Chinese coins or other coins with specific symbolism. The position of the coins, heads or tails, or the numerical value of the coins can all be considered in the interpretation.

Shell Divination: Shell divination involves casting or tossing shells and interpreting their positions or patterns to gain insights or answers. Hoodoo practitioners often work with cowrie shells, which have their own symbolic meanings. The shells' orientations, patterns, or positions are considered during the interpretation.

Water Scrying: Water scrying involves using a bowl or basin of water as a scrying tool. The practitioner gazes into the water's surface and observes any images, symbols, or visions that appear. These can be interpreted to gain insights, receive messages, or understand the energies surrounding a situation.

Remember, divination techniques can vary among practitioners, so it's important to find the ones that resonate with you and practice them with respect and intention.

Astrology in Hoodoo

Astrology is one of the many tools used in Hoodoo divination. It involves studying the positions and movements of celestial bodies and their influence on human affairs. In Hoodoo, astrology is used to gain insights, understand the energies at play, and determine auspicious or inauspicious times for various actions. Astrology in Hoodoo can be practiced through various techniques, including:

Natal Chart Analysis: A natal chart is a snapshot of the sky at the moment of an individual's birth. Hoodoo practitioners may analyze a person's natal chart to gain insight into their personality traits, strengths, weaknesses, and potential life events. This information helps in understanding how the individual can navigate their life path and make informed choices.

Electional Astrology: Electional astrology is the practice of selecting the most favorable astrological conditions for specific actions or events. Hoodoo practitioners may consult astrological charts to determine the best time for performing rituals, workings, starting new ventures, or making important decisions. They consider planetary aspects, moon phases, and other astrological factors to maximize the chances of success.

Planetary Metaphysics: Hoodoo incorporates planetary correspondences to enhance workings and rituals. Each planet is associated with specific energies, attributes, and intentions. Hoodoo practitioners may align their intentions with the corresponding planetary energy by performing rituals or workings during specific planetary hours or days. For example, they may work with Mars energy for courage and protection or Venus's energy for love and beauty.

Lunar Metaphysics: The moon plays a significant role in Hoodoo practices. Hoodoo practitioners pay attention to the moon phases and the energy they bring. Different moon phases, such as the new moon, waxing moon, full moon, and waning moon, carry distinct energies that can be utilized in workings, rituals, or manifestation practices.

By incorporating astrology into Hoodoo practices, practitioners can gain deeper insights into the energies at play and align their work with the cosmic forces. It helps them make informed decisions, choose auspicious timings, and harness the celestial energies to enhance their workings or rituals.

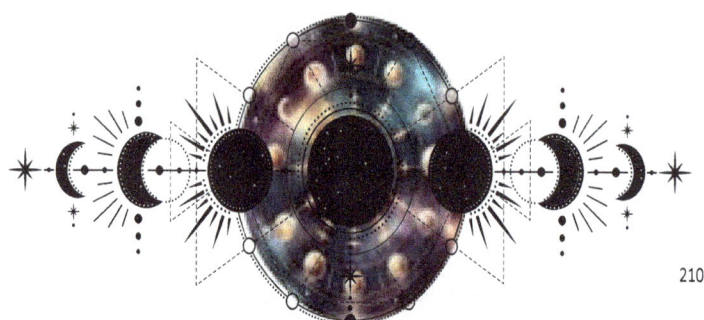

The Moon & The Sun

The moon and the sun hold significant symbolism and energy in Hoodoo. Here's how they are used, and some rituals associated with them:

Moon in Hoodoo:

The New Moon:
The new moon represents beginnings, setting intentions, and new opportunities. It is a time for planting seeds and starting fresh.

Ritual: During the new moon, Hoodoo practitioners may perform rituals for manifestation, setting goals, or starting new projects. They may write down their intentions, light candles, and perform works to attract what they desire.

Full Moon:
The full moon represents abundance, heightened energy, and culmination. It is a time for amplifying intentions and releasing negativity.

Ritual: Hoodoo practitioners may use the full moon energy for charging objects, crystals, or tools. They perform rituals for manifestation, divination, and cleansing. They may create moon water by placing a container of water under the moonlight and use it for cleansing or spiritual baths.

Waning Moon:
The waning moon represents release, banishing, and letting go. It is a time for removing obstacles and negative influences.

Ritual: Hoodoo practitioners may perform rituals to banish negative energies, bad habits, or unwanted situations during the waning moon. They may write down what they wish to release and burn it, symbolizing the letting go of those things.

Sun in Hoodoo:

Solar Energy:
The sun represents vitality, energy, and power. It is associated with strength, success, and enlightenment.

Ritual: Hoodoo practitioners may harness the energy of the sun for empowerment, protection, and success. They may perform rituals or works during sunrise or use solar symbols in their altar setups to invoke the sun's energy. Burning candles or herbs associated with the sun can also be part of these rituals.

Please note that specific rituals and practices in Hoodoo can vary among practitioners. It is important to approach these rituals with respect, understanding, and personal adaptation to align with your beliefs and intentions.

Bodies of Water in Hoodoo

Bodies of water hold significant symbolism and spiritual power in Hoodoo. Diverse types of water, such as river water, ocean water, and lake water, are used for various purposes. Here is a detailed description of their significance and usage in Hoodoo:

River Water:
River water symbolizes movement, cleansing, and renewal. It is associated with flowing energy and represents a continuous stream of spiritual power.

Usage: River water is commonly used for cleansing and purification rituals in Hoodoo. It is believed to wash away negative energies, remove spiritual impurities, and bring about a fresh start. Hoodoo practitioners may collect river water and use it in spiritual baths, floor washes, or to sprinkle around their home to cleanse the space and invite positive influences.

Ocean Water:
Ocean water represents vastness, strength, and abundance. It embodies the powerful and ever-changing energy of the sea.

Usage: Ocean water is used for its potent and expansive energies. Hoodoo practitioners may collect ocean water and use it in rituals or workings related to prosperity, abundance, and attracting opportunities. It can be added to bathwater or used in spiritual cleansings to bring about a sense of empowerment, clarity, and success. Some practitioners also use ocean water for protection rituals, as the ocean is seen as a natural barrier against negativity.

Lake Water:
Lake water represents stillness, reflection, and tranquility. It embodies a sense of serenity and connection to the spiritual realms.

Usage: Lake water is often used for spiritual work related to intuition, dreamwork, and divination. Hoodoo practitioners may collect lake water to enhance their psychic abilities or to anoint tools used for divination, such as tarot cards or pendulums. It can also be used as an offering to spirits or ancestors during rituals or placed on an altar to create a calm and receptive atmosphere.

When using water in Hoodoo practices, it is essential to approach it with reverence and gratitude. Collecting water from natural sources should be done respectfully and with permission, adhering to any local regulations or guidelines. Additionally, it is important to consider the quality and cleanliness of the water used, especially if it will be used for personal or internal purposes.

Dirt in Hoodoo

In Hoodoo, distinct types of dirt are used for their symbolic and spiritual properties. Here are a few common types of dirt used in Hoodoo, along with their significance and instructions on how to use them:

Graveyard Dirt:

Graveyard dirt is collected from cemeteries and holds powerful energy associated with ancestors, spirits, and the cycle of life and death.

Usage: Graveyard dirt is often used in rituals for protection, communication with spirits, and ancestral work. It can be sprinkled around a space or added to mojo bags, talismans, or work jars to invoke the guidance and protection of ancestors. Hoodoo practitioners may also use graveyard dirt in rituals related to justice, revenge, or cursing, although these practices should be approached with caution and ethical considerations.

Crossroads Dirt:

Crossroads dirt is collected at the intersection of two roads and is believed to contain potent energy and the ability to open pathways.

Usage: Crossroads dirt is used in rituals for decision-making, opportunities, and spiritual crossroads. It can be incorporated into works or charms to clear obstacles, open new paths, or bring about significant changes. Hoodoo practitioners may sprinkle crossroads dirt at the threshold of their home or business to attract new opportunities or to draw in beneficial energies from different directions.

Red Brick Dust:

Red brick dust is finely ground red bricks and is believed to possess protective and boundary-setting properties.

Usage: Red brick dust is used for creating spiritual barriers, protection, and boundary work in Hoodoo. It is commonly used to create a protective line or circle around a space, such as a home or ritual area.

To use red brick dust in Hoodoo:

1. Collect or purchase red bricks.
2. Break the bricks into small pieces or grind them into a fine powder using a mortar and pestle or a grinder.
3. Cleanse and consecrate the red brick dust by passing it through incense smoke or sprinkling it with a few drops of a protective oil, such as basil or frankincense oil.
4. Choose the area you wish to protect, such as your home or ritual space.
5. Sprinkle the red brick dust in a line or circle around the area, visualizing a strong and impenetrable barrier forming.
6. While sprinkling the dust, you can recite a prayer or affirmation, focusing on your intentions for protection and boundary-setting.

Magnetic Sand:
Magnetic sand, also known as lodestone grit or iron filings, is believed to possess magnetic and attracting properties.

Usage: Magnetic sand is used for attracting love, money, or opportunities. It can be placed in a mojo bag, sprinkled on candles, or added to work jars to enhance attraction and draw positive energies towards you. Some practitioners also use magnetic sand to "feed" their lodestones, which are natural magnets used in Hoodoo for their powerful magnetic properties.

Road Opener Dirt:
Road Opener dirt is a mixture of dirt collected from crossroads, along with other herbs and ingredients associated with clearing obstacles and opening new paths.

Usage: Road Opener dirt is used in rituals and works to remove blockages, open new opportunities, and clear the way for success. It can be sprinkled in front of a doorway or added to bathwater to cleanse and remove obstacles. Hoodoo practitioners may also use Road Opener dirt in mojo bags or work jars to attract new possibilities and remove any barriers to progress.

Bank Dirt:
Bank dirt is often used in Hoodoo to enhance workings and rituals related to financial matters.

To Use Bank Dirt in Hoodoo:
1. Money drawing workings: Bank dirt is often incorporated into money drawing workings to enhance their effectiveness. It can be sprinkled around candles, added to mojo bags or talismans, or used as a component in work jars or sachets.
2. Wealth and prosperity rituals: Bank dirt can be used in rituals focused on attracting wealth and abundance. It can be sprinkled on altars or mixed with other ingredients such as herbs, oils, or crystals to create a wealth-drawing mixture.
3. Business success workings: Bank dirt is believed to have a connection with financial institutions and the energy of success. It can be used in works or rituals aimed at boosting the success and prosperity of a business or career.
4. Money altar or workspace setup: Some practitioners choose to create a dedicated money altar or workspace using bank dirt as a foundation. This can be a space where offerings, petitions, or affirmations related to financial goals are made.

When using dirt in Hoodoo practices, it is important to collect it respectfully and with permission, adhering to any local regulations or guidelines. Additionally, it is essential to consider the cleanliness and quality of the dirt, especially if it will be used for personal or internal purposes.

Container Workings

Jars are commonly used in Hoodoo as a container for various workings, ingredients, and intentions. They are believed to create a contained and focused energy that can enhance the effectiveness of the work:

Honey Jar Working: A honey jar is used to sweeten a specific person or situation towards you. It involves placing the personal concerns (such as a photo, name paper, or hair) of the targeted individual in a jar filled with honey, along with other ingredients like herbs or oils. The jar is then sealed and placed on an altar or in a hidden location to enhance the working over time.

Vinegar Jar Working: A vinegar jar is used for the purpose of souring or breaking up a relationship or situation. It typically involves placing the names or photos of the parties involved, along with other items like chili peppers or black mustard seeds, into a jar filled with vinegar. The jar is then shaken or agitated regularly to intensify the effects and create discord or separation.

Protection Jar Working: A protection jar is created to ward off negative energies, entities, or influences. It involves combining various protective herbs, crystals, or personal items into a jar and sealing it tightly. The jar can be buried on your property, placed near entrances or windows, or kept on an altar as a protective charm.

Money Jar Working: A money jar is designed to attract financial abundance and prosperity. It typically involves placing symbols of wealth, such as coins, herbs like cinnamon or bay leaves, and a petition or affirmation for financial success, into a jar. The jar is then sealed and placed on an altar or in a prominent area to draw in money and opportunities.

Remember, these are just a few examples of jar container works in Hoodoo, and there are many variations and personal adaptations based on individual needs and intentions.

The Ring Shout

The ring shout in Hoodoo is a traditional African American religious practice. It involves forming a circle and moving in a counterclockwise direction while singing, clapping, and stomping. It's a powerful and energetic ritual that is believed to connect with ancestors and invoke spiritual energy. It's a beautiful expression of faith and community in Hoodoo traditions.

Let's dive into a more detailed step-by-step breakdown of what typically happens during a ring shout in Hoodoo:

The participants gather in a circle, creating a sacred space where the shout will take place.

The leader of the shout, often called the "shout leader," sets the rhythm by clapping their hands or using a drum. This establishes the heartbeat of the shout.

As the rhythm takes hold, the participants begin to move in a counterclockwise direction, creating a circular motion. This movement symbolizes the cyclical nature of life and spirituality.

As they move, the participants engage in call-and-response singing. The shout leader leads the group in singing spiritual songs, and the rest of the participants respond with their voices, creating a powerful harmonious sound.

Alongside the singing, the participants stomp their feet and clap their hands in sync with the rhythm. This physical expression of energy adds to the intensity and power of the shout.

As the shout progresses, the energy and intensity continue to build. The rhythm may quicken, and the movement and singing become more fervent.

The shout serves as a means of connecting with ancestors and spiritual forces. Participants may call upon the spirits of their ancestors, seeking their guidance, protection, and blessings.

The shout reaches its peak when the energy is at its highest. This is a moment of deep spiritual connection, where participants may feel a sense of unity, transcendence, and divine presence.

After the peak, the shout gradually winds down. The energy subsides, and the participants may enter a state of reflection, gratitude, and reverence for the experience they shared.

Remember, the specific steps and variations of a ring shout can vary depending on the Hoodoo tradition and the community involved. Each shout is a unique expression of spirituality, culture, and community.

Additional Rituals

Before embarking on your journey to become a Hoodoo practitioner, it is important to understand the significance of preparation and setting the right intentions. Hoodoo rituals are powerful tools that can bring about positive change and manifestation in your life. However, it is essential to approach them with caution and respect for the energy they harness.

In this section, we will explore a collection of rituals I have created to be simple and easy to aid you on your spiritual path. Please feel free to adapt the rituals to fit your spiritual practice. These rituals are not presented in any particular order, as each one serves a unique purpose and can be practiced independently. However, as mentioned earlier in this book it is worth noting that before engaging in any ritual, it is important to create a sacred space.

So, as a quick reminder, I just want to let you know this can be done by cleansing the area with sage or other purifying herbs, lighting candles, and playing soft, soothing music. Creating a sacred space helps to create a focused and peaceful environment for your rituals.

One of the most common rituals in Hoodoo practice is the use of candles. Candles are believed to carry the energy of fire and can be used to manifest desires, bring about healing, and provide protection. Another important aspect of Hoodoo rituals is the use of herbs and roots. Herbs and roots have long been used in spiritual practices for their healing and magical properties. In addition to candles and herbs, the use of oils and powders is also common in Hoodoo practice. Oils and powders are believed to carry the essence of specific intentions and can be used to anoint candles, objects, or even yourself. Lastly, the importance of intention and visualization in Hoodoo rituals. Your intention is the driving force behind any ritual, and visualization helps to amplify that intention.

I also light a white candle and have a glass of water next to it to invite in my ancestors or spirits to my sacred space before starting any ritual. (This is just a personal practice I think is worth mentioning.)

Throughout this section, I will provide step-by-step instructions for each ritual. Just keep in mind all of the rituals in this book are built for customization. These rituals are purposely made to be simple and easy to understand. If you are an advanced practitioner please feel free to make these rituals more advanced based on your already developed practice.

Remember, Hoodoo is a personal and intuitive practice, so feel free to adapt these rituals to suit your own needs and preferences. Now that we have reset the foundation for understanding Hoodoo rituals, let's dive into the wonderful world of changing circumstances.

Journey Back to the Divine

This ritual is created for love ones who are in hospice or are ready to take their journey back to the spiritual realm. This will help them cross over in peace. I created this ritual for a dear friend. I hope it will help those who need it.

"Dear [Higher Power/Divine Spirit/Universe], I humbly come before you with a heavy heart, seeking your guidance and comfort during this challenging time. As [name] prepares to transition from this earthly life, I ask for your divine presence to surround them with love, peace, and serenity. May their journey be gentle and free from pain, and may they find solace in the embrace of your divine light. Grant them strength and courage, and let them know that they are deeply loved and cherished. May their soul find eternal rest and may their spirit find its way to a place of everlasting peace. In your name, I pray. Ashe.

Instructions

1. Find a quiet and peaceful space where you can perform the ritual. If they are in a medical facility just make sure it's quiet and nurses know not to disturb you.
2. Place 12 white candles in a safe holder or dish. These candles represent 444 . 444 is often associated with peace and tranquility. This number serves as a reminder to seek inner peace, trust in divine guidance, and release any worries or anxieties. It embraces the feeling of calmness and is a reminder that your loved one is being supported on their journey towards the divine.
3. Light the candles, focusing on its gentle glow and the intention of creating a calming atmosphere.
4. Place a glass of water near your loved one, and talk to them as they join in the ritual with you, whether in spirit or in consciousness.
5. Take a few deep breaths and center yourself.
6. Apply a few drops of lavender essential oil to your palms and gently rub them together. Then rub a few drops on your loved one's chest.
7. Close your eyes and inhale the soothing scent of the lavender oil, allowing it to relax your mind and body.
8. As you continue to breathe deeply, visualize a peaceful and serene energy surrounding you and your loved one.
9. Offer prayers (suggested prayer above or or positive affirmations for their comfort and well-being.)
10. Sit quietly for a few moments, embracing the calmness and sending of the healing energy from you, the candles, the water, and your prayers.
11. When you're ready, extinguish the candles, expressing gratitude for the tranquility it brought. (or you may leave them burning until they are completely burned out.)
12. To complete this ritual read the Psalms for peaceful transitions, I suggest Psalm 23 because it is often utilized for peaceful transitions. This Psalm is known as the "Shepherd's Psalm" and is believed to bring comfort, guidance, and a sense of calm during times of transition or loss. It can be recited or incorporated into prayers, rituals, or work to invoke a peaceful and gentle transition for the individual involved.

Self- Love Ritual

Ingredients:

1. Pink candle
2. Purple candle
3. Love Powder (ingredients: rose petals, lavender, cinnamon)
4. Love Oil (ingredients: rose essential oil, jasmine essential oil, almond oil)
5. A small dish or plate
6. Matches or a lighter

Instructions

1. Begin by creating a sacred space for your ritual. Cleanse the area with sage or other purifying herbs, light candles, and play soft, soothing music.
2. Take the pink candle and carve your name or initials into it, representing yourself. As you carve, visualize yourself surrounded by love and acceptance.
3. Take the purple candle and carve the word "love" into it. This candle represents the love you are seeking to cultivate within yourself.
4. Take the Love Powder and sprinkle a small amount onto the dish or plate. Use your fingers to mix the powder and infuse it with your intention for self-love.
5. Take the Love Oil and anoint both the pink and purple candles with a few drops of oil. As you do this, visualize the oil infusing the candles with love and self-acceptance.
6. Light the pink candle, representing yourself, and say a prayer or affirmation for self-love. You can use the following example or create your own: "Divine love surrounds me and fills my heart. I am worthy of love and acceptance. I embrace my true self with compassion and kindness. I am deserving of all the love and happiness that comes my way. So mote it be."
7. Light the purple candle, representing the love you are seeking to cultivate within yourself, and say a prayer or affirmation for attracting love. You can use the following example or create your own: "I am a magnet for love and positive relationships. I attract love and acceptance into my life. I radiate love from within and attract love in return. I am open to receiving love in all its forms. So mote it be."
8. Sit in meditation for a few moments, visualizing yourself surrounded by a loving, pink and purple energy. Feel the love and acceptance flowing through you, filling every cell of your being.
9. Allow the candles to burn down completely or extinguish them safely if you need to leave the space. Keep the Love Powder and Oil in a safe place for future rituals or use.

Remember, this is just an example ritual, and you can personalize it to suit your own preferences and intentions. Feel free to modify the ingredients, prayers, or affirmations to align with your specific needs and desires.

Road Opener

Ingredients:

1. Yellow candle
2. Road Opener Oil (ingredients: lemongrass essential oil, bergamot essential oil, olive oil)
3. Road Opener Herb Blend (ingredients: bay leaves, cinnamon sticks, ginger root)
4. Singing bowl or bell
5. Matches or a lighter

Instructions

1. Begin by creating a sacred space for your ritual. Cleanse the area with sage or other purifying herbs, light candles, and play soft, soothing music.
2. Take the yellow candle and carve the word "obstacles" into it. This candle represents the obstacles and blockages that you wish to remove from your path.
3. Take the Road Opener Oil and anoint the yellow candle with a few drops of oil. As you do this, visualize the oil clearing away any obstacles and opening up new opportunities for you.
4. Take the Road Opener Herb Blend and sprinkle a small amount onto the dish or plate. Use your fingers to mix the herbs and infuse them with your intention to clear your path.
5. Light the yellow candle, representing obstacles, and say a prayer or affirmation for removing obstacles. You can use the following example or create your own: "I release any obstacles that stand in my way. I am open to new opportunities and possibilities. I embrace the path of growth and success. I am ready to move forward with ease and grace. So mote it be."
6. Sit in meditation for a few moments, visualizing the yellow candle burning away the obstacles in your path. Feel a sense of freedom and clarity as you envision a clear and open road ahead.
7. After the meditation, take the singing bowl or bell and gently strike or ring it. Allow the sound to fill the space, vibrating and clearing any stagnant energy. If using a bell, you can also walk around the room, ringing the bell in each corner to further clear the energy.
8. Take a moment to express gratitude for the clearing and opening of your path. Thank the universe, your guides, or any higher power you believe in for their support and guidance.
9. Allow the candle to burn down completely or extinguish it safely if you need to leave the space. Keep the Road Opener Oil and Herb Blend in a safe place for future rituals or use.

Remember, this is just an example ritual, and you can personalize it to suit your own preferences and intentions. Feel free to modify the ingredients, prayers, or affirmations to align with your specific needs and desires.

Stop Gossiping

Ingredients:

1. Red candle
2. White candle
3. Clove (whole or powdered)
4. Cinnamon (whole or powdered)
5. Stop Gossip Oil (ingredients: lemon essential oil, clove powder, eucalyptus essential oil, olive oil)
6. A small dish or plate
7. Matches or a lighter

Instructions

1. Begin by creating a sacred space for your ritual. Cleanse the area with sage or other purifying herbs, light candles, and play soft, soothing music.
2. Take the red candle and carve the word "stop the gossip" into it. This candle represents the negative energy of gossip that you wish to stop.
3. Take the white candle and carve the word "peace" into it. This candle represents the peaceful energy that you wish to cultivate in your relationships.
4. Take the clove and cinnamon and sprinkle a small amount onto the dish or plate. Use your fingers to mix the spices and infuse them with your intention to stop gossiping.
5. Take the Stop Gossip Oil and anoint both the red and white candles with a few drops of oil. As you do this, visualize the oil creating a protective barrier around you, preventing gossip from affecting you.
6. Light the red candle, representing gossip, and say a prayer or affirmation for stopping gossip. You can use the following example or create your own: "I release the need to engage in gossip. I choose to speak words of kindness and understanding. I create a shield of protection around me, deflecting gossip and negativity. I am a source of peace and harmony. So mote it be."
7. Light the white candle, representing peace, and say a prayer or affirmation for cultivating peaceful relationships. You can use the following example or create your own: "I invite peace and harmony into my relationships. I choose to communicate with love and compassion. I release any negative energy that may lead to gossip. I am a source of positivity and understanding. So mote it be."
8. Sit in meditation for a few moments, visualizing yourself surrounded by a peaceful, white light. Feel the negative energy of gossip being replaced by a sense of calm and tranquility.
9. Allow the candles to burn down completely or extinguish them safely if you need to leave the space. Keep the clove, cinnamon, and Stop Gossip Oil in a safe place for future rituals or use.

Remember, this is just an example ritual, and you can personalize it to suit your own preferences and intentions. Feel free to modify the ingredients, prayers, or affirmations to align with your specific needs and desires.

Simple Court Case Victory

Ingredients:
1. Green candle
2. Purple candle
3. Bay leaves
4. Frankincense resin or incense
5. Court Case Oil (ingredients: basil essential oil, bergamot essential oil, olive oil)
6. A small dish or plate
7. Matches or a lighter

Instructions
1. Begin by creating a sacred space for your ritual. Cleanse the area with sage or other purifying herbs, light candles, and play soft, soothing music.
2. Take the green candle and carve the word "victory" into it. This candle represents the outcome you desire in your court case.
3. Take the purple candle and carve the word "justice" into it. This candle represents the fair and just resolution of your court case.
4. Take the bay leaves and place them on the dish or plate. As you do this, visualize the bay leaves symbolizing the strength and success you seek in your court case.
5. Light the green candle, representing victory, and say a prayer or affirmation for success in your court case. You can use the following example or create your own: "I call upon the energies of victory and success. I am confident in my abilities and the strength of my case. I attract positive outcomes and favorable rulings. I am supported by the universe and guided towards victory. So mote it be."
6. Light the purple candle, representing justice, and say a prayer or affirmation for a fair and just resolution in your court case. You can use the following example or create your own: "I invoke the power of justice and fairness. I trust in the legal system to deliver a just outcome. I am surrounded by truth and integrity. I am protected by the forces of justice. So mote it be."
7. Take the Court Case Oil and anoint both the green and purple candles with a few drops of oil. As you do this, visualize the oil amplifying the energies of victory and justice in your court case.
8. Light the frankincense resin or incense and let the smoke fill the space. As the smoke rises, visualize it carrying your intentions and prayers to the universe.
9. Sit in meditation for a few moments, visualizing the candles burning brightly and the bay leaves radiating success and strength. See yourself standing in the courtroom, confident and supported, as the case unfolds in your favor.
10. Allow the candles to burn down completely or extinguish them safely if you need to leave the space. Keep the bay leaves and Court Case Oil in a safe place for future rituals or use.

Remember, this is just an example ritual, and you can personalize it to suit your own preferences and intentions. Feel free to modify the ingredients, prayers, or affirmations to align with your specific needs and desires.

Criminal Court Case Victory

Ingredients:
1. 12 candles (choose colors that resonate with you for victory and justice, such as green, purple, or white)
2. Court Case Oil (ingredients: calendula essential oil, basil essential oil, bergamot essential oil, olive oil)
3. Courthouse dirt (collected from the area around a courthouse)
4. Herbs for justice (such as Solomon's seal, angelica root, or bay leaves)
5. Victory Powder (ingredients: cinnamon, frankincense, myrrh, and other herbs associated with victory)
6. River water (collected from a clean and flowing river)
7. A small dish or plate
8. Matches or a lighter
9. A Bible or a copy of Psalm 35

Instructions

1. Begin by creating a sacred space for your ritual. Cleanse the area with sage or other purifying herbs, light candles, and play soft, soothing music.
2. Take the 12 candles and arrange them in a circle, evenly spaced apart. Each candle represents a different aspect of your court case, such as evidence, witnesses, or the judge. Choose colors that resonate with you for victory and justice. Write each name, evidence, witness, or judge on the candles based on your situation..
3. Take the Court Case Oil and anoint each candle with a few drops of oil. As you do this, visualize the oil infusing the candles with the energy of victory and justice.
4. Take the courthouse dirt and sprinkle a small amount onto the dish or plate. Place the dish in the center of the circle of candles. The courthouse dirt symbolizes the influence and power of the legal system in your case.
5. Take the herbs for justice and sprinkle them around the dish of courthouse dirt. As you do this, visualize the herbs amplifying the energy of justice and fairness in your court case.
6. Light each candle, starting from the north and moving clockwise around the circle. As you light each candle, state your intention for that aspect of your court case. For example, "I light this candle for the truth to be revealed" or "I light this candle for a fair and just judgment."
7. Take the Victory Powder and sprinkle a small amount onto the dish of courthouse dirt. Use your fingers to mix the powder and herbs together, infusing them with your intention for victory in your court case.
8. Take the river water and pour a small amount into the dish of courthouse dirt and Victory Powder. As you do this, visualize the water washing away any obstacles or negativity in your court case, leaving a clear path to victory.
9. Open the Bible or the copy of Psalm 35 and read it aloud, focusing on the verses that speak of justice and victory. You can also recite your own prayer or affirmation for justice and victory in your court case.
10. Sit in meditation for a few moments, visualizing the candles burning brightly, the herbs and powder infusing the space with powerful energy, and the river water cleansing and purifying your court case.
11. Allow the candles to burn down completely or extinguish them safely if you need to leave the space. Dispose of the remaining materials from the ritual in a respectful manner, such as burying them in the earth or scattering them in flowing water.

Remember, this ritual and requires careful consideration and respect for the ingredients and practices involved. Give back to the earth for everything that is taken through libations or coins. It's important to personalize the ritual to suit your own beliefs and intentions. Feel free to modify the ingredients, prayers, or affirmations to align with your specific needs and desires.

Purchasing a New Home

Ingredients:

1. Dirt from the property (collected from the area where the new home will be)
2. Railroad spikes (collect safely and within the laws of your state)
3. White candle
4. Green candle
5. Sage or other purifying herbs
6. Anointing oil (such as olive oil or a specific oil for home blessings)
7. A small dish or plate
8. Matches or a lighter

Instructions

1. Begin by creating a sacred space for your ritual. Cleanse the area with sage or other purifying herbs, light candles, and play soft, soothing music.
2. Take the dirt from the property and place it on the dish or plate. This dirt represents the foundation and connection to the land where your new home will be built.
3. Take the railroad spikes and arrange them in a circle around the dish of dirt. The railroad spikes symbolize strength, stability, and protection for your new home.
4. Light the white candle, representing purity and cleansing. Use the flame of the candle to purify the dirt and railroad spikes, passing them through the smoke of the candle.
5. Take the green candle, representing growth and abundance, and anoint it with the anointing oil. As you do this, visualize the energy of prosperity and success flowing into the candle.
6. Light the green candle and place it in the center of the dish of dirt. As the candle burns, visualize the light and energy radiating outwards, filling the space with positive vibrations.
7. Close your eyes and take a few deep breaths. Visualize yourself signing the closing documents for your new home with ease and confidence. See the sale being finalized and the keys to your new home in your hands.
8. Say a prayer or affirmation, expressing gratitude for the opportunity to purchase your new home and asking for blessings and protection for your future in the new space. You can use the following example or create your own: "Divine Spirit, I am grateful for the opportunity to purchase this new home. I ask for your blessings and protection as I embark on this new chapter of my life. May this home be a place of love, joy, and abundance. May it bring me peace and prosperity. I thank you for guiding me on this journey. So mote it be."
9. Sit in meditation for a few moments, visualizing your new home filled with happiness, love, and positive energy. See yourself enjoying the space, making memories, and feeling a sense of belonging.
10. Allow the candles to burn down completely or extinguish them safely if you need to leave the space. Take the dish of dirt and railroad spikes and bury them in the ground of your new property, symbolically grounding the energy and connection to the land.

Remember, this ritual requires careful consideration and respect for the ingredients and practices involved. Give back to the land through libations or coins when you take from it. It's important to personalize the ritual to suit your own beliefs and intentions. Feel free to modify the ingredients, prayers, or affirmations to align with your specific needs and desires.

New Job or Promotion

Ingredients:

1. Parchment paper
2. Green candle (for prosperity and abundance)
3. Purple candle (for spiritual power and success)
4. White candle (to honor ancestors and seek their guidance)
5. Job or promotion-related oils (such as Success Oil or Money Drawing Oil)
6. Job or promotion-related herbs (such as bay leaves, cinnamon, or basil)
7. A small dish or bowl
8. Matches or a lighter

Instructions

1. Find a quiet and comfortable space where you can perform the ritual without interruptions. Cleanse the area by smudging with sage or any other cleansing method you prefer.
2. Place the green candle on the left side, the purple candle on the right side, and the white candle in the center.
3. Take a moment to connect with your ancestors and seek their guidance. You can say a prayer or simply speak from your heart, expressing your intention to find a new job or receive a promotion. Ask for their support and assistance in your endeavor.
4. Take the parchment paper and write your intention in clear and concise language. For example, you can write, "I attract a new job that aligns with my highest good and brings me prosperity and success." Be specific about the qualities and aspects you desire in your new job or promotion.
5. Take the job or promotion-related oils and anoint each candle from the bottom to the top, focusing on your intention. As you do this, visualize yourself already in the desired job or position, feeling fulfilled and successful.
6. Light each candle, starting with the white candle in the center.
7. Sprinkle a small amount of the job or promotion-related herbs onto the parchment paper. These herbs can enhance the energy and intention of your ritual. For example, bay leaves can bring success and protection, cinnamon can attract abundance, and basil can bring luck and prosperity.
8. Carefully light the parchment paper using the white candle flame. As it burns, visualize your intention being released into the universe, knowing that it will manifest in the perfect way and at the perfect time.
9. Express gratitude to your ancestors, the universe, and any spiritual guides or deities you work with. Thank them for their support and assistance in manifesting your desired job or promotion.
10. Let the candles burn down completely or extinguish them if you need to leave the space. If you choose to extinguish the candles, relight them in subsequent rituals until your intention is manifested.

Remember, this is just an example ritual. Feel free to adapt and personalize it according to your beliefs and practices. It's important to approach any ritual with respect, sincerity, and a clear intention.

Banishment Containment

Ingredients:
1. A small glass jar with a lid
2. Black candle (for banishing and protection)
3. Paper and pen
4. Scissors
5. Salt or black salt
6. Protective herbs (such as sage, rosemary, or bay leaves)
7. Personal belongings or a photo of the person you want to banish (optional)
8. Matches or a lighter

Instructions
1. Find a quiet and comfortable space where you can perform the ritual without interruptions. Cleanse the area by smudging with sage or any other cleansing method you prefer.
2. Cleanse the glass jar by washing it with warm water and a mild soap, and smoke. Dry it thoroughly before use.
3. Take the paper and pen, and write the name of the person you want to banish. Be as specific as possible. If you have personal belongings or a photo of the person, you can place them inside the jar as well.
4. Cut the paper into small pieces, making sure each piece has the person's name on it.
5. Take the protective herbs and hold them in your hands. Visualize a protective energy surrounding you and the person you want to banish. Infuse the herbs with this energy and intention.
6. Start by placing a layer of salt or black salt at the bottom of the jar. This will create a protective barrier. Then, add a layer of the charged herbs. Repeat this layering process until the jar is almost full.
7. Place the small pieces of paper with the person's name on top of the herb layers. As you do this, visualize the person's negative energy and influence being trapped and contained within the jar.
8. Close the jar tightly with the lid. You can also seal it further by dripping black candle wax around the lid or using a black ribbon to tie it shut. This will symbolize the binding and containment of the person's energy. (or do both)
9. Place the black candle on top of the sealed jar. Light the candle, focusing on your intention to banish the person from your life. Visualize their negative influence dissipating and being replaced with positive energy and protection.
10. Speak your intention out loud, stating that you are banishing the person's negative energy and influence from your life. Be firm and assertive in your words.
11. Allow the black candle to burn down completely. As it burns, visualize the person's energy being transformed and released, no longer affecting you.
12. Once the candle has burned out, you can choose to bury the jar in a secluded place, throw it into a body of water, or simply place it in a hidden spot where it won't be disturbed. This symbolizes the permanent removal of the person's energy from your life.

Remember, this is just an example ritual. Feel free to adapt and personalize it according to your beliefs and practices. It's important to approach any ritual with respect, sincerity, and a clear intention. Please check the laws in your state before tossing your working into a body of water.

Strengthen A Marriage

Ingredients:

1. A small glass jar with a lid
2. Pink or red candle (for love and passion)
3. Paper and pen
4. Scissors
5. Rose petals or/and other love-related herbs (such as lavender or jasmine)
6. Small personal items or photos representing you and your partner
7. Matches or a lighter

Instructions

1. Find a quiet and comfortable space where you can perform the ritual without interruptions. Cleanse the area by smudging with sage or any other cleansing method you prefer.
2. Cleanse the glass jar by washing it with warm water and a mild soap, and smoke. Dry it thoroughly before use.
3. Take the paper and pen, and write your intention for strengthening your marriage. Be as specific as possible, focusing on the qualities and aspects you want to enhance in your relationship.
4. Cut the paper into small pieces, making sure each piece has a part of your intention written on it.
5. Take the rose petals or/and other love-related herbs and hold them in your hands. Visualize a loving and harmonious energy surrounding you and your partner. Infuse the herbs with this energy and intention.
6. Start by placing a layer of the charged herbs at the bottom of the jar. This will symbolize the foundation of love and passion in your marriage. Then, add a layer of the small personal items or photos representing you and your partner. Repeat this layering process until the jar is almost full.
7. Place the small pieces of paper with your intention on top of the herb and personal item layers. As you do this, visualize your intention for a strong and loving marriage being infused into the jar.
8. Close the jar tightly with the lid. You can also seal it further by dripping pink or red candle wax around the lid or using a pink or red ribbon to tie it shut. (or both) This will symbolize the sealing and protection of your marriage.
9. Place the pink or red candle on top of the sealed jar. Light the candle, focusing on your intention to strengthen your marriage. Visualize the flame representing the love and passion between you and your partner.
10. Speak your intention out loud, stating that you are strengthening your marriage and deepening the love and connection between you and your partner. Express your gratitude for your relationship and the growth you will experience together.
11. Allow the pink or red candle to burn down completely. As it burns, visualize the love and passion in your marriage growing stronger and radiating out into the world.
12. Once the candle has burned out, place the jar in a prominent and sacred space in your home. This can be on an altar, a shelf, or any place where it will be seen and honored. Whenever you need a reminder of your intention, you can hold the jar, visualize your desired outcome, and send love and positive energy to your marriage.

Remember, this is just an example ritual. Feel free to adapt and personalize it according to your beliefs and practices. It's important to approach any ritual with respect, sincerity, and a clear intention.

Cord Cutting

Ingredients:
1. Two black candles (for protection and banishing)
2. Twine or string
3. Scissors
4. Black salt or black pepper (for banishing and protection)
5. Protective oil (rosemary essential oil, frankincense essential oil, angelica root essental oil and olive oil)
6. Banishing powder (black salt, cayenne pepper, nettle leaf, garlic powder, and rue)
7. Matches or a lighter

Instructions

1. Find a quiet and comfortable space where you can perform the ritual without interruptions. Cleanse the area by smudging with sage or any other cleansing method you prefer.
2. Place the two black candles in front of you, with enough space between them to tie the twine or string.
3. Cut a piece of twine or string long enough to comfortably tie around your wrists.
4. Pass the twine through the smoke of the black candles, visualizing any negative or unwanted energy being cleansed and removed.
5. Take a moment to reflect on the relationship or situation you want to release and cut ties with. Formulate a clear intention in your mind, focusing on the aspects you want to let go of and the freedom you seek.
6. Hold the twine in your hands and state your intention out loud. Then, tie the twine around your wrists, symbolizing the connection you want to sever.
7. Take the protective oils and anoint each black candle from the bottom to the top, focusing on your intention to banish and protect yourself. As you do this, visualize any negative or unwanted energy being repelled and replaced with positive and protective energy.
8. Sprinkle a small amount of the banishing powders around the area where the candles are placed. This will enhance the banishing and protective energy of the ritual.
9. Light the black candles, focusing on your intention to cut ties and release any negative or unwanted connections. As the candles burn, visualize the cords that bind you to the relationship or situation being severed and dissipated.
10. Recite a prayer or affirmation that aligns with your intention. Here's a suggested prayer: "Divine Spirit, I call upon your guidance and protection in this moment. I release and cut ties with [name of person or situation]. I release any negative energy, attachments, or influences that no longer serve my highest good. I reclaim my power and freedom. I am strong, protected, and free. Thank you for your support and guidance. So mote it be."
11. Take the scissors and carefully cut the twine or string that is tied around your wrists. As you do this, visualize the cords being severed and the energy being released.
12. Allow the black candles to burn down completely or extinguish them using a candle snuffer or by pinching the flame. As you do this, visualize the energy of the relationship or situation being fully released and transformed.
13. Take the cut twine and any remnants of the ritual (such as ashes or wax) and dispose of them in a way that feels appropriate to you. This can be burying them in the earth, throwing them into flowing water, or simply placing them in a sealed bag and discarding them.

Remember, this is just an example ritual. Feel free to adapt and personalize it according to your beliefs and practices. It's important to approach any ritual with respect, sincerity, and a clear intention.

Spiritual Woman

In the depths of her soul, she found her way,
A spiritual woman, embracing her African American sway.
With ancestors whispers and spirits as her guide,
She broke free from chains, no longer confined.

Like the wind, she soared, untamed and wild,
Her spirit dancing, a free spirited child.
And in her heart, the power of the big cat roared,
Strength and courage, her essence fully restored.

Trials she faced, but never did she yield,
For she knew her roots were a mighty shield.
With African rhythms pulsing through her veins,
She triumphed with resilience, breaking all chains.

So let her story inspire, let her spirit ignite,
A woman empowered, shining so bright.
Reconnected to her roots, she found her true power,
A spiritual journey, triumphant every hour.

—Rootworker Kye

Closing Remarks

In closing my book, I want to emphasize that the stories I have shared and the lessons I have learned throughout the years are deeply personal to me. I understand that each person's spiritual path is unique and individualized. What resonates with one may not resonate with another, and that is perfectly okay. Spirituality is a personal journey, and no two journeys will ever be the same.

It is crucial to remember that this book is not intended to be a self-righteous guide or a declaration of perfection. We all stumble, make mistakes, and succumb to our emotions from time to time. But the beauty lies in the fact that we can always start anew, make amends, and strive to become better versions of ourselves.

Hoodoo, at its core, is about the journey itself. It is about seeking and discovering our purpose within our unique paths. It is not always an easy road, but the challenges and obstacles we face along the way are what shape us and help us grow. I sincerely hope that this book serves as a guiding light on your own spiritual journey.

I know I repeated myself often in this book, but I wanted to make sure certain aspects of Hoodoo and my journey were completely understood. I also know how reading a book with so much information can be too much, and sometimes you miss things. So, I made sure to repeat important aspects throughout this work.

May it provide you with insight, inspiration, and encouragement to find your purpose and embrace the path that resonates with your soul. Remember, you are capable of incredible transformation and the power to create positive change lies within you. May you embark upon this journey with an open heart and a willingness to learn and grow.

My Hoodoo

START UP JOURNAL

Introduction

Welcome to your Hoodoo Journal! This journal is a sacred tool that will help you record your path of spiritual growth, self-discovery, and personal empowerment. Journaling is an essential practice when you're on a spiritual journey. It allows you to document your experiences, insights, and dreams so that you don't forget the valuable lessons and messages they hold. This journal is specifically designed to help you capture and preserve the important aspects of your spiritual journey. In this journal, you will find different sections that cater to various aspects of your Hoodoo practice.

The 'Thoughts' section provides a space for you to reflect on your thoughts, emotions, and observations as you navigate the realms of metaphysics and spirituality. Use this section to delve deep into your inner world and gain clarity and understanding.

The 'Holistic Recipes' section is dedicated to recording the recipes and remedies that you discover along your Hoodoo journey. From herbal concoctions to spiritual baths, this section will serve as a treasure trove of knowledge, ensuring that you never forget the powerful rituals and potions that have brought you healing and transformation.

The 'Rituals' section is where you can document the rituals and workings that you perform. Whether it's a candle ritual, a protection working, or a manifestation ceremony, this section will help you keep track of your practices and their outcomes. It's a testament to your growth and a source of inspiration for future rituals.

Dreams hold profound wisdom and guidance from the spiritual realm. That's why the 'Dream Journal' section is included in this journal. Use it to record your dreams, decipher their meanings, and explore the messages they bring. Your dream journal will become a portal to the subconscious, revealing hidden truths and offering guidance on your spiritual path.

Remember, this journal is just the beginning of your Hoodoo journey. It is a tool to get you started and to help you build a strong foundation for your practice. May this journal be a constant companion and a source of inspiration, guidance, and transformation as you delve into the mysteries of Hoodoo and unlock the hidden depths of your own spiritual potential.

Embrace the magic within you and let your journey begin!

My Thoughts

YOUR SPIRITUAL JOURNEY

My Thoughts

Date:

My Hoodoo Journal

My Thoughts

Date:

My Thoughts

Date:

My Hoodoo Journal

My Thoughts

Date:

My Thoughts

Date:

My Thoughts

Date :

My Thoughts

Date:

My Thoughts

Date:

My Hoodoo Journal

My Thoughts

Date:

My Hoodoo Journal

My Thoughts

My Hoodoo Journal

Date:

My Thoughts My Hoodoo Journal

Date:

My Thoughts

Date:

My Thoughts

Date:

My Thoughts

Date.

My Hoodoo Journal

My Thoughts

Date:

My Thoughts

Date:

My Thoughts

Date :

My Thoughts

Date:

My Hoodoo Journal

My Thoughts

Date:

My Hoodoo Journal

My Thoughts

Date:

My Thoughts

My Hoodoo Journal

Date:

My Thoughts

Date:

My Hoodoo Journal

My Thoughts

Date:

… My Thoughts

Date:

My Hoodoo Journal

My Thoughts

My Hoodoo Journal

Date:

My Recipes

HOLISTIC RECIPES

Holistic Recipe

RECIPE NAME: ....
RECIPE TYPE: ....

INGREDIENTS:

- ....
- ....
- ....
- ....
- ....
- ....
- ....
- ....
- ....

DIRECTIONS: ....

....
....
....
....
....
....
....
....
....

NOTES:

Holistic Recipe

RECIPE NAME: ....
RECIPE TYPE: ....

INGREDIENTS:

- ....
- ....
- ....
- ....
- ....
- ....
- ....
- ....
- ....

DIRECTIONS: ....

....
....
....
....
....
....
....
....

NOTES:

Holistic Recipe

RECIPE NAME:
RECIPE TYPE:

INGREDIENTS:

-
-
-

-
-
-

-
-
-

DIRECTIONS:

NOTES:

Holistic Recipe

RECIPE NAME: ....
RECIPE TYPE: ....

INGREDIENTS:

- ....
- ....
- ....
- ....
- ....
- ....
- ....
- ....
- ....

DIRECTIONS: ....
....
....
....
....
....
....
....

NOTES:

Holistic Recipe

RECIPE NAME: ....
RECIPE TYPE: ....

INGREDIENTS:

- ....
- ....
- ....
- ....
- ....
- ....
- ....
- ....
- ....

DIRECTIONS: ....

....

....

....

....

....

....

....

....

NOTES:

Holistic Recipe

RECIPE NAME: ....
RECIPE TYPE: ....

INGREDIENTS:

- ....
- ....
- ....
- ....
- ....
- ....
- ....
- ....
- ....

DIRECTIONS: ....

....

....

....

....

....

....

....

NOTES:

Holistic Recipe

RECIPE NAME: ....
RECIPE TYPE: ....

INGREDIENTS:

- ....
- ....
- ....

- ....
- ....
- ....

- ....
- ....
- ....

DIRECTIONS: ....

....

....

....

....

....

....

....

....

NOTES:

Holistic Recipe

RECIPE NAME: ....
RECIPE TYPE: ....

INGREDIENTS:

- ....
- ....
- ....
- ....
- ....
- ....
- ....
- ....
- ....

DIRECTIONS: ....

....
....
....
....
....
....
....
....

NOTES:

Holistic Recipe

RECIPE NAME: ....
RECIPE TYPE: ....

INGREDIENTS:

- ....
- ....
- ....

- ....
- ....
- ....

- ....
- ....
- ....

DIRECTIONS: ....

....

....

....

....

....

....

....

NOTES:

Holistic Recipe

RECIPE NAME: ....
RECIPE TYPE: ....

INGREDIENTS:

- ....
- ....
- ....
- ....
- ....
- ....
- ....
- ....
- ....

DIRECTIONS: ....
....
....
....
....
....
....
....

NOTES:

Holistic Recipe

RECIPE NAME: ....
RECIPE TYPE: ....

INGREDIENTS:

- ....
- ....
- ....
- ....
- ....
- ....
- ....
- ....
- ....

DIRECTIONS:

....

....

....

....

....

....

....

....

NOTES:

Holistic Recipe

RECIPE NAME: ....
RECIPE TYPE: ....

INGREDIENTS:

- ....
- ....
- ....
- ....
- ....
- ....
- ....
- ....
- ....

DIRECTIONS: ....

....
....
....
....
....
....
....
....

NOTES:

Holistic Recipe

RECIPE NAME: ....
RECIPE TYPE: ....

INGREDIENTS:

- ....
- ....
- ....

- ....
- ....
- ....

- ....
- ....
- ....

DIRECTIONS: ....

....

....

....

....

....

....

....

NOTES:

Holistic Recipe

RECIPE NAME: ....
RECIPE TYPE: ....

INGREDIENTS:

- ....
- ....
- ....
- ....
- ....
- ....
- ....
- ....
- ....

DIRECTIONS: ....

....

....

....

....

....

....

....

NOTES:

Holistic Recipe

RECIPE NAME: ....
RECIPE TYPE: ....

INGREDIENTS:

- ....
- ....
- ....

- ....
- ....
- ....

- ....
- ....
- ....

DIRECTIONS: ....

....

....

....

....

....

....

....

NOTES:

My Rituals

WORKINGS & RITUALS

Ritual or Working's Name: Date:

Purpose

Photo:

Ingredients

Directions

Notes

My Hoodoo Journal

Ritual or Working's Name: _____ Date: _____

Purpose
_____

Photo:

Ingredients

_____	_____
_____	_____
_____	_____
_____	_____

Directions
_____
_____
_____
_____
_____
_____

Notes
_____
_____
_____
_____

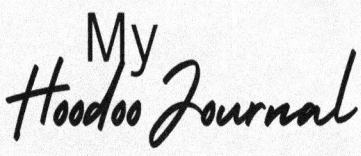

Ritual or Working's Name: Date:

Purpose

Photo:

Ingredients

Directions

Notes

Ritual or Working's Name: _____ Date: _____

Purpose
_____

Ingredients

Photo:

Directions
_____
_____
_____
_____
_____
_____
_____

Notes
_____
_____
_____

Ritual or Working's Name: Date:
_____

Purpose
_____

Photo:

Ingredients

_____	_____
_____	_____
_____	_____
_____	_____
_____	_____

Directions
_____
_____
_____
_____
_____
_____

Notes
_____
_____
_____

My Hoodoo Journal

Ritual or Working's Name: _____   Date: _____

Purpose
_____

Ingredients

_____	_____
_____	_____
_____	_____
_____	_____
_____	_____

Photo:

Directions

_____
_____
_____
_____
_____
_____
_____

Notes

_____
_____
_____

Ritual or Working's Name: _____ Date: _____

Purpose
_____

Ingredients

_____	_____
_____	_____
_____	_____
_____	_____
_____	_____

Photo:

Directions
_____
_____
_____
_____
_____
_____
_____

Notes
_____
_____
_____

Ritual or Working's Name: _____   Date: _____

Purpose
_____

Ingredients

_____	_____
_____	_____
_____	_____
_____	_____
_____	_____

Photo:

Directions
_____
_____
_____
_____
_____
_____
_____
_____

Notes
_____
_____
_____

Ritual or Working's Name: _____ Date: _____

Purpose
_____

Ingredients

Photo:

Directions
_____
_____
_____
_____
_____
_____
_____

Notes
_____
_____
_____
_____

Ritual or Working's Name: _____ Date: _____

Purpose
_____

Ingredients

Photo:

Directions
_____
_____
_____
_____
_____
_____
_____

Notes
_____
_____
_____
_____

Ritual or Working's Name: Date:

Purpose

Photo:

Ingredients

Directions

Notes

My Hoodoo Journal

Ritual or Working's Name: Date:
_____

Purpose

_____

Photo:

Ingredients

_____	_____
_____	_____
_____	_____
_____	_____
_____	_____

Directions

_____
_____
_____
_____
_____
_____
_____

Notes

_____
_____
_____

Ritual or Working's Name: Date:

Purpose

Photo:

Ingredients

Directions

Notes

Ritual or Working's Name: _____ Date: _____

Purpose
_____

Photo:

Ingredients

Directions
_____
_____
_____
_____
_____
_____
_____
_____

Notes
_____
_____
_____
_____

My Hoodoo Journal

Ritual or Working's Name: _____ Date: _____

Purpose
_____

Photo:

Ingredients

_____	_____
_____	_____
_____	_____
_____	_____
_____	_____

Directions
_____
_____
_____
_____
_____
_____
_____

Notes
_____
_____
_____
_____

Ritual or Working's Name: Date:

Purpose

Photo:

Ingredients

Directions

Notes

My Dreams

RECORD TO REMEMBER

My
Hoodoo Journal

Dream Journal

Title: _____ Date: _____

Mood/Emotion Tracker
○ ○ ○ ○ ○
VERRY SAD ⟷ VERY HAPPY

Space for Creativity
(DOODLES, ILLUSTRATION, TEXT, ETC)

What colors did you see?

What animals or objects?

Most important parts:

I don't want to forget:

Dream Journal

My
Hoodoo Journal

Dream Journal

Title: _____ Date: _____

Mood/Emotion Tracker

○ ○ ○ ○ ○

VERRY SAD ⟷ VERY HAPPY

Space for Creativity
(DOODLES, ILLUSTRATION, TEXT, ETC)

What colors did you see?

What animals or objects?

Most important parts:

I don't want to forget:

Dream Journal

My Hoodoo Journal

Dream Journal

Title: _____ Date: _____

Mood/Emotion Tracker

○ ○ ○ ○ ○

VERRY SAD ⟷ VERY HAPPY

What colors did you see?

What animals or objects?

Most important parts:

I don't want to forget:

Space for Creativity
(DOODLES, ILLUSTRATION, TEXT, ETC)

Dream Journal

My Hoodoo Journal

Dream Journal

Title: _____ Date: _____

Mood/Emotion Tracker

○ ○ ○ ○ ○

VERRY SAD ⟷ VERY HAPPY

Space for Creativity
(DOODLES, ILLUSTRATION, TEXT, ETC)

What colors did you see?

What animals or objects?

Most important parts:

I don't want to forget:

299

Dream Journal

My
Hoodoo Journal

Dream Journal

Title: _____   Date: _____

Mood/Emotion Tracker

○ ○ ○ ○ ○

VERRY SAD ⟷ VERY HAPPY

Space for Creativity
(DOODLES, ILLUSTRATION, TEXT, ETC)

What colors did you see?

What animals or objects?

Most important parts:

I don't want to forget:

Dream Journal

My
Hoodoo Journal

Dream Journal

Title: _____ Date: _____

Mood/Emotion Tracker

○ ○ ○ ○ ○

VERRY SAD ⟷ VERY HAPPY

Space for Creativity
(DOODLES, ILLUSTRATION, TEXT, ETC)

What colors did you see?

What animals or objects?

Most important parts:

I don't want to forget:

303

Dream Journal

My
Hoodoo Journal

Dream Journal

Title: _____ Date: _____

Mood/Emotion Tracker

○ ○ ○ ○ ○

VERRY SAD ⟷ VERY HAPPY

Space for Creativity
(DOODLES, ILLUSTRATION, TEXT, ETC)

What colors did you see?

What animals or objects?

Most important parts:

I don't want to forget:

305

Dream Journal

My
Dream Journal
Hoodoo Journal

Title: _____   Date: _____

Mood/Emotion Tracker
○ ○ ○ ○ ○

VERRY SAD ⟷ VERY HAPPY

Space for Creativity
(DOODLES, ILLUSTRATION, TEXT, ETC)

What colors did you see?

What animals or objects?

Most important parts:

I don't want to forget:

Dream Journal

My
Hoodoo Journal

Dream Journal

Title: _____ Date: _____

Mood/Emotion Tracker

○ ○ ○ ○ ○

VERRY SAD ⟷ VERY HAPPY

Space for Creativity
(DOODLES, ILLUSTRATION, TEXT, ETC)

What colors did you see?

What animals or objects?

Most important parts:

I don't want to forget:

Dream Journal

My
Hoodoo Journal

Dream Journal

Title: _____ Date: _____

Mood/Emotion Tracker

○ ○ ○ ○ ○

VERRY SAD ⟷ VERY HAPPY

Space for Creativity
(DOODLES, ILLUSTRATION, TEXT, ETC)

What colors did you see?

What animals or objects?

Most important parts:

I don't want to forget:

311

Dream Journal

My
Hoodoo Journal

Dream Journal

Title: _____ Date: _____

Mood/Emotion Tracker

○ ○ ○ ○ ○

VERRY SAD ⟷ VERY HAPPY

Space for Creativity
(DOODLES, ILLUSTRATION, TEXT, ETC)

What colors did you see?

What animals or objects?

Most important parts:

I don't want to forget:

313

Dream Journal

My
Hoodoo Journal

Dream Journal

Title: _____ Date: _____

Mood/Emotion Tracker

○ ○ ○ ○ ○

VERRY SAD ⟷ VERY HAPPY

Space for Creativity
(DOODLES, ILLUSTRATION, TEXT, ETC)

What colors did you see?

What animals or objects?

Most important parts:

I don't want to forget:

Dream Journal

My
Hoodoo Journal

Dream Journal

Title: _____ Date: _____

Mood/Emotion Tracker
○ ○ ○ ○ ○
VERRY SAD ⟷ VERY HAPPY

Space for Creativity
(DOODLES, ILLUSTRATION, TEXT,ETC)

What colors did you see?

What animals or objects?

Most important parts:

I don't want to forget:

Dream Journal

My
Hoodoo Journal

Dream Journal

Title: _____   Date: _____

Mood/Emotion Tracker

○ ○ ○ ○ ○

VERRY SAD ⟷ VERY HAPPY

What colors did you see?

What animals or objects?

Space for Creativity
(DOODLES, ILLUSTRATION, TEXT, ETC)

Most important parts:

I don't want to forget:

Dream Journal

My
Hoodoo Journal

Dream Journal

Title: _____   Date: _____

Mood/Emotion Tracker

○ ○ ○ ○ ○

VERRY SAD ⟷ VERY HAPPY

Space for Creativity
(DOODLES, ILLUSTRATION, TEXT, ETC)

What colors did you see?

What animals or objects?

Most important parts:

I don't want to forget:

Dream Journal

About the Author

Kyesha Burns, known as Rootworker Kye and affectionately called Medusa, is a highly skilled and passionate practitioner of Hoodoo, a spiritualist, writer, and spiritual educator hailing from the beautiful landscapes of Arkansas.

With a magnetic personality and a wealth of knowledge, Kyesha captivates her audience with her unique blend of professionalism and entertainment. As a devoted mother of five, Kyesha brings her nurturing energy and deep-rooted wisdom to her practice. Her journey into the mystical arts began over a decade ago, and she has since become a revered figure in the spiritual community. Specializing in rootwork, Kyesha's expertise lies in the powerful art of harnessing the natural energies of herbs, crystals, and other sacred tools to manifest desired outcomes.

With her Bachelor of Fine Arts degree in Creative Writing for the Entertainment Industry, Kyesha's innate storytelling abilities shine through in her work. She weaves captivating narratives into her consultations, workshops, and writings, making spiritual exploration an enlightening and engaging experience. Kyesha's insatiable curiosity and thirst for knowledge led her to pursue a Master Degree in Innovation and Entrepreneurship. This unique blend of creativity and business acumen fuels her entrepreneurial venture, Medusa by Kye. At her Hoodoo shop, she offers an extensive range of handmade products, spiritual consultations, and workshops that empower individuals to embrace their own spiritual paths.

In addition to her expertise in rootwork and Hoodoo, Kyesha is a gifted Conjurer card reader, utilizing ancestral cards and playing cards to unveil profound insights. She also practices dream divination and astral travel, delving into the realms of the subconscious and beyond to unlock hidden truths and guidance. Kyesha's ultimate goal is to live life in alignment with her purpose, radiating joy and creating a legacy that her children can be proud of. With her warm-hearted approach and unwavering commitment to helping others, Kyesha wishes everyone luck on their personal journeys, offering her support and guidance every step of the way.

For more information about Kyesha and her offerings, visit her website at www.medusabykye.com, where the enchantment of her spiritual expertise awaits.

www.ingramcontent.com/pod-product-compliance
Lightning Source LLC
Chambersburg PA
CBHW051618010526
44119CB00008B/198